50
big ideas
you really need to know

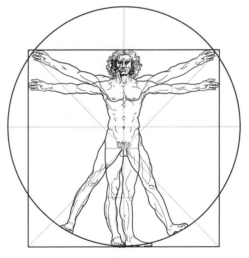

Ben Dupré

Quercus

Contents

Introduction

'Greater than the tread of mighty armies is an idea whose time has come.'
The French novelist Victor Hugo understood the combination of substance and
timing that come together to form an idea that really shakes things up – that is
destined to be big. But bigness can come in many guises: big and beautiful, big
and ugly, big and scary. Ideas can be big in all these ways and so may be admirable,
despicable or intimidating. Ideas of all these kinds are represented here.

The aim of philosophy, Adam Smith suggested, is 'to lay open the concealed
connections that unite the various appearances of nature'. In the light of such
lofty ambitions, it is little surprise that philosophers have provided some of
the most spacious of big ideas. A selection of these, covering two-and-a-half
millennia from Platonism to existentialism, is included here. No less profound is
philosophy's frequent adversary and occasional ally, religion – a spiritual path
to a different kind of truth. Faith, soul and other central ideas of religion are
fundamental in understanding how people judge the value and meaning of life.
At the same time, positions taken in opposition to religion, such as atheism
and secularism, have forged new and distinctive perspectives on the world.

The American humorist Will Rogers's joke about communism being like
prohibition – 'it's a good idea but it won't work' – is at least half wrong on both
counts: for better or for worse, communism is probably the most successful
political ideology ever to be planned on paper and realized in fact. Communism
is joined here by other seminal ideologies, including conservatism, liberalism and
republicanism. Much darker is the legacy of some other political ideas, notably
fascism and racism, which have left an indelible stain on human history.

In the last part of the book transformative ideas are drawn from the arts and
science. The artistic trajectory of human culture is traced through dominant
movements such as classicism, romanticism and modernism. On first encounter,
scientific ideas such as relativity and quantum mechanics may appear forbidding,
but their overall architecture is accessible and awesome. One cannot help but
marvel at minds that could encompass such things.

There are many wonderful ideas in this book and some dreadful ones too. If the
reader is not left with some sense of awe, the fault is surely mine: the ideas are
still big, it's just the writing that got smaller. Many thanks to my unflappable
editor-cum-designer, Nick Hutchins, and for the support and friendship of my
publisher, Richard Milbank, whose bright idea this was in the first place. Finally,
thanks to my own four best and brightest ideas, who huddle together ever closer
in the diminishing space left by my expansion.

01 Platonism

'The safest general characterization of the European philosophical tradition is that it consists of a series of footnotes to Plato.' While undoubtedly more pithy than true, the fact that a philosopher of the stature of A.N. Whitehead could make such a claim points to the astonishing awe in which later philosophers have held Plato, a citizen of Athens who was born nearly 2500 years ago.

'The chief error in philosophy is overstatement,' Whitehead pointed out earlier in his *Process and Reality* (1929) – ironically, at least in relation to the above-quoted remark, which is manifestly an exaggeration. But while Whitehead may fail to give subsequent Western philosophy its due, it is unquestionably true that Plato cast a huge shadow over later thinkers and that many of them developed and refined their ideas in creative interaction with or reaction to those of Plato.

In the course of some 35 dialogues, written over half a century, we see a range of doctrines – ethical, political, aesthetic, among others – evolving and maturing, and the term 'Platonism' may refer to some or all of these ideas. At the core of his philosophy, however, is a strikingly original metaphysical theory that assumes the existence of a realm of eternal and unchanging realities, distinct from the shifting world of everyday experience. These entities are both the cause of everything and the source of all value and meaning, and exploring their transcendent nature and the manner in which we gain knowledge of them is the most distinctive part of Plato's philosophy. Accordingly, it is this aspect of his work that can most precisely be called Platonic, and it is by extension from this peculiar conception of ultimate reality that the name 'Platonism' is sometimes

timeline

c.429 BC	399 BC	347 BC
Plato born in Athens of an aristocratic family	Socrates, Plato's mentor and spokesman in the dialogues, executed	Death of Plato

applied to other theories that are realist (idealist) in character. These typically assert that abstract entities, especially mathematical ones, exist outside time and space, independently of our perception or experience of them.

The theory of Forms   The motivation for Plato's extreme realism is dissatisfaction with what purports to be knowledge of the world around us, where everything is imperfect and changeable. How can we know what tallness is when a tall person is short next to a tree? Or what redness is when an apple that appears red in daylight looks black in the dark? Such things, Plato concludes, are the objects not of knowledge but of opinion or conjecture. What is known must be perfect, eternal and unchanging, and since nothing in our everyday experience (in the 'realm of becoming') fits this description, there must be a transcendent 'realm of being' where there are perfect and unchanging models or paradigms. These are what Plato calls 'Forms' or 'Ideas', and it is by virtue of imitating or copying them that things in our experience are the way they are. So, for instance, it is by copying the Form of Justice that all particular just actions are just.

And how, we may wonder, do we gain knowledge of these transcendent Forms, if all that is available to us through our senses is poor imitations or copies? Plato's surprising answer is that we must have come to know the Forms when we were in some earlier state and that what we are engaged in now is a process not of learning but of recollection. On this basis Plato develops a thoroughgoing dualism, in which our immortal souls exist prior to occupying physical bodies. It is the process of embodiment that encumbers the soul and causes it to forget the knowledge that it gained from previous direct contact with Forms in the realm of being.

> We ought to fly away from earth to heaven as quickly as we can; and to fly away is to become like God, as far as this is possible; and to become like him is to become holy, just, and wise.

Plato, *Theaetetus*, c.369 BC

6th century AD
Boethius initiates medieval controversy over nature of universals

1929
Publication of *Process and Reality* by English philosopher A.N. Whitehead

Plato's cave

Plato's complex and many-layered conception of knowledge and truth is illustrated by the most famous of the many images and analogies he used: the Allegory of the Cave. The essence of the story, which appears in his greatest and most influential work, *The Republic*, is as follows:

'Imagine you have been imprisoned all your life in a dark cave. Your hands and feet are shackled and your head restrained so that you can only look at the wall straight in front of you. Behind you is a blazing fire, and between you and the fire a walkway on which your captors carry statues and all sorts of objects. The shadows cast on the wall by these objects are the only things you and your fellow prisoners have ever seen, all you have ever thought and talked about. Now suppose that you are released from your shackles and free to walk around the cave. Dazzled at first by the fire, you will gradually come to see the situation of the cave properly and to understand the origin of the shadows that you previously took to be real. And finally you are allowed out of the cave and into the sunlit world outside, where you see the fullness of reality illuminated by the brightest object in the skies, the Sun.'

As usually interpreted, the cave represents 'the realm of becoming' – the visible world of our everyday experience, where everything is imperfect and constantly changing and where ordinary people, symbolized by the chained captives, live a life based on conjecture and illusion. The prisoner released to roam within the cave attains the most accurate view of reality possible within this deceptive world, but it is only when he moves outside the cave, into 'the realm of being', that he comes to a full understanding of the intelligible world of truth. This realm is populated by perfect and eternal objects of knowledge, the Forms, and overarching them all is the Form of the Good, represented by the Sun, which bestows on the others their ultimate meaning and reality.

The problem of universals Plato's theory of Forms may seem far-fetched, but one of the chief problems that it seeks to address – the so-called problem of universals – has been a dominant theme in philosophy, in some guise or other, ever since. In the Middle Ages the philosophical battle lines were drawn up between the Realists (or Platonists) on one side, who believed that universals such as redness and tallness existed independently of particular red and tall things; and the Nominalists on the other, who held that they were mere names or labels that were attached to objects to highlight particular similarities between them.

The same basic distinction still resonates throughout many areas of modern philosophy. So a realist position holds that there are entities 'out there' in the world – physical things or ethical facts or mathematical properties – that exist independently of our knowing or experiencing them. So, on this view, the business of (say) mathematics is not devising proofs involving entities that are in some sense constructed in the minds of mathematicians; rather, it is a matter of *discovering* truths about pre-existing entities. Opposed to this kind of view, other philosophers, known as anti-realists, put forward proposals in which there is a necessary and internal link or relation between what is known and our knowledge of it. The basic terms of all such debates were set up over 2000 years ago by Plato, one of the first and most thoroughgoing of all philosophical realists.

Platonic love

The idea with which Plato is most closely associated in the popular imagination – the pre-eminence of non-physical or 'platonic' love – flows naturally from the sharp contrast he draws in his philosophy between the world of the intellect and the world of the senses. In the dialogue *Phaedrus*, Plato explains how the true lover is impassioned by a divinely inspired love of intellectual beauty, to be found only in the Form of the Good. The soul of such a lover is famously compared to a chariot in which the charioteer, symbolizing reason, steers a pair of winged horses, representing our sensual and spiritual appetites, towards ultimate truth. Much subsequent religious thinking has been coloured by Plato's elevation of mind over body and by his idea that moral excellence resides in having a well-ordered soul in which the pure intellect keeps the lowly physical appetites in check.

the condensed idea
Towards transcendent reality

02 Aristotelianism

To medieval scholars Aristotle was 'the Philosopher'. In reputation and influence he so clearly surpassed all others – even Plato – that no more precise designation was needed; in Dante's *Inferno* he is simply 'the master of those who know'. Skilfully fused with Christian theology in a 13th-century synthesis achieved principally by Thomas Aquinas, Aristotelianism soon became established as the new dogma. For the following three centuries the Greek philosopher's authority went almost unchallenged in medieval Europe and his hand was felt in every area of intellectual activity.

Such was the respect accorded to Aristotle that his philosophy (or, sometimes, what passed for his philosophy) was often accepted and followed unquestioningly, to such a degree that in time it came to impede progress, stifling original and unorthodox thinking. Such slavish adherence eventually brought about a reaction, and outright rejection of the Aristotelian world view was a prime motive in the intellectual and scientific revolution that erupted in 16th-century Europe. Yet, while Aristotle's star was certainly eclipsed in the succeeding period, his influence never entirely disappeared, and in recent decades there has been a renewed appreciation of the many and deep insights his philosophy offers. In the area of moral thinking, in particular, his legacy has helped to inspire a distinctive approach known as 'virtue ethics'.

The term 'Aristotelian' can, of course, describe all or any of the doctrines set forth by Aristotle, the famous Greek philosopher who studied under Plato, taught Alexander the Great, and founded a highly influential philosophical school (the Lyceum) in 4th-century Athens. Today, however, Aristotelianism is most often mentioned in connection with

timeline

384 BC	367–347 BC	335 BC	322 BC
Aristotle born in Stagira, a Greek colony in Macedonia	Studies at Plato's Academy in Athens	Founds the Lyceum in Athens	Death of Aristotle

Virtue ethics

For most of the last 400 years, moral philosophers have tended to focus primarily on actions, not agents – on the sort of things we should *do* rather than the sort of people we should be. Typically, this has involved devising principles on which moral obligation allegedly depends and then formulating rules that guide us to behave in accordance with those principles. Over the last half century, however, a number of philosophers have become dissatisfied with this approach and, inspired mainly by Aristotle's ethics, have shifted attention back to character and virtues. The result is a new approach known as 'virtue ethics'.

According to the usual Greek account, the highest good for man and the ultimate purpose of human activity is *eudaimonia* – usually translated as 'happiness' but better captured by the broader concept of 'flourishing' or 'well-being'. The main issue, then, is not 'What is the right thing to do [in such and such circumstances]?' but 'What is the best way to live?' In Aristotle's view, the essence of man is the ability to reason – in particular, the use of practical reason to determine the best way to live; and *eudaimonia* consists in 'the active exercise of the soul's faculties [i.e. rational activity] in conformity with virtue or moral excellence'. Living virtuously is a matter of being or becoming the kind of person who, by acquiring wisdom through proper practice and training, habitually behaves in appropriate ways in the appropriate circumstances. In other words, having the right kind of character and dispositions, natural and acquired, issues in the right kind of behaviour. This attractive insight has lost none of its potency in the course of over 2000 years.

the Scholastic philosophical tradition that was established by Aquinas and other so-called 'Schoolmen' of the medieval period. Scholasticism undeniably owed a huge debt to Aristotle, but somewhat ironically, his increasingly dogmatic supporters, in their anxiety to defend him, came over time to display deeply conservative tendencies that were greatly at odds with the true spirit of his work.

Student and master It is sometimes said, simplistically, that Aristotle's philosophy developed in reaction to that of his teacher, Plato.

AD 529	1266	16th–17th century
Emperor Justinian closes the pagan schools	Aquinas begins *Summa Theologiae*, the pinnacle of medieval Scholasticism	Modern world view of Copernicus, Galileo *et al* replaces Aristotelian conception

In fact, the relationship between the two is considerably more complex. The younger philosopher is both more systematic than his master and has a far wider range, making significant and often foundational contributions in physics, biology, psychology, politics, ethics, metaphysics, rhetoric, aesthetics, logic, and more besides. While Plato has his head (almost literally) in the clouds, Aristotle keeps his feet very firmly on the ground; while Plato is otherworldly and abstract, proposing a transcendental realm of ultimate reality where alone true knowledge is attainable, Aristotle is stubbornly down to earth and concrete. Always respectful of common sense, he finds a full and sufficient reality in the ordinary world of experience, insisting that genuine knowledge can be acquired here (and only here) by diligent research and inquiry. He is tirelessly empirical and practical in his methods: he gathers evidence; carefully sorts and classifies it; subjects it to methodical and systematic analysis; and then, in a rational, logical and judiciously inductive manner, draws generalized conclusions in the light of his investigations.

The Scholastic synthesis Aristotle's influence was sustained for several centuries after his death first by his own school, the Lyceum, and then by the work of various editors and commentators, but he largely fell from view after AD 529, when the emperor Justinian closed the pagan schools in Athens and Alexandria. The medieval revival of interest in Aristotle's work in the West was encouraged initially through Latin translations of Arabic texts and commentaries on Aristotle, notably those by Avicenna and Averroës. It was then mainly due to the efforts of two Dominican friars – Albertus Magnus and his pupil Thomas Aquinas – that Aristotle became established as a mainstay of the burgeoning European universities.

Partly in reaction to the transcendental abstractions of Neoplatonist theologians, Aquinas set out to fashion a single philosophy that accommodated many aspects of Aristotelian rationalism within Christian

Scarce anything can be more absurdly said in natural philosophy than that which now is called Aristotle's *Metaphysics*; nor more repugnant to government than much of that he hath said in his *Politics*; nor more ignorantly, than a great part of his *Ethics*.

Thomas Hobbes, 1651

‘Linnaeus and Cuvier have been my two gods . . . but they were mere schoolboys to old Aristotle.’

Charles Darwin, 1882

theology. He broadly assimilated Aristotle's physics (account of physical objects); dynamics (analysis of place and motion); epistemology (views on the acquisition of intellectual knowledge); and cosmology (a universe built out of four elements – air, earth, fire and water – with a stationery earth surrounded by concentric crystal spheres holding the planets). Aquinas's Five Ways (proofs of God's existence) were all indebted to some degree to Aristotelian arguments. Above all, in shaping his naturalistic version of Christianity, he – like Aristotle but in opposition to the Neoplatonists – was anxious to defend the notion of humans as agents genuinely responsible for their own actions.

The very success of Aquinas's synthesis proved in the end to be its undoing. Aristotelianism quickly established itself as unquestioned dogma, and some of the more speculative parts in particular, such as Aristotle's conception of the universe, became increasingly vulnerable to attack as scientific knowledge advanced. His essentially teleological account of nature – the idea that biological organisms, systems and processes are ultimately explicable in terms of their aims or purposes – remained the orthodox view long after its foundations had been substantially undermined by advances in astronomy, mechanics and elsewhere. Aristotelians often did little to help their own cause, stubbornly choosing to defend the least defensible parts of Aristotle's philosophy. In 1624 the Parliament of Paris decreed that 'on pain of death no person should either hold or teach any doctrine opposed to Aristotle'. In a final irony, at the climax of the scientific revolution, one of the principal charges against Aristotelianism was its obscurantism and dogmatism; by this time the ancient Greek's insistence on empirical and scientific methodology had apparently been long forgotten.

the condensed idea
'The master of those who know'

03 The golden rule

The golden rule, popularly captured in the proverb 'Do as you would be done by', is one of the most ubiquitous of all moral principles. The underlying notion, appealing to the most basic human ethical sense, is expressed in some form or other in virtually every religious tradition, while few moral philosophers have failed either to invoke the rule or at least to remark on its relation to principles of their own.

The universal appeal of the golden rule is partly due to its sheer generality. Thus, according to particular taste and need, its dominant facets may be variously seen to include reciprocity, impartiality and universality. The rule's artless simplicity is also its weakness, however, making it an apparently easy target for cynics and sophisticates, who question how much practical guidance or good can be gained from its observance.

Whip that you may be whipped At the heart of the golden rule is a demand for consistency, but the egoist can consistently pursue his own self-interest and show no inconsistency in recommending that others do likewise. People take their pleasures in various ways, and the non-masochistic majority should be wary of the masochist who firmly adheres

> **What you do not wish for yourself, do not do to others . . . As you yourself desire standing, then help others achieve it; as you yourself desire success, then help others attain it.**
>
> **Confucius,** *c.*500 BC

timeline

1785

Kant defines categorical imperative in *Groundwork of the Metaphysics of Morals*

1863

J.S. Mill claims the golden rule for utilitarianism

to the golden rule. Yet when we try defining and refining the rule, we risk sapping its force. We may wish to specify the context and circumstances in which the rule is to apply, but if we are *too* specific, the rule begins to lose the universality that is a large part of its appeal.

Rather than seeing the golden rule as some kind of moral panacea, it is more fruitful to regard it as an essential ingredient, a necessary part of the foundations of our ethical thinking: a demand not only for consistency, but for fairness; the requirement that you seek imaginatively to put yourself in some else's position, that you show to others the kind of respect and understanding that you would hope to receive yourself. As such, the golden rule is a useful antidote to the kind of moral myopia that often afflicts people when their own close interests are at stake.

> **So in everything, do unto others as you would have them do unto you, for this sums up the law and the prophets.**
>
> **Jesus**, *c.* AD 30

JFK and the golden rule

A notably effective appeal to the golden rule was made in June 1963 by US president John F. Kennedy. In a televised address to the American people, at a time when racial tensions were spilling over into overt violence and civil unrest, Kennedy argued passionately against segregation and discrimination on grounds of race:

'The heart of the question is whether all Americans are to be afforded equal rights and equal opportunities, whether we are going to treat our fellow Americans as we want to be treated. If an American, because his skin is dark, cannot eat lunch in a restaurant open to the public, if he cannot send his children to the best public school available, if he cannot vote for the public officials who will represent him, if, in short, he cannot enjoy the full and free life which all of us want, then who among us would be content to have the color of his skin changed and stand in his place?'

Impelled by Kennedy's appeal to fairness and, six months later, by the trauma of his assassination, Congress passed into law in 1964 some of the most radical and sweeping civil rights legislation in US history.

Kant's categorical imperative The great German philosopher Immanuel Kant claimed that the golden rule lacked the rigour to qualify as a universal law, yet its imprint is clearly visible in the fundamental principle – the so-called categorical imperative – that underlies his whole ethical system. Indeed, Kantian ethics can be seen as the project of fashioning a version of the golden rule that is binding on all agents following the dictates of reason.

> **Hurt no one so that no one may hurt you.**
>
> Muhammad, c. AD 630

To explain what a categorical imperative is, Kant first tells us what it is not, by contrasting it with a *hypothetical* imperative. Suppose I tell you what to do by issuing an order (an imperative): 'Stop smoking!' Implicitly, there is a string of conditions that I might attach to this command – 'if you don't want to ruin your health', for instance, or 'if you don't want to waste your money'. Of course, if you are unconcerned about your health and money, the order carries no weight with you and you need not comply. With a categorical imperative, by contrast, there are no ifs attached, implicit or explicit. 'Don't lie!' and 'Don't kill people!' are injunctions that are not hypothesized on any aim or desire that you may or may not have and must be obeyed as a matter of duty, unconditionally and regardless of the consequences. A categorical imperative of this kind, unlike a hypothetical imperative, constitutes a fundamental principle of morality, or moral law.

In Kant's view, beneath every action there is an underlying rule of conduct, or maxim. Such maxims can have the *form* of categorical

Do as I say, not as I do

The essence of the golden rule is moral consistency, and it is the flouting of this – not practising what you preach – that makes hypocrisy so obnoxious. The basic objection to the adulterous vicar who eulogizes the sanctity of marriage or the politician who takes a backhander while fulminating against financial impropriety is inconsistency: between their stated opinions and the beliefs that are evinced by their behaviour; between the importance they claim to attach to certain propositions and the indifference that one can infer from their actions.

imperatives, however, without qualifying as moral laws, because they fail to pass a test, which is itself a supreme or overarching form of categorical imperative and is clearly imbued with the spirit of the golden rule:

> 'Act only in accordance with a maxim that you can at the same time will to become a universal law.'

In other words, an action is morally permissible only if it accords with a rule that you can consistently and universally apply to yourself and others. For instance, we might propose a maxim that it is permissible to lie. But lying is only possible against a background of (some level of) truth-telling – if everyone lied all the time, no one would believe anyone – and for that reason it would be self-defeating and in some sense irrational to wish for lying to become a universal law. The requirement of universality thus rules out certain kinds of conduct on purely logical grounds.

Universalizability Amongst recent philosophers, one of the most influential champions of the golden rule has been the English philosopher R.M. Hare. Taking as his starting point the eminently Kantian insight that moral terms have a prescriptive element – they tell us what to do or how to behave – Hare's ethical theory ('prescriptivism') proposes that the essence of moral terms is that they are action-guiding; saying that killing is wrong is equivalent to giving and accepting a command – 'Don't kill!'. The essential feature of ethical judgements that distinguishes them from other kinds of command is, in Hare's view, that they are 'universalizable': if I issue a moral injunction, I am thereby committed to holding that that injunction should be obeyed by anyone (including myself) in relevantly similar circumstances; in other words, I must comply with the golden rule.

> **In the golden rule of Jesus of Nazareth, we read the complete spirit of the ethics of utility.**
>
> **J.S. Mill, _Utilitarianism_, 1863**

the condensed idea
Do as you would be done by

04 Altruism

A little after 09:00 on 11 September 2001, minutes after the lethal impact of United Airlines Flight 175, a small group of terrified survivors huddled in the wrecked sky lobby on the 78th floor of the World Trade Center's South Tower. Some had suffered terrible burns; all were traumatized by the appalling chaos and carnage surrounding them: they were praying for help but in fact – unwittingly, in the doomed tower – were merely awaiting death. Suddenly, out of nowhere, a young man appeared, stripped to his T-shirt and wearing a red bandana to shield his nose and mouth. Quickly taking charge, he guided the dazed survivors to an open stairwell, which was shrouded in smoke and debris. Fifteen floors below, he left those whose lives he had saved (including a young black woman he had carried on his back) and headed back up to repeat his heroics in the inferno above.

Six months later the body of 24-year-old equities trader and volunteer firefighter Welles Crowther was recovered in the main lobby of the South Tower. Within a few weeks he had been identified by two women who owed their lives to him as the 'man in the red bandana'. He had apparently been setting off on yet another rescue mission at the moment he was crushed by the collapsing tower. When the extent of his courage became clear, his mother spoke of her pride in his 'sense of duty to help others', while his father expressed a hope of the legacy his son might leave: 'If Welles's story helps people to think of others, then God bless them, God bless him.'

timeline

It is noteworthy that both of Crowther's parents singled out their son's selfless regard for others. Alongside his great courage, he gave an extraordinary display of altruism: a willingness to set the interests and welfare of others above his own – to the ultimate degree of sacrificing his own life. It would be offensive to our ordinary sense of morality to suggest that the young man's behaviour was motivated in any way by self-interest, as the excellence of his actions would thereby be diminished. Yet the notion of pure altruism has been philosophically perplexing since antiquity. Several of the sophists – philosophers for hire – who locked horns with Plato's Socrates glibly assumed that benevolence to others was apparent only and that the true motive, if you scratched beneath the surface, was always self-interest. Many more recent thinkers have argued either that people are, as a matter of fact, motivated by concern for their own interests (psychological egoism); or that their behaviour *should* be guided by such concerns (ethical egoism). Thus Thomas Hobbes, for instance, takes it for granted that people in the 'state of nature' will be in constant conflict with others to further their own ends; while Friedrich Nietzsche condemns charity and altruistic behaviour as manifestations of the slave morality by which the weak have subdued the strong. And particularly over the last century and a half, since the revolutionary work of Charles Darwin, these many philosophical doubts have been reinforced by biological ones.

> **Of the voluntary acts of every man, the object is some good to himself.**
>
> **Thomas Hobbes, 1651**

> **Men often act knowingly against their interest.**
>
> **David Hume, 1740**

Do the good die young? Humans are by no means the only animals to exhibit altruistic (or apparently altruistic) behaviour. Certain kinds of monkeys and deer, for instance, give alarm calls or signs as a warning to other members of their group that a predator is nearby, even though by doing so they risk danger to themselves. In social insects such as bees and ants, certain castes do not (and cannot) breed, devoting themselves entirely to the well-being of the colony. It doesn't matter that such behaviour is typically instinctive rather than deliberate; the important point is that it has the effect of promoting others' interests at the expense of the agent.

1887–8	1859	11th Sept. 2001
Nietzsche attacks altruism's role in emasculating the true self	Darwin explains evolution by natural selection in the *Origin of Species*	9/11 attack on New York's World Trade Center

The difficulty of accommodating such behaviour within the framework of Darwin's theory of evolution is clear enough. The principal mechanism by which Darwinian evolution proceeds is natural selection – the 'survival of the fittest': animals that are endowed with qualities that allow them to survive longer and produce more offspring (on average) are 'selected' by nature; and hence those beneficial qualities (to the extent that they are inheritable) tend to survive and become more common in the population. In such circumstances we expect animals to behave in ways that enhance their own life prospects, not those of others. No forms of behaviour could be *less* likely than altruism and self-sacrifice to enhance an agent's survival prospects, so we might predict that animals disposed to act altruistically would be at a great selective disadvantage and would rapidly be eliminated from the population by their more selfish fellows. Darwin himself, well aware of the problem, summed it up in his *Descent of Man* (1871):

> 'It is extremely doubtful whether the offspring of the more sympathetic and benevolent parents . . . would be reared in greater number than the children of selfish and treacherous parents . . . He who was ready to sacrifice his own life, rather than betray his comrades, would often leave no offspring to inherit his noble nature.'

A tyranny against nature

One of the most virulent and influential attacks on altruism (and conventional morality in general) was launched by the German philosopher Friedrich Nietzsche near the end of the 19th century. He regarded benevolence as a 'tyranny against nature' – an inversion or perversion of the natural order. Spurred on by the Christian church and driven by resentment and jealousy, the weak and the ugly have initiated a 'slave revolt' against the strong and the beautiful. Cowed by morality's weapons of guilt and blame, the best and noblest of humanity unwittingly connive in their own oppression and enslavement, blinded to their true and natural goal – the will to power.

> **Nature's stern discipline enjoins mutual help at least as often as warfare. The fittest may also be the gentlest.**
>
> **Theodosius Dobzhansky, 1962**

Looking after one's own An explanation of this puzzle begins
to emerge when we recognize that it does not necessarily have to be the
'offspring of the benevolent parents' that carry altruistic tendencies into
the next generation: it may be sufficient for cousins and other relatives to
do so. In other words, it is not the survival of an altruistic individual that
matters, provided that the genetic material that contributed to its altruistic
disposition survives, and this can be achieved
through relatives that share some of the same
genes. For natural selection to operate in this way,
through so-called 'kin selection', we would expect
altruistic individuals to favour relatives as
beneficiaries of their altruistic behaviour, and this
has indeed been confirmed by research.

> **'The weak and ill-constituted shall perish: first principle of our philanthropy.'**
>
> **Friedrich Nietzsche, 1888**

Nobody who believes in Darwinian evolution (and that includes virtually
every biologist on the planet) would deny that humans are the products
of evolutionary processes, so mechanisms such as kin selection offer
explanations of how altruistic behaviour may have evolved in humans.
The problem, of course, is that biological altruism of this kind is not 'pure'
or 'real' altruism at all: it is a way of explaining behaviour that benefits
others in terms of the agent's (ultimate) self-interest – or at least in terms
of its genes' interest. And if this is the *only* way of explaining altruistic
behaviour, it is obvious that 'real' altruism – behaviour that benefits others
irrespective of, or in opposition to, the agent's interests – cannot exist in a
Darwinian world.

Deep-rooted intuitions, not to mention cases like the story of Welles
Crowther, may lead us to balk at such a conclusion. Like David Hume, we
are likely to protest that 'The voice of nature and experience seems plainly
to oppose the selfish theory' – the idea that human benevolence can be
reduced ultimately to self-interest. Large areas of human behaviour are
hard to explain in purely evolutionary terms, and to pretend otherwise is to
ignore the subtle role played by cultural and other influences. Nevertheless,
the lessons of biology may leave us with an uncomfortable sense of the
degree to which self-interest underlies what we ordinarily think of as
benevolent and altruistic behaviour.

the condensed idea
Selfless or selfish?

05 Liberty

'Is life so dear, or peace so sweet, as to be purchased at the price of chains and slavery? Forbid it, Almighty God! I know not what course others may take; but as for me, give me liberty or give me death!' So, famously, Patrick Henry expressed his preference for death over loss of liberty, as in March 1775 he implored his fellow Virginians to take up arms against the British in order to win independence.

Few since have seriously demurred from Henry's view. Certainly no US president has done so: not Abraham Lincoln, who on the battlefield at Gettysburg in 1863 invoked the spirit of a 'new nation, conceived in Liberty'; nor John F. Kennedy, who in 1961 pledged to 'pay any price, bear any burden . . . to assure the survival and the success of liberty'; nor George W. Bush, who vowed 40 years later that his 'war on terror' would bring 'an age of liberty, here and across the world'. Generally this most basic of political ideals – liberty or freedom – is accorded a degree of importance commensurate with the great hardships endured to win it: struggles against the dominance of religions that were ready to kill those who questioned their orthodoxies; against the power of absolute monarchies supposedly sanctioned by divine right; against slavery, prejudice and ignorance; against the subjection of women; against the victimization of political dissidents; and much more besides.

Almost no-one doubts that liberty is one of the most basic human rights, and many would say that it is a right worth fighting for and, if necessary, dying for. Yet, in spite of the broad consensus on its importance, there is surprisingly little agreement about the nature of liberty.

Berlin's two concepts of liberty The most influential recent analysis of liberty is due to the great 20th-century political philosopher

timeline

July 1776	July 1789	Aug. 1789	1859
US Declaration of Independence	Fall of the Bastille	French revolutionaries' Declaration of the Rights of Man and of the Citizen	Publication of J.S. Mill's *On Liberty*

Isaiah Berlin. At the heart of his study of liberty lies a crucial distinction between positive and negative freedom.

We often think of freedom as being the absence of any external restriction or coercion: you are free so long as there is no obstacle preventing you from doing what you want to do. This is the kind of freedom that Berlin calls 'negative freedom'. However, no one can enjoy unfettered freedom in this sense without encroaching on the freedom of others, so when people live together in societies, some degree of compromise is needed to prevent liberty turning into licence. The compromise generally sanctioned by classical liberals, of whom the Victorian philosopher J.S. Mill is a prime example, is the so-called 'harm principle'. This stipulates that individuals should be permitted to act in any way that does not bring harm to others; only where such harm is done is society justified in imposing restrictions. In some such way we can define an area of private liberty that is sacrosanct and immune to outside interference and authority.

> **What freedom means is being allowed to sing in my bath as loudly as will not interfere with my neighbour's freedom to sing a different tune in his.**
>
> **Tom Stoppard, 2002**

Suppose a person has liberty in this negative sense, but lacks the resources (money, education, social status, etc.) to act on it. Is such a person really free in a full and meaningful sense? In seeking to transform such purely formal freedom to something more real and substantial, we may come to endorse forms of intervention that belong more properly to Berlin's positive version of liberty. While negative freedom is freedom *from* external interference, positive freedom is usually characterized as freedom *to* achieve certain ends – in other words, as a form of empowerment that allows individuals to fulfil their potential and to reach a state of personal autonomy and self-mastery.

Whereas negative freedom is essentially interpersonal, existing as a relation *between* people, positive freedom, by contrast, is intrapersonal –

Nov. 1863	Oct. 1958	Jan. 1961	Sept. 2001
Abraham Lincoln delivers Gettysburg Address	Isaiah Berlin gives lecture entitled 'Two Concepts of Liberty'	John F. Kennedy delivers Inaugural Address	George W. Bush delivers 'war on terror' speech before Congress

something that develops and is nurtured *within* an individual. It presupposes some sort of division of the self into higher and lower parts, where the attainment of freedom is marked by the triumph of the (morally, rationally) preferable higher self. It was in part due to this concept of a divided self, which Berlin felt was implicit in the positive understanding of liberty, that he was so wary of it. Once those in authority take the paternalistic view that people have a 'better side' that needs to be encouraged – and a worse side that needs to be suppressed – it is a short step for the powerful to assume the right 'to ignore the actual wishes of men or societies, to bully, oppress, torture in the name, and on behalf, of [people's] "real" selves'. Marching beneath the banner of (positive) freedom, government turns to tyranny, setting a particular goal for society and prioritizing a certain way of life for its citizens. Berlin's own deep distrust of positive freedom was fuelled by the enormities of the 20th century (especially the totalitarian horrors of Stalin's Soviet Union), but others have taken a more favourable view of its potential for personal transformation and self-realization.

> ‘Those who have ever valued liberty for its own sake believed that to be free to choose, and not to be chosen for, is an inalienable ingredient in what makes human beings human.’
>
> **Isaiah Berlin, 1969**

Liberty's troubled defence   On 28 October 1886 one of the world's most iconic artefacts – *Liberty Enlightening the World*, more commonly known as the Statue of Liberty – was formally dedicated in New York harbour. Presented to the United States by the people of France, it was an entirely fitting gift, for the two countries had long been linked by a shared concept of liberty that had underpinned their two momentous revolutions in the last quarter of the 18th century. The US Declaration of Independence of 1776, founded on the natural-rights theory of government devised by John Locke and others, proclaimed the 'self-evident' truth that 'all men are . . . endowed by their Creator with certain unalienable Rights [and] that among these are Life, Liberty and the pursuit of Happiness'. Just 13 years later this document, together with the Enlightenment theory that underlay it, became the inspiration for the Declaration of the Rights of Man and of the Citizen issued by the French revolutionaries.

Liberty, in company with justice and democracy, has since become the principal and unquestioned yardstick by which the so-called 'liberal democracies' of the West are measured. There is some oddity, at least, in the elevation of the USA and France to the position of historical antecedent and paradigm for such political systems. Liberty's antithesis, slavery, remained legal in the USA for nearly a century after it won its independence, while the three ideological pillars of the French Revolution – liberty, equality and fraternity – were never fully or permanently realized in revolutionary France itself. The 'serene and blessed liberty' proclaimed by a Parisian newspaper at the Fall of the Bastille in 1789 had been transformed, in the space of just four years, to Robespierre's Reign of Terror, in which all political opposition was swept aside and some 17,000 suspected counter-revolutionaries were guillotined.

Intellectual freedom

In his *On Liberty* of 1859, John Stuart Mill gives a passionate defence of freedom of speech and expression. He warns us of the dangers of a culture of prejudice and intellectual repression, in which questioning and criticism of received opinion is discouraged and 'the most active and inquiring intellects' are afraid to enter into 'free and daring speculation on the highest subjects'. In a similar spirit Immanuel Kant had earlier protested that the intellect needs liberty (a liberty that he found sadly lacking) in order to achieve full maturity: 'Nothing is required for enlightenment except freedom; and the freedom in question is the least harmful of all, namely, the freedom to use reason publicly in all matters.'

The French revolutionaries' excuse for their total disregard for civil liberties at the height of the Terror in 1793–4 was the threat of counter-revolution at home and the menace of foreign armies abroad. Sadly, subsequent liberal democracies, copying the French model rather than improving on it, have habitually responded to the emergency of war or to the threat of terrorism by trampling over time-honoured laws and enacting repressive ones in their stead. In September 2001, in the wake of the 9/11 attacks on New York and Washington, US president Bush declared a 'war on terror' – 'civilization's fight . . . the fight of all who believe in progress and pluralism, tolerance and freedom' – but over the following years the casualties of this war included civil liberties and human rights. The abuse and torture of prisoners by US military personnel at Abu Ghraib in Iraq and the detention and treatment of so-called 'enemy combatants' at Camp X-Ray in Guantanamo Bay, Cuba, are merely the latest examples of the tired claim that liberty's best defender is illiberality.

> **❝O liberty! what crimes are committed in thy name!❞**
>
> **Madame Roland (before her execution by guillotine), 1793**

the condensed idea
Something worth dying for?

06 Tolerance

'We ought to be tolerant of one another, because we are all weak, inconsistent, liable to fickleness and error. Shall a reed laid low in the mud by the wind say to a fellow reed fallen in the opposite direction: "Crawl as I crawl, wretch, or I shall petition that you be torn up by the roots and burned?"'

So Voltaire concludes the article on tolerance in his *Philosophical Dictionary* of 1764. Appealing to principles of individual liberty and freedom of thought, the French writer gives a classic statement of one of the most characteristic of Enlightenment virtues. 'Think for yourselves and let others enjoy the privilege to do so too,' as Voltaire neatly sums it up elsewhere.

The practice of toleration and its attendant virtue, tolerance, are so ingrained in liberal thinking that we perhaps take for granted their significance both in the operation of well-ordered states and in the relations between right-minded individuals. Such a ready assumption should not blind us to how poorly toleration is realized in the real world. Members of the major religions – Muslim, Christian, Hindu, Jew – are at each other's throats in numerous countries, quite unwilling to tolerate their opponents or their religious beliefs. The situation is little better when it comes to non-religious differences, where people are divided by skin colour, ethnic origins, sexual preferences and lifestyle choices, amongst many other things. It is invariably the case that these examples of intolerance and bigotry – as they would be described by tolerant liberals – would not be acknowledged as such by their perpetrators. Indeed, there are difficulties with the notion of toleration, historical and conceptual, that have led some to doubt whether this Enlightenment virtue *par excellence* is straightforwardly enlightened or virtuous.

> **I disapprove of what you say, but I will defend to the death your right to say it.**
>
> **Voltaire (as paraphrased by Evelyn Beatrice Hall), 1906**

timeline

1689
Locke's *Letter Concerning Toleration* argues for separation of church and state

1764
Enlightenment view of tolerance given in Voltaire's *Philosophical Dictionary*

The paradox of toleration Much of the difficulty concerning the concept of tolerance is caused by a troublesome paradox that lies at its core. Broadly speaking, tolerance is a disposition to put up with things (or people) of which one disapproves, in situations where one has the capacity to intervene but chooses not to. The disapproval involved can lie anywhere on a spectrum from mild distaste to strong aversion, and the level of tolerance is proportionate to the degree of disapproval. In other words, you need to display a high degree of toleration to restrain yourself from intervening in something that you find highly distasteful. The paradox arises when tolerance is considered to be a virtue (as it usually is) and the objectionable beliefs or practices themselves are held to be in some sense morally wrong or bad. On this reading, it is virtuous – it is a morally good thing – to let something morally bad happen; and the worse it is, the more virtuous you are in putting up with it. But how can it be good to let a bad thing happen? If you can stop it happening (which by definition you can), surely you should?

> **Human diversity makes tolerance more than a virtue; it makes it a requirement for survival.**
> **René Dubos, 1981**

One way out of the paradox is clear enough. We need to show that there are reasons for toleration robust enough to outweigh those that urge intervention; to show that it would actually be wrong *not* to tolerate what is wrong. In the classical liberal tradition, the most influential demonstration of this kind was given by John Stuart Mill, who suggests that the grounds for toleration that 'trump' those for intervention are human diversity, which is inherently valuable, and respect for human autonomy – the capacity that allows individuals to make their own choices in life. In his essay *On Liberty* (1859), he argues that a person's

> 'own mode of laying out his existence is the best, not because it is the best in itself, but because it is his own mode. Human beings are not like sheep; and even sheep are not undistinguishably alike. A man cannot get a coat or a pair of boots to fit him, unless they are either made to his measure, or he has a whole warehouseful to choose from: and is it easier to fit him with a life than with a coat . . .?'

1859

J.S. Mill's *On Liberty*
argues for tolerance in
light of human autonomy

1995

UNESCO issues Declaration
of Principles on Tolerance

Religious toleration In modern liberal, pluralist societies tolerance is underpinned by the value given to autonomy and to the individual's right to make up their own mind and form their own opinions. There are limits to toleration, of course, but in general people are permitted to do and think what they like, provided that their actions and beliefs do not harm others. The harm in question usually involves injury to someone else's autonomy, so toleration does not have to extend to theft or murder, for instance, nor to the many less flagrant infringements of others' rights. But harm can come in many forms, and what harm could be greater, in the view of (say) a devout Christian, than the soul's damnation and forfeiture of eternal life? An appeal to autonomy – to a person's right to shape his own destiny – is neither here nor there, if the destiny in question

Harmony in difference

Born of centuries of religious schism and strife and baptised in unknown quantities of human blood, tolerance now stands as one of the pillars of liberal theory. In 1995 the United Nations Educational, Scientific and Cultural Organization (UNESCO) issued its Declaration of Principles on Tolerance, elevating this much-disputed disposition to the status of guiding principle in the establishment of global peace and harmony:

'Tolerance is respect, acceptance and appreciation of the rich diversity of our world's cultures, our forms of expression and ways of being human. It is fostered by knowledge, openness, communication, and freedom of thought, conscience and belief. Tolerance is harmony in difference . . . the virtue that makes peace possible, [it] contributes to the replacement of the culture of war by a culture of peace . . .

Tolerance is the responsibility that upholds human rights, pluralism (including cultural pluralism), democracy and the rule of law.

It involves the rejection of dogmatism and absolutism . . .

The practice of tolerance . . . means that one is free to adhere to one's own convictions and accepts that others adhere to theirs. It means accepting the fact that human beings, naturally diverse in their appearance, situation, speech, behaviour and values, have the right to live in peace and to be as they are . . .

In the modern world, tolerance is more essential than ever before. It is an age marked by the globalization of the economy and by rapidly increasing mobility, communication, integration and inter-dependence, large-scale migrations and displacement of populations, urbanization and changing social patterns. Since every part of the world is characterized by diversity, escalating intolerance and strife potentially menaces every region . . .'

is everlasting damnation. A little bit of persecution is a small price to pay for an eternity of paradise.

The idea that tolerance should extend to matters of religion would have appeared strange, if not intolerable, to most people in 17th-century Europe. In accordance with its claim to be the one true faith, Christianity was inherently intolerant of other religions and equally unwilling to accept schisms and heresies within its own ranks. Indeed, up until the 17th century and beyond, the debate over toleration was largely driven by and restricted to religious matters. The Wars of Religion in which Protestant and Catholic tore Europe apart in their eagerness to shed each other's blood were driven principally by the theologically inspired intolerances of those who had no doubt that it was their right and duty to crush religious dissent and to impose orthodoxy. Desperate to end the seemingly interminable conflict, various post-Reformation thinkers began to ask whether human knowledge could encompass the divine will with sufficient certitude to justify persecution, while others questioned the possibility of using coercion to change beliefs (or at least to change them in such a way as to make them pleasing to God). A more pragmatic line of argument pointed to the all-enveloping civil strife caused by intolerance and urged tolerance as a matter of political expediency. However, such down-to-earth reasoning was never likely to persuade those standing high on religious principle.

> **❝I affirm that the magistrate's power extends not to the establishing of any articles of faith, or forms of worship, by the force of his laws.❞**
>
> **John Locke, 1689**

One of the best-known contributions to the debate over religious toleration is John Locke's *Letter Concerning Toleration* (1689), and it is this document that has done more than any other to shape the modern liberal perspective. Locke agrees that voluntary conviction of a kind required by God cannot be enforced by compulsion, but his main purpose is to 'distinguish exactly the business of civil government from that of religion'. He insists that it is none of the state's business to interfere in the 'care of souls' and that in this area the application of its penalties is 'absolutely impertinent'. The mischief, in Locke's view, lies in the confusion of the functions of church and state, and his insistence on strictly separating them has provided one of the central pillars of modern liberal society.

the condensed idea
A troubled and paradoxical virtue

07 Scepticism

Given the current rate of progress, it is probably only a matter of time before human technology reaches a level of sophistication such that it can create incredibly sophisticated computer simulations of human minds and of worlds for those minds to inhabit. Maintaining such simulated worlds will require relatively tiny computer resources – a single laptop of the future could be home to thousands or millions of simulated minds – so in all probability simulated minds will vastly outnumber biological ones. The quality of the simulation will be so high that the experiences of biological and simulated minds will be indistinguishable, so the latter will be totally unaware that they are simulated. But they will be wrong. We, of course, know that we are not computer-simulated minds living in a simulated world . . .

Or do we? That is certainly what we *would* think, but how could we possibly tell? How do we know that such computer expertise has not already been attained and such minds already simulated? Indeed, given the logic of the scenario outlined above, it is in fact much more likely than not that we are already living in just such a simulated world.

Of vats and virtual worlds Serious food for thought, prepared according to a recipe devised in 2003 by the Swedish philosopher Nick Bostrom. Bostrom's simulation argument (simplified here) is not the first argument to raise the possibility that what we believe about ourselves and our world is grossly mistaken. In 1981 the US philosopher Hilary Putnam told a celebrated story of an evil scientist who removes a person's brain and places it in a vat of nutrients, where it is connected to a super-powerful

timeline

5th century BC	c.300 BC	AD 1637
Socrates' dialectic method undermines opponents' dogmatic positions	Pyrrho of Elis counsels tranquillity through suspension of belief	Descartes turns scepticism against the sceptics

computer that gives the person – or is that the brain? – the impression that everything is perfectly normal. It sounds like a nightmare, the stuff of science fiction, but of course that is exactly what you would say if you *were* a brain in a vat. The point is that it is hard to see how you could know for certain that you are not, and if you cannot rule out the possibility, all the things you think you know will turn out to be false. And if that's possible – just possible – you don't really know anything at all, do you?

Scenarios of the kind envisaged by Putnam and Bostrom have always been powerful weapons in the arsenal of the philosophical sceptic. As a philosophical position, scepticism sets out to challenge our claims to knowledge. We think that we know all sorts of things, but how and on what grounds can we defend those claims? Our supposed knowledge of the world is based on perceptions gained through our senses, but are not such perceptions always prone to error? Can we ever be sure that we are not hallucinating or dreaming, or that our memory is not playing tricks? If the experience of dreaming is indistinguishable from our waking experience, we can never be certain, in any particular case, that something we think to be the case is in fact the case – that what we take to be true is in fact true. There is always, it seems, the possibility that we are brains bobbing about in vats or virtual avatars in a computer-simulated reality.

> **Every passion is mortified by it [sceptical philosophy], except the love of truth; and that passion never is, nor can be, carried to too high a degree.**
>
> **David Hume, 1748**

The Greek sceptics Since its origins in ancient Greece, scepticism has typically developed as a strategy against forms of dogmatism that claim, in a particular area or in general, to have established a definitive view of how things stand in the world and/or in heaven. Anticipating concerns that were to re-emerge 2000 years later, Greek scepticism was motivated primarily by the seemingly unbridgeable gulf between appearance and reality – by the fact that our means of engaging with the world always leave us at one remove from truth and that it is always possible in principle to present counterexamples against any claim to knowledge. Though far from sceptical himself, Plato's Socrates employs a probing dialectical

1748	1981	2003
Hume suggests that 'natural instinct' will save us from sceptical despair	Hilary Putnam paints brain-in-a-vat scenario	Simulation argument suggests that we may be living in a virtual world

method that seems capable of undermining any dogmatic claim made by his contemporaries, and the scepticism that could be inferred from his claim that wisdom lies in awareness of one's own ignorance left a deep impression on his successors. The most influential sceptic, known to us only through the writings of others, was Pyrrho of Elis, who was active around 300 BC. His response to the essentially provisional nature of truth-claims – to the fact that questions of knowledge could never be finally decided – was to counsel suspension of belief whence came a tranquillity that would be proof against the disappointment inevitable in the frustrated search for certainty.

From doubt to certainty? Scepticism resurfaced with particular vigour in the 15th and 16th centuries, when the first stirrings of the scientific revolution led people to question the proper basis of knowledge and the validity of theological truth. In a deep historical irony, the man who stepped forward to dispel sceptical doubts once and for all succeeded only in pushing scepticism to the centre of the stage and ensuring that its defeat would remain one of the central tasks of subsequent philosophy.

The Frenchman René Descartes was himself at the vanguard of the new science sweeping through Europe in the 17th century, and it was his ambitious plan to cast aside the tired dogmas of the medieval world and to 'establish the sciences' on the firmest of foundations. To this end his plan was to turn scepticism against the sceptics by adopting the most rigorous 'method of doubt'. Not content to pick out the odd rotten apple (to use his own metaphor), he empties the barrel of beliefs completely, discarding any that are open to the slightest degree of doubt. In a final twist, he imagines an evil demon (the clear ancestor of Putnam's brain in a vat) whose sole object is to deceive him, and so ensures that even the apparently self-evident truths of geometry and mathematics are no longer certain.

Stripped of every belief that could conceivably be doubted, Descartes desperately casts about for some foothold, some firm ground on which to rebuild the edifice of human knowledge:

> 'I noticed that while I was trying to think everything false, it was necessary that I, who was thinking this, was something. And observing that this truth, 'I am thinking, therefore I exist' [*cogito ergo sum*], was so firm and sure that all the most extravagant suppositions of the sceptics were incapable of shaking it, I decided that I could accept it without scruple as the first principle of the philosophy I was seeking.'

Hume's mitigated scepticism

The fierce sceptical attack on Descartes's project of establishing the new science on foundations of certainty eventually mellowed, in the following century, into a constructive, 'mitigated' scepticism that was especially due to the Scottish naturalist philosopher David Hume. Hume saw no means of evading the conclusions of full-blown scepticism (or Pyrrhonism, as he called it) and famously claimed that our beliefs about the world could be justified neither by inductive reasoning nor by causal necessity; the perceived patterns and uniformity in nature were, in his view, merely a matter of habit and custom. But he thought that our human nature would inevitably preserve us from complete doubt and lead us back to the beliefs of common sense, however unfounded: 'Philosophy would render us entirely Pyrrhonian, were not Nature too strong for it.' The upshot was a new approach to science and the acquisition of knowledge that was empirical and pragmatic; an intellectual modesty informed by a recognition that human faculties and the deliverances of reason are severely limited.

After he has dug down to bedrock, the rebuilding phase of Descartes's enterprise proves to be remarkably straightforward. Founded on belief in a non-deceiving God who will guarantee the veracity of our senses, the world is swiftly restored and the task of reconstructing our knowledge on a sound and sceptic-proof basis can begin. The force of Descartes's famous *cogito* has been continuously debated ever since, but most of his critics, contemporary and modern, have been unconvinced by his attempt to climb out of the sceptical hole that he had so adroitly dug for himself. He had summoned up the spectre of scepticism in order to exorcize it, but he signally failed to put it to rest and left later philosophers in thrall to its spell.

the condensed idea
The scourge of dogma

08 Reason

'The gods plant reason in mankind, of all good gifts the highest.' So said the tragic poet Sophocles in the 5th century BC, echoing an age-old view of the centrality of reason and rationality to mankind's understanding of itself and its position in the world. Sophocles' fellow Greeks generally concurred. Pythagoras, a shadowy figure from the 6th century BC, fell under the spell of numbers and their relations and is one of earliest thinkers known to venerate the powers of reason. Plato, in the 4th century BC, thought that the exercise of reason was the highest human good, as did his pupil Aristotle, who argued that reason was the very essence of a person – the aspect that set humans apart from other animals – and that its proper function was the key to man's well-being and happiness.

Reason lost none of its allure in the modern period, and from the 17th century it became enshrined as the supreme human attribute in the Enlightenment, which was accordingly known also as the Age of Reason. But there has been less agreement about the precise role of reason in the proper functioning of humans. In particular, reason has often been opposed to sensory perception and experience, broadly interpreted, as the most appropriate means of acquiring knowledge of how things stand in the world and how best humans should conduct themselves in it.

Rationalism and empiricism The Age of Reason was so called because its pioneers, first in England and a little later in Scotland and in continental Europe, saw themselves as raising the torch of reason to dispel the shadows of prejudice and superstition that had enveloped (as they

timeline

6th century BC	c.441 BC	c.350 BC
Pythagoras recognizes power of reason in discerning numerical relations	Sophocles' *Antigone* performed in Athens	Aristotle argues that reason sets humans apart from other animals

supposed) the previous medieval period. Henceforth, beliefs would be tested and approved on the touchstone of reason, rather than on the basis of clerical authority or tradition. The progress of science suggested, in general, that the world was intelligibly structured and that its secrets would be revealed by the power of rational thought. One of the greatest figures of the Enlightenment, the German philosopher Immanuel Kant, saw the new age as mankind's emergence from its infancy – a period of immaturity in which people lacked the 'resolve and courage to use [their reason] without the guidance of another'.

From early in the Enlightenment, however, there were signs of a rift between rationality and rationalism. Rationality – which required that beliefs be based on a proper evaluation of available evidence, that alternative explanations be considered, and so on – was widely accepted as the defining virtue of the age. In contrast, rationalism – the more specific view that reason is in some way a uniquely privileged means of apprehending certain fundamental truths – was immediately contentious. Descartes had founded his philosophical project on the rock of rational certainty, which was reached by reason alone and from which he hoped to corroborate all knowledge, including knowledge derived from the senses. The primacy he gave to reason in the acquisition of knowledge was broadly accepted by the other so-called Continental rationalists, Leibniz and Spinoza, but central aspects of his thesis were opposed by the British empiricists, Locke, Berkeley and Hume. Of the latter, Hume was most prominent in the task of limiting the scope of rationality, denying that it had an essential role in

Rationalism is a hideous monster when it claims for itself omnipotence. Attribution of omnipotence to reason is as bad a piece of idolatry as is worship of stock and stone believing it to be God. I plead not for the suppression of reason, but for a due recognition of that in us which sanctifies reason.

Mahatma Gandhi, 1926

AD **1637**	**1739–40**	**1781**	**1785**
Descartes extols reason as the ultimate guarantor of knowledge	Hume argues in *Treatise of Human Nature* that reason is slave of passions	In *Critique of Pure Reason* Kant expounds rationalist theory of knowledge	In *Groundwork* Kant argues that reason is the key determinant of moral action

the normal, empirical (experience-based) processes by which beliefs are formed. He also insisted that reason's part in deciding moral questions was secondary to that of 'sympathy' or human sentiment.

Slave of the passions?

The extent to which matters of right and wrong are subject to rational assessment has long been a bone of contention between rationalists and empiricists. As in the theory of knowledge, Kant and Hume are among the leading protagonists.

In his *Treatise of Human Nature* (1739–40), Hume gives a subjectivist account of morality. He argues that you will never find the vice in a supposedly vicious act 'till you turn your reflection into your own breast, and find a sentiment of disapprobation, which arises in you, towards this action. Here is a matter of fact; but 'tis the object of feeling, not of reason. It lies in yourself, not in the object.' All humans are naturally moved by a 'moral sense' or 'sympathy', which is essentially a capacity to share the feelings of happiness or misery of others; and it is this sentiment, rather than reason, that ultimately provides the motive for our moral actions. Reason is essential in understanding the consequences of our actions and in planning how to achieve our moral aims, but it is itself inert and unable to provide any impetus to action: in Hume's famous phrase, 'reason is, and ought only to be the slave of the passions'.

In his *Groundwork for the Metaphysics of Morals* (1785) Kant opposes the kind of position taken by Hume, defending the rationalist claim that pure reason, rather than feeling, custom or authority, informs and directs the will of a moral agent. Beneath every action, he argues, there is an underlying rule of conduct, or maxim, and such maxims qualify as moral laws if they accord with the fundamental standard of rationality, the so-called 'categorical imperative': 'Act only in accordance with a maxim that you can at the same time will to become a universal law.' In other words, an action is morally permissible only if it follows a rule that you can consistently and universally apply to yourself and others. We might, for instance, propose a maxim that it is permissible to lie or steal, but lying and stealing only make sense against a background of respect for truth and property, so it would be irrational to wish for them to become universal laws. For Kant, then, self-consistency is the acid test of morality, and such a principle can be apprehended by reason alone.

The most influential attempt to expound a rationalist theory of knowledge was made by Kant in his *Critique of Pure Reason* (1781). In a consciously grandiose move which he likened to Copernicus' revolution in astronomy, Kant set out to show that all previous philosophy had been done back to front: the underlying assumption had been that 'all our knowledge must conform to objects' – and for that reason it had failed – so he now suggested that the assumption be reversed and objects made to conform to our knowledge. There are, he argues, certain concepts or categories of thought, such as substance and causation, which we cannot learn from the world but which we are required to use in order to make sense of it. We can be certain that our logic and mathematics (for instance) will not become invalidated in the light of experience precisely because the patterns and conformities on which they are based have been abstracted from our own minds and imposed on the 'great blooming, buzzing confusion' of perceptions. And it is precisely this capacity to impose order and structure on this chaos of sensation that constitutes our powers of reasoning, or rationality.

The lure of mathematics

For rationalists who believe that reason is able to grasp truths that lie beyond the reach of sensory perception, the field of mathematics has always had a particular fascination. It appears to offer a paradigm of knowledge – a realm of abstract objects where insights are available only by means of rational inquiry. Thoroughgoing empiricists cannot let this go unchallenged, of course, so they either deny that the facts of mathematics can be known in this way or try to show that its conclusions are essentially tautologous or trivial. The latter course usually takes the form of arguing that the supposedly abstract facts of mathematics are actually human constructs and that mathematical thinking is at root a matter of convention: in the end there is consensus, not discovery; formal proof, not substantial truth.

the condensed idea
Master or slave of
the passions?

09 Punishment

'As one reads history . . . one is absolutely sickened, not by the crimes that the wicked have committed, but by the punishments that the good have inflicted; and a community is infinitely more brutalized by the habitual employment of punishment than it is by the occasional occurrence of crime.' In the jaunty guise of Marxist aesthete in *The Soul of Man under Socialism* (1891), Oscar Wilde elegantly captures what is perhaps the central paradox of society's uneasy relationship with crime and punishment. In meting out punishment and inflicting harm, the state's representatives knowingly cross normal ethical boundaries and in some sense emulate the depravity of the punished. In so doing, they apparently risk sullying the very name of civilization.

A central function of civilized society, most would agree, is to defend the rights of its citizens: to protect them from arbitrary treatment and harm, to allow them full political expression, to guarantee their freedom of speech and movement, and so on. So what business is it of society to deliberately inflict harm on its citizens, to exclude them from the political process, and to restrict their liberty to speak and move freely? For this is the prerogative that the state takes upon itself when it punishes its citizens for breaching the rules that it has itself, willy-nilly, imposed upon them.

From a philosophical point of view, then, the problem of punishment is to explain and justify the state apparently stooping to the level of the criminal in the very act of punishing him. In addressing this question, penologists generally follow two quite distinct lines of argument. Some stress the beneficial consequences that follow from punishing wrongdoers,

timeline

1789
Bentham argues that 'all punishment in itself is evil'

1823
Gaols Act, promoted by Elizabeth Fry, improves UK prison conditions

such as deterrence and protection of society. Others argue that punishment is a good thing in itself, as a form of retribution or as a statement of society's disapproval, irrespective of other benefits it may bring.

Just deserts It is a commonly held view that people should get what they deserve: just as they should benefit from behaving well, so they should suffer for behaving badly. The idea of retribution – that people should pay a price (for instance, in loss of liberty) for their wrongdoing – sits comfortably with this intuition. There may also be a perception that wrongdoing creates a kind of imbalance in society and that the moral equilibrium is restored by the wrongdoer 'repaying his debt' to the state. An offender is under an obligation not to break society's rules in order to gain an unfair advantage, and by doing so he incurs a penalty (a debt or due) which must be paid. The financial metaphor can neatly be extended to demand a fair transaction – that the severity of the penalty should match the severity of the crime.

> **If he who breaks the law is not punished, he who obeys it is cheated. This, and this alone, is why lawbreakers ought to be punished: to authenticate as good, and to encourage as useful, law-abiding behaviour.**
>
> **Thomas Szasz, 1974**

The idea that 'the punishment should fit the crime' gets support from the *lex talionis* (law of retaliation) of the Hebrew bible: 'an eye for an eye, a tooth for a tooth'. This implies that crime and punishment should be equivalent not only in severity but also in kind. Defenders of the death penalty, for instance, often plead that the only proper reparation for the taking of life is the loss of life. The point is less persuasive in the case of some other crimes, and few would suggest that rapists, for instance, should be raped (though in practice many are). This biblical support for the retributive theory gets to the heart of the main problem that it must address: the *lex talionis* is explicitly the work of a 'vengeful God', but in

1840
Modern concept of parole first introduced in Australian penal colonies

1891
Oscar Wilde's *The Soul of Man under Socialism* published

2007
China responsible for c.40% of confirmed executions worldwide

2008
Death penalty in use in 36 of 50 US states

order to keep a footing on the moral high ground, the retributivist must prevent retribution sliding into revenge. The idea that some crimes 'cry out' for punishment is sometimes dressed up as the notion that punishment expresses society's disgust or outrage at a particular act, but when retribution is thus stripped down to little more than an urge for vengeance, it scarcely appears adequate as a justification for punishment.

A necessary evil The idea that punishment is in any absolute sense a good thing is denied by those who focus instead on its social consequences. Indeed, Jeremy Bentham, the pioneer of classical utilitarianism, writing towards the end of the 18th century, was in no doubt that it is a thoroughly bad thing: 'All punishment is mischief: all punishment in itself is evil.'

> **'Does capital punishment tend to the security of the people? By no means. It hardens the hearts of men, and makes the loss of life appear light to them.'**
>
> **Elizabeth Fry, 1848**

From his perspective, punishment is at best a *necessary* evil: bad because it adds to the sum of human unhappiness; justified only in so far as the benefits it brings outweigh the unhappiness it causes. Nor is this a purely theoretical position, as the eminently practical 19th-century prison reformer Elizabeth Fry makes clear: 'Punishment is not for revenge, but to lessen crime and reform the criminal.'

In the case of serious offences, where public safety is at risk, the need for punishment in the form of incapacitation is hard to contest. To give an obvious example, a murderer who is incarcerated will not reoffend so long as he remains locked up. Another utilitarian ground on which punishment is supposedly justified is deterrence, but the case for this is not so easily made. On the face of it, it seems perverse to say that someone should be punished, not for the crime he has committed, but in order to deter others from offending in a similar way. There are also doubts over its effectiveness, in that studies suggest that the principal deterrent is not punishment but fear of capture.

The other main strand in utilitarian thinking about punishment is reform or rehabilitation of the criminal. There is an obvious attraction, to the liberal-minded at least, in the idea of seeing punishment as a form of therapy whereby offenders are re-educated and reformed in such a way that they can become full and useful members of society. Incentives for prisoners to behave well, such as the parole system, are examples of this kind of thinking in practice, but in general there are serious doubts over the ability of penal systems – most current systems, at least – to achieve this kind of benign outcome.

It is easy to pick holes in theories of punishment that invoke specific beneficial consequences – to cite cases where an offender does not present a danger to the public or does not need reform, or whose punishment would not have any deterrent value. Utilitarian theorists tend to adopt an inclusive approach, proposing a range of possible benefits that punishment may bring, without suggesting that all of them apply in every case. A few have gone even further and produced truly hybrid accounts, in which some space is also allowed for some element of retribution.

The death penalty

Proponents of capital punishment argue that it is right for the most serious crimes to be punished by the severest penalty. The supposed benefits, such as deterrence and protection of the public, are often mentioned, but most of those in favour would not seek to justify it on that basis alone: they think it is an appropriate response that reflects society's revulsion at the offence committed. Opponents counter by pointing out that the deterrent value is doubtful at best, that life imprisonment affords equal protection to the public, and that the very institution of capital punishment debases society. A powerful argument against the death penalty – the certainty that innocent people have been and will continue to be executed – is hard to resist. It might be argued that some offenders would regard death as preferable to a life behind bars and hence that they should be given the option of execution. On the other hand, if the aim of the judiciary is to inflict the heaviest possible punishment on those guilty of the most heinous crimes, the same argument could be used to justify keeping them alive in order to prolong their suffering.

the condensed idea
A necessary evil?

10 Materialism

'These people do not sit on the beach and listen to the steady roar of the pounding surf. They sit on the beach and listen to the aperiodic atmospheric compression waves produced as the coherent energy of the ocean waves is audibly redistributed in the chaotic turbulence of the shallows . . . They do not observe the western sky redden as the sun sets. They observe the wavelength distribution of incoming solar radiation shift towards the longer wavelengths as the shorter are increasingly scattered away from the lengthening atmospheric path they must take as terrestrial rotation turns us slowly away from their source.'

A humorous picture, perhaps, but there is a serious purpose behind Canadian-born philosopher Paul Churchland's 1979 vision of a future comprehended by science. In time, Churchland argues, as our scientific understanding advances, 'folk psychology' – our ordinary ways of thinking and expressing our mental lives, in terms of beliefs, desires, intentions and so on – will fall out of the picture, to be replaced by accurate concepts and descriptions drawn principally from neuroscience.

In company with most of today's philosophers and scientists, Churchland is a materialist (or physicalist). Impressed by the undeniable successes of science, he believes that the world and everything in it, including human beings, are composed of matter; that the universe is exclusively physical and explicable, in principle at least, purely in terms of physical laws and processes. One consequence of this is that nothing can be non-physical: there is no place for the spiritual or supernatural (including gods), nor for minds and mental phenomena to the extent that these are considered to

timeline

1640s	1710	1949
Descartes makes definitive statement of mind–body dualism	Bishop Berkeley propounds his immaterialist theory	Gilbert Ryle gives classic exposition of (logical) behaviourism

> **Nobody has the slightest idea how anything material could be conscious. Nobody even knows what it would be like to have the slightest idea about how anything material could be conscious. So much for the philosophy of consciousness.**
>
> **Jerry Fodor, US philosopher, 1992**

lie outside the physical realm. It is true that Churchland's 'eliminative materialism', so called from its ambition to jettison the concepts of folk psychology altogether, puts him at the radical end of materialist views. Yet the problem that he seeks to address is one faced by any materialist. We are all immediately conscious of our consciousness and of the rich array of mental phenomena with which it is populated. How can this teeming mental life, essentially subjective and private, possibly be accommodated within a purely physical account of the world – the kind of account, that is, that would be given by science, which is essentially objective, non-perspectival and publicly accessible?

Difficult relations Advances in neuroscience have established beyond doubt that mental and physical states are intimately related. With the exception of eliminativists like Churchland, who regard mental concepts as some sort of primitive, soon-to-be-obsolete constructs, materialists agree, broadly, that conscious experience emerges from, or is somehow determined by, electrochemical activity within the mass of neural fibres that constitutes the brain. Views differ considerably, however, on the nature of this 'emergence'.

At one time many materialists believed that a particular mental state could in principle be *identified* with a particular brain state, so that pain, for instance, might be correlated directly with the excitation of a certain set of neural fibres; pain, on this view, would not be some kind of by-product of a particular brain event – it would be (identical to) that brain event. However, so-called 'multiple realizability' – the recognition that a single mental state can be produced by several different physical states – put paid

1950s	**1974**	**1979**
Functionalism emerges as response to difficulties facing behaviourism	Thomas Nagel asks 'What is it like to be a bat?'	Eliminative materialism set forth by Paul Churchland

The idealist turn

One important motivation behind materialism is the severity of the difficulties facing the kind of mind–body dualism associated with the 17th-century French philosopher René Descartes. The relation between the two distinct realms of mental substance and material substance that he proposed is so deeply mysterious that there is an obvious appeal in adopting a monistic approach – in insisting that there is only one kind of 'stuff' in the world. While most have supposed that the one stuff in question is matter, a few have taken the other, idealist path, claiming that reality consists in nothing but minds and ideas.

The best-known idealist is the 18th-century Irish bishop, George Berkeley, who was fearful that if our perception of the world were limited (as he assumed it was) to 'resemblances, or ideas of things without', there would never be any way of verifying that these ideas actually resembled the external things themselves. There would always be a 'veil of perception' between us and the external world; we would be trapped in a world of representations, and the way would be open for the most extreme scepticism. Berkeley's surprising solution was to deny that there is an external, physical world – to claim that there is nothing behind the veil, and that reality consists in the ideas themselves. It is unfortunate for Berkeley that he is probably best remembered today for Samuel Johnson's famous though uncomprehending rebuttal of his immaterialist theory, recorded in Boswell's *Life of Johnson*: 'Striking his foot with mighty force against a large stone, [he exclaimed] "I refute it *thus*."'

to such naive identity theories. Today, materialists sometimes introduce a non-symmetrical dependency relation called 'supervenience', according to which the mental supervenes on the physical in the sense that the former is wholly determined by the latter, yet the latter could occur without the former. A parallel might be drawn with the aesthetic qualities of objects, which are determined by certain underlying physical features of the objects, yet remain distinct from those features. Without further elucidation, however, it seems that the notion of supervenience merely relocates the problem, rather than solving it.

Amongst recent materialists, probably the most influential and widely held view on the relation between mind and body is functionalism, a theory that grew out of an earlier, flawed position known as behaviourism (basically, the thesis that mental phenomena could be translated, without loss of content, into kinds of behaviour or dispositions to behaviour).

According to the functionalist account, mental states are functional (not physical) states: a certain mental state is identified as such by virtue of the role or function it has in relation to various inputs (the causes that typically bring it about), the effects it has on other mental states, and various outputs (the effects it typically has on behaviour). A significant problem for functionalism (as for behaviourism before it) is that it casts no light on mental states themselves and focuses purely on their relations to one another and to inputs (various kinds of stimuli) and outputs (various kinds of behaviour). In effect, functionalism says nothing about consciousness *per se* and so fails to address what is, for most people, the aspect that is most in need of explanation.

> **Without consciousness the mind–body problem would be much less interesting. With consciousness it seems hopeless.**
>
> **Thomas Nagel, US philosopher, 1974**

On being a bat

The lingering unease that many feel with materialist attempts to analyse our mental life and consciousness in purely physical terms was brilliantly captured by US philosopher Thomas Nagel in his 1974 paper 'What is it like to be a bat?' However hard I try to put myself in a bat's position – if I imagine myself flapping around in the dark, hanging upside down by my feet in an attic, catching moths by echo-location, etc. – I can never get beyond 'what it would be like for *me* to behave as a bat behaves. But that is not the question. I want to know what it is like for a *bat* to be a bat.' Nagel's point is that there is a 'subjective character of experience' – something that it is to *be* a particular organism, something it is like *for* the organism – that is always missing from materialist accounts. 'It is a mystery,' he concludes, 'how the true character of experiences could be revealed in the physical operation of that organism.' But that is all that science has to offer.

the condensed idea
Matter over mind

11 Relativism

'Today, having a clear faith is often labelled as fundamentalism. Whereas relativism, that is, letting oneself be "tossed here and there, carried about by every wind of doctrine", seems the only attitude that can cope with modern times. We are building a dictatorship of relativism that does not recognize anything as definitive and whose ultimate goal consists solely of one's own ego and desires.'

On 18 April 2005, the day before his election as Pope Benedict XVI, Cardinal Joseph Ratzinger delivered a sermon in which he traced social and moral disintegration, marked by practices such as same-sex marriage and abortion, to the spread of relativism. The certainty of faith, which 'opens us up to all that is good and gives us the knowledge to judge true from false', was being usurped, in his opinion, by a corrosive belief that any point of view is as good as another and hence that it is impossible to reach absolute truth on any matter. The result was a false and anarchic sense of freedom that had descended into moral, and especially sexual, licentiousness.

> **What is morality in any given time or place? It is what the majority then and there happen to like, and immorality is what they dislike.**
>
> **Alfred North Whitehead, 1953**

While the soon-to-be-new pope's conservative agenda is clear enough, he nevertheless accurately diagnoses the social and political significance of a way of thinking that has become widespread, particularly in liberal Western democracies. From the facile judgement on almost any issue that 'it's all relative', it has been commonly inferred that 'anything goes', and in recent decades there has been no shortage of libertarians who have adopted this as their mantra in opposing traditional or reactionary forces, religious and other.

timeline

6th century BC	5th century BC
Darius the Great of Persia shows (according to Herodotus) sensitivity to relativism	Extreme relativist Protagoras is defeated by Plato's Socrates

One man's meat . . . While relativism may provoke extreme positions, as in the example above, the need for some degree of moral and cultural relativism has been recognized for thousands of years. The historian Herodotus, writing in the 5th century BC, tells the story of a party of Greeks at the court of Darius, king of Persia, who were appalled at the suggestion that they might eat the dead bodies of their fathers; they were then confronted with members of a tribe, the Callatians, who followed just such a practice, only to discover that the Callatians were no less disgusted by the Greek habit of burning their dead. The historian then approvingly quotes the poet Pindar's saying that 'Custom is king of all': it is not a matter of one side being right and the other wrong – each group has its own code of customs and traditions, and judgements about their behaviour should not be made without regard to that code.

It is from such cases of cultural diversity that the fully fledged relativist argues that in general there are no absolute or universal truths: *all* moral appraisals should only be made relative to the social norms of the groups involved. The relativist's proposal is, in effect, that we treat moral judgements as if they were aesthetic ones. If you say you like oysters and I do not, we agree to differ: something is right or true for you but not for me. In such cases, if you sincerely say what you like, you cannot be wrong – it is true (for you). In the same way, the relativist argues, if we (as a society) approve of capital punishment, it is morally right (for us), and it is not something that we can be wrong about. And just as we would not try to persuade people to stop liking oysters or criticize them for doing so, so in the moral case persuasion or criticism would be out of place.

Moral disagreement The problem, of course, is that our moral lives are full of argument and censure. We habitually take strong positions on matters such as capital punishment, and we frequently change our minds over time. The out-and-out relativist would have to say that one thing was right for some people but not others, and right for us at one time but not at another. In the case of issues such as genocide, slavery, female circumcision and legal infanticide, this might be a bitter pill for the relativist to swallow.

AD **1962**

Kuhn's idea of paradigm shifts suggests that science is not immune to relativism

2005

Pope Benedict XVI decries the 'dictatorship of relativism'

Scientific relativism

In *The Structure of Scientific Revolutions* (1962) the American philosopher Thomas Kuhn challenged the conventional view of scientific progress as a cumulative process in which each generation of scientists builds on the discoveries of its predecessors. Instead, he suggested that the history of science was one of fitful and intermittent progress punctuated by revolutionary crises known as 'paradigm shifts'. A central feature of his picture is that scientific change is culturally embedded in a whole host of historical and other factors. Though Kuhn himself was keen to distance himself from a relativistic reading of his work, such an account of how science develops casts doubt on the idea that the aim of science is to discover objectively true facts about how things are in the world. For what sense does it make to talk of objective truth when each scientific community sets its own standards of evidence and proof and then filters everything through a web of existing assumptions and beliefs? The usual view is that the truth of a scientific theory is a matter of how well it stands up alongside neutral and objective observations about the world. But what if there are no 'neutral' facts and no neat line between theory and data? What if, as Kuhn's work suggests, every observation is 'theory-laden'?

The failure of relativism to take any serious account of aspects that are clearly characteristic of our actual moral lives is usually seen as a decisive blow against it, but relativists may try to turn it to their advantage. Perhaps, they argue, we should *not* be so judgemental and critical of others; we should be *more* tolerant, open-minded and sensitive to other customs and practices. Relativism encourages tolerance and open-mindedness, they suggest, while non-relativists are just bigots, impatient of practices other than their own. But this is a caricature: there is in fact no incompatibility between taking a generally tolerant view of things and yet maintaining that on some matters other people or other cultures have got it wrong. Indeed, a frustration facing the relativist is that it is only the *non*-relativist who can hold up tolerance and cultural sensitivity as universal virtues!

Getting knowledge in perspective Strong or radical relativism quickly ties itself in knots. Is the claim that all claims are relative itself relative? Well, it has to be, to avoid self-contradiction; but if it is, it means that my claim that all claims are absolute is true *for me*. And this kind of incoherence rapidly infects everything else, to the extent that relativists cannot, consistently and without hypocrisy, maintain the validity of their own position. The self-refuting nature of full-blown relativism was spotted in its infancy by Plato, who swiftly showed up the inconsistencies in the relativist position adopted by the sophist Protagoras, in the dialogue that bears his name. The crucial point is that rational discussion depends on sharing *some* common ground; we have to agree on *something* in order to communicate meaningfully.

> **Man is the measure of all things.**
> **Protagoras, 5th century BC**

The absurdity of full-blown relativism has meant that insights offered by its more moderate versions are sometimes overlooked. The most important lesson of relativism is that knowledge itself is perspectival: our take on the world is always from a certain perspective or point of view; there is no external vantage point from which we can observe the world 'as it really is'. This point is often explained in terms of conceptual schemes or frameworks: put simply, we can only get an intellectual grasp on reality from within our own conceptual framework, determined by a complex combination of factors including our culture and history. But the fact that we cannot step outside our own conceptual scheme and take an objective view of things – a 'god's-eye view' – does not mean that we cannot get to know anything. A perspective has to be a perspective on *something*, and by sharing and comparing our different perspectives we can hope to bring our various beliefs into relief and to achieve a fuller and more rounded picture of the world.

the condensed idea
Anything goes?

12 Utilitarianism

Kirk is certain to die within a week but is being kept alive on a life-support system. His heart and kidneys happen to be a perfect match for Scottie and Bones, who are certain to die before him if they do not get the transplants they need but who have excellent prospects of recovery if they do. There are no other suitable donors on the *Enterprise*. Is it right to let Kirk die – or perhaps even to kill him – in order to save Scottie and Bones? On the one hand, it seems clear that the net outcome of letting Kirk die is beneficial; on the other, we may feel that choosing to let someone die, or killing them, is wrong, however good the consequences may be.

> **Nature has placed mankind under the governance of two sovereign masters, pain and pleasure. It is for them alone to point out what we ought to do.**
>
> **Jeremy Bentham, 1789**

Many philosophers have been attracted to the idea that it is the consequences of our actions that should be considered when we assess whether those actions are right or wrong (an approach known as 'consequentialism'). Utilitarianism, the most influential of consequentialist theories, is the more specific view that actions should be judged right or wrong to the extent that they increase or decrease human well-being or 'utility'. Scenarios like the Kirk case may seem far-fetched, but in fact situations that are similar in morally relevant ways arise all the time. Politicians, for instance, are obliged to make many decisions about the use of public money and priorities in the health service that cause the death of innocent people. If the sum of human well-being is accepted as the appropriate standard, as utilitarians suggest, there appears to be some prospect of reaching and justifying such decisions on a rational basis.

timeline

late 18th century

Bentham lays the foundations of classical utilitarianism

The experience machine

In 1974 the US philosopher Robert Nozick devised a thought experiment that challenges the assumption that lies at the very heart of utilitarianism. Imagine an 'experience machine' that could create for you a life in which all your fondest desires and ambitions would be fully realized. Once plugged into the machine, you will have no idea that you are plugged in – you will think that everything is real, that everything is actually happening. You have the chance to exchange a real life of inevitable frustrations and unfulfilled dreams for a virtual existence of unbroken success and unalloyed pleasure. 'Would you plug in?' Nozick asks. 'What else can matter to us, other than how our lives feel from the inside?' 'Quite a lot' is his answer. In spite of the obvious attractions, most people, he supposes, would reject the offer. The reality of life, its *authenticity*, is important to us: we want to do certain things, not only experience the pleasure of doing them. Yet, if pleasure were the only thing affecting our well-being, if it were the sole constituent of the good life, surely we would not make this choice. There must, then, be things apart from pleasure that we consider intrinsically valuable. But if Nozick's intuitions are sound, then utilitarianism, at least in its classical manifestation, must be false.

The classic formulation of utilitarianism was given by its founder Jeremy Bentham in the late 18th century. For him, utility lay solely in human pleasure or happiness, and his theory is sometimes summarized as the promotion of 'the greatest happiness of the greatest number'. One of the chief recommendations of utilitarianism for Bentham was that it apparently promised a rational and scientific basis for moral and social decision-making, in contrast to the chaotic and incoherent intuitions on which so-called natural rights and natural law were based. To this end, he proposed a 'felicific calculus', according to which the different amounts of pleasure and pain produced by different actions could be measured and compared; the right action on a given occasion could then be determined by a (supposedly) simple process of addition and subtraction.

1861
Mill's essay *Utilitarianism* defends and elaborates Bentham's theory

1974
Nozick's experience machine questions the basis of utilitarianism

'Better to be Socrates dissatisfied' Critics were quick to point out just how narrow a conception of morality Bentham had given. By supposing that life had no higher end than pleasure, he had apparently left out of the reckoning all sorts of things that we would normally count as inherently valuable, such as knowledge, honour and achievement. It was, as his younger contemporary and fellow utilitarian J.S. Mill recorded the accusation, 'a doctrine worthy only of swine'. Bentham himself, a bluff egalitarian splendidly unmoved by his theory's rougher edges, confronted the accusation head-on: 'Prejudice apart,' he declared, 'the game of push-pin is of equal value with the arts and sciences of music and poetry.' In other words, if a greater overall quantity of pleasure was produced by playing a popular game, that game was indeed more valuable than the more refined pursuits of the intellect.

> **Actions are right in proportion as they tend to promote happiness, wrong as they tend to produce the reverse of happiness.**
>
> **J.S. Mill, 1861**

Mill himself was uncomfortable with Bentham's forthright conclusion and sought to modify utilitarianism to deflect the critics' charge. While Bentham had allowed only two variables in measuring pleasure – duration and intensity – Mill introduced a third, quality, thereby creating a hierarchy of 'higher and lower pleasures'. According to this distinction, some pleasures, such as those of the intellect and the arts, are by their nature more valuable than base physical ones, and by giving them greater weight in the calculus of pleasure, Mill was able to conclude that it was 'better to be a human being dissatisfied than a pig satisfied; better to be Socrates dissatisfied than a fool satisfied'. This accommodation was made at some cost, however. One of the apparent attractions of Bentham's scheme – its simplicity – was clearly diminished. More seriously, Mill's notion of different *kinds* of pleasure seems to require some criterion other than pleasure to tell them apart. If something other than pleasure is a constituent of Mill's idea of utility, it is questionable whether his theory remains strictly utilitarian at all.

Utilitarianism today The classical utilitarianism of Bentham and Mill has since been modified in many ways, but the basic idea remains as influential today as ever. More recent variants typically recognize that human happiness depends not only on pleasure but also on the satisfaction of a wide range of desires and preferences.

Beyond the call of duty?

One criticism often levelled at utilitarianism is that it is simply too demanding. Suppose you decided to give away most of your money to the poor. Others would doubtless be impressed by your generosity, but they probably wouldn't feel obliged to follow your example. Yet, looking at it from a utilitarian perspective, if charity on such a lavish scale promotes general utility – which it very likely would – how can it *not* be the right thing to do? Some radical utilitarians accept the full implications of their theory and advise that we should alter our ways of life accordingly. But such extreme demands go against the grain of our ordinary moral thinking and are bound to mark most of us down as moral failures.

Extraordinary acts of this kind – acts of astonishing bravery or generosity, for instance – are usually the province of the hero or the saint: people who have a personal sense of duty, of what it is right for *them* to do, without any expectation that others will or should follow their example. But most forms of utilitarianism are rigidly impersonal, and so tend to underestimate the importance of personal aims and commitments and an agent's sense of his or her own moral integrity.

There are also different views on how utilitarianism is to be applied to actions. According to *direct* or *act* utilitarianism, each action is assessed directly in terms of its own contribution to utility. In contrast, according to *rule* utilitarianism, an appropriate course of action is determined by reference to various sets of rules which will, if generally followed, promote utility. For instance, killing an innocent person might in certain circumstances lead to the saving of many lives and hence increase general utility, so for the act utilitarian this would be the right course of action. However, *as a rule*, killing innocent people decreases utility, so the rule utilitarian might hold that the same action was wrong, even though it might have beneficial consequences on a particular occasion.

the condensed idea
The greatest happiness principle

13 Existentialism

'Usually existence hides itself. It is there, around us, in us, it is *us*, you can't say two words without mentioning it, but you can never touch it . . . If anyone had asked me what existence was, I would have answered, in good faith, that it was nothing, simply an empty form which was added to external things without changing anything in their nature. And then all of a sudden, there it was, clear as day: existence had suddenly unveiled itself. It had lost the harmless look of an abstract category: it was the very paste of things . . . The diversity of things, their individuality, were only an appearance, a veneer. This veneer had melted, leaving soft, monstrous masses, all in disorder – naked, in a frightful, obscene nakedness.'

Towards the end of Jean-Paul Sartre's novel *Nausea* (1938), the main protagonist, Antoine Roquentin, undergoes a horrid epiphany as he discovers at last the cause of the nausea, the 'sweetish sickness', with which he has been afflicted by contact with everybody and everything around him. Stripping away the false veneer – the colours, tastes and smells – that conceals the raw, undifferentiated mass of being beneath, he is appalled and overwhelmed by the brute fact of existence: existence that is bloated, cloying, repulsive – 'existence everywhere, infinitely, in excess, for ever and everywhere . . . a fullness which man can never abandon.' Choked with rage and disgust at its grossness, Roquentin shouts 'Filth! what rotten filth!' and shakes himself to 'get rid of this sticky filth, but it held fast and there was so much, tons and tons of existence'.

Anguish caused by the sheer, physical burden of existence lies at the heart of the existentialist vision. For the French intellectual Sartre, existentialism's

timeline

1840s	1880s–90s
Kierkegaard's writings address many of the basic concerns of existentialism	Nietzsche's ideal *Übermensch* flourishes in unshackled existential freedom

best-known exponent, existence is a palpable fact, a force that 'must invade you suddenly, master you, weigh heavily on your heart like a great motionless beast'. But while existence itself is cloying and oppressive, it is also quite contingent, a chance affair: you are but you might not have been – your being is pure accident. There is no God, in Sartre's view, to provide any explanation or reason for our existence; and equally there is no given purpose to life. The universe is indifferent to our aspirations, and this is the cause of the inevitable existential anxiety. But this very fact also gives us a freedom – a freedom to make choices for ourselves and a responsibility to engage in the world and to take on projects and commitments that alone can forge meaning for us. Thus 'condemned to be free', we are responsible for creating purpose for ourselves and validating our lives through the choices we make.

> **Man is condemned to be free; because once thrown into the world, he is responsible for everything he does.**
> Jean-Paul Sartre, 1946

Existentialist roots Existentialism was always as much a mood or an attitude as a philosophy in the strict sense, and it remained a somewhat loose bundle of diverse ideas and concepts. The shared emotional tone that lies at its core was prompted in part by a realization of the pointlessness of the human condition – its 'absurdity' – in the sense that we are thrust, products of chance without reason or purpose, into an uncaring world which is itself beyond rational explanation. Existential broodiness was perfectly in tune with the mood of despondency and anxiety that coloured the decades following the Second World War, and it is popularly thought of as (primarily) a 20th-century phenomenon. This perception was reinforced by the figure of Sartre himself, who (with the French writer Albert Camus) became the popular face of existentialism. Sartre's intellectual and literary skills combined perfectly to give expression to a movement that straddled the conventional boundaries between academia and popular culture.

1927	**1938**	**1942**	**1943**
Heidegger's *Being and Time* casts its spell on subsequent existentialists	Sartre's novel *Nausea* published	Camus's essay *The Myth of Sisyphus* explores the doctrine of the absurd	Sartre's most significant philosophical work, *Being and Nothingness,* published

In spite of the popular perception, much of the theoretical groundwork for existentialism was in fact carried out by the German philosopher Martin Heidegger, with whom Sartre studied in the 1930s. Heidegger himself – a highly controversial figure whose reputation is clouded by his Nazi connections – was heavily indebted to intellectuals of the previous century, especially to the Danish philosopher Søren Kierkegaard.

> **'Dread is the dizziness of freedom which occurs when . . . freedom gazes down into its own possibility, grasping at finiteness to sustain itself.'**
>
> **Søren Kierkegaard, 1848**

It was Kierkegaard who first insisted that human life could be understood only from the first-personal perspective of the 'ethically existing subject'; and it was he who first impregnated the word 'existence' with a richness of meaning that signified a distinctively human mode of being. For him, existence as a 'real subject' is not something to be taken for granted but is an achievement: it is impossible to 'exist without passion'; realizing our full potential as individuals, with a proper sense of our own identity, calls for an active engagement of the will: a commitment to make choices that forge long-term interests and give an ethical framework to our lives. In the end, the essential commitment, in Kierkegaard's view, is the 'leap of faith' by which we bind ourselves in a relationship with God.

Existence precedes essence Kierkegaard was the first to diagnose the *Angst* or 'dread' that is caused by our awareness of the vicissitudes or contingencies of fortune and that finally drives our commitment (as Kierkegaard sees it) to become 'Christlike' in the choice of life we lead. Similar concerns, allied to a decisive rejection of God, led Friedrich Nietzsche to extol the idealized *Übermensch*, or 'superman', who revels in, rather than fears, such existential freedom. Heidegger followed Kierkegaard in focusing on the rich and charged fact of existence as the characteristic quality of human life (a mode of being he terms *Dasein*). We cannot avoid a practical concern about the nature of our own existence, for, as Heidegger famously comments, human beings are the only beings to whom being is an issue. Like Kierkegaard, he uses the term *Angst* to describe the anxiety we experience when we become conscious that we are responsible for the structure of our own existence. How we measure up to the challenge of this responsibility determines the shape and fullness of our lives.

Heidegger's central insight, then, is that there is no fixed essence that gives shape to human life beyond the goals that we actively commit

The absurd

Central to the existentialist view of the human condition is the notion of absurdity. The universe is irrational in the sense that there is no rational explanation for it, nor is there a God to guide it; hence any value or meaning in human existence comes from within, imposed by humans themselves. The brute fact of existence is accidental and, in itself, pointless or (in the existentialists' sense) 'absurd'. Albert Camus captures existentialism's central dilemma in his essay *The Myth of Sisyphus* (1942): 'Man finds himself face to face with the irrational. He feels within himself his longing for happiness and for reason. The absurd is born of this confrontation between the human need and the unreasonable silence of the world.' Cast into the world without external guidance or purpose, individuals are obliged to seek meaning for themselves by affirming the value of such things as freedom and creativity. This underlying sense of bewilderment and dislocation in an obscurely menacing universe provides the background to the 'theatre of the absurd', in which Samuel Beckett, Jean Genet and others experimented with novel and often bizarre uses of language and silence.

ourselves to and which give substance to our existence. This is captured in the existentialists' famous slogan, 'Existence precedes essence', which in Sartre's hands is moulded into the claim that we are what we choose to be – in other words, that we are products of the significant choices we make for ourselves. We create an essence for ourselves and by so doing also create meaning in our lives. It is in this context that Sartre introduces the notion of 'bad faith' to describe the manner of existence of those who fail to recognize their responsibility to take up their freedom and create value in their lives by shaping their own essence. Such people live, in Heidegger's phrase, 'inauthentically' – they pass their lives without acknowledging or accepting the potential that is available to them and thus subsist in an existence that is stripped of purpose and all that is most distinctively human.

the condensed idea
Condemned to be free

14 Evil

Bad people do bad things, and if the people and the things are bad enough, we may call both of them 'evil'. Various other words may be used to describe such behaviour – wicked, depraved, vicious – and all suggest that a specifically moral boundary has been crossed. But the word 'evil' carries a special and distinct connotation, a sort of metaphysical baggage gathered during its long and ancient association with religion.

Standing in a grand cosmic opposition as the antithesis of good, evil is intimately tied up with the idea of sin, the transgression of divine law. The implied offence against God (or gods) is often personified in the agency of a devil or devils. In the Christian tradition, for instance, the supreme embodiment of evil is Satan, the arch enemy of God, whose minions, or demons, enter humans to incite or inflict various kinds of evil.

What makes evil evil? On the face of it, the close link between evil and sin offers a ready solution to the problem of identifying evil – saying what evil *is*. Something is wrong, in this view, simply because it is an offence against God's law: morality is based on divine command; good is good and evil is evil for the simple reason that God has ordained that it should be so. And as the word of God is preserved in the bible and other sacred texts, we have a detailed record of God's pleasures and displeasures and hence an authoritative source of guidance on what we should and shouldn't do.

There is no doubt that for most people throughout most of history, some such account of morality, of good and evil, has been accepted without question. There are, nevertheless, significant difficulties with this view.

timeline
4th century BC
'Euthyphro dilemma' posed by Plato

Is it unlucky to be bad?

To what degree is the evil that we impute to people and their actions a matter of luck? We can only display the good and bad points of our characters if circumstances provide us with opportunities to do so: to this extent we are all at the mercy of luck. We may think that we would never have displayed the evil depravity of Nazi guards at Auschwitz, but of course we will never know that for sure. All we can say for certain is that we are very fortunate that we will never have to find out.

First, there is the familiar problem that the various religious texts through which God's will is made known to humans, contain many conflicting and/or unpalatable messages. At the very least, it is a challenge to use God's known views to construct an acceptable and internally coherent moral system. A second problem, casting doubt on the nature of divine authority, was first raised by Plato some 2400 years ago in his dialogue *Euthyphro*. Suppose that good and evil are based on what is pleasing or displeasing to God. Is what is evil evil because God dislikes it, or does God dislike it because it is evil? If the former, clearly God's preferences might have been different – God *might* have liked genocide (say), and if he had, genocide would be all right; so morality is little more than blind obedience to an arbitrary authority. And if the latter – if God dislikes evil because it is evil – the fact that evil is evil is clearly independent of God; God, in this case, is simply redundant. In matters of morality, then, God is either arbitrary or irrelevant: an unhappy conclusion for those who would ground morality in this way.

> **Evils can never pass away, for there must always remain something which is antagonistic to good.**
>
> **Plato, 4th century BC**

5th century AD

St Augustine argues that God is perfect, yet permits evil

13th century

Aquinas presents definitive medieval account of evil

The problem of evil There are questions, then, over the foundations of good and evil and God's relation to them. Perhaps even more damaging is the so-called 'problem of evil' – the difficulty of reconciling the fact of evil occurring in the world with the existence of God as usually conceived.

Manifestly, the world is full of evil: famine, murder, earthquake, disease – millions of people's futures blighted, young lives needlessly snuffed out, children left orphaned and helpless, agonizing deaths of young and old alike. If you could click your fingers and put an end to all this misery, you would have to be a heartless monster not to do so. Yet there is supposed to be a being that *could* sweep it all aside in an instant, a being that is unlimited in its power, knowledge and moral excellence: God. How can such evil exist side by side with a god who has, by definition, the capacity to put an end to it?

The problem arises as a consequence of certain qualities that are usually thought by believers to be part of the essence of God. As conventionally conceived, God is . . .

- omniscient: he (or she or it) knows everything;
- omnipotent: he is able to do anything;
- omnibenevolent: he desires to do every good thing.

From this it appears to follow that God is fully aware of all the evil (pain and suffering) in the world; that he is able to prevent it; and that he wishes to do so. But this flatly contradicts the reality of evil in the world. So, unless we simply deny that there is any such evil, we must conclude either that there is no God or that he does not possess one or more of his supposedly essential properties: he doesn't know what is going on, doesn't care, or can't do anything about it.

Is it possible to explain how evil and God, with all his properties intact, can in fact co-exist after all? The usual suggestion is that there are 'morally sufficient reasons' why God, while remaining a being of perfect moral excellence, might not always choose to eliminate suffering. The idea is that it is in some sense in our interests – it is good for us – that God should allow evil to happen in the world.

So exactly what interests are served, what greater goods are to be gained, at the price of human suffering? Probably the most powerful answer to this question is the so-called 'free will defence', according to which suffering on

The free will defence

The presence of evil in the world offers the most serious challenge to the idea that there is an all-powerful, all-knowing and all-loving god. Historically, the most influential argument used to counter this challenge – to show that there are sufficient reasons why a morally perfect god might yet choose to allow evil to exist – is the so-called 'free will defence'. Human free will, it is argued, is a divine gift of enormous value; our freedom to make genuine choices allows us to live lives of real moral worth and to enter into a deep relationship of love and trust with God. However, God could not have made this gift to us without the risk of our abusing it – of our misusing our freedom to make the wrong choices. It was a risk worth taking and a price worth paying, but God could not have

eliminated the possibility of moral baseness without depriving us of a greater gift – the capacity for moral goodness.

The most obvious difficulty that confronts the free will defence is the existence in the world of *natural* evil. Even if we accept that free will is a possession so precious that it is worth the cost in so-called 'moral evil' – the bad and vicious things brought about when people use their freedom to make wrong choices – what possible sense can we make of naturally occurring evil? How would God have undermined or diminished our free will in any way if he had suddenly wiped out the HIV virus, haemorrhoids, mosquitoes, flash floods and earthquakes?

earth is the price we pay – and a price worth paying – for our freedom to make genuine choices in our actions (see box). Another important idea is that true moral character and virtue are forged on the anvil of human suffering: it is only by overcoming adversity, helping the oppressed, opposing the tyrant (etc.) that the real worth of the saint and the hero is able to shine forth. However, such arguments may begin to look shallow when set against the sheer arbitrariness and scale of human suffering. Not only is the amount of suffering out of all proportion with what might reasonably be required for purposes of character-building; the greater part of the world's evil is visited upon the blameless while the vicious go unscathed.

> **If all evil were prevented, much good would be absent from the universe.**
>
> **Thomas Aquinas, c.1265**

the condensed idea
Is evil good for us?

15 Fate

The idea that there is some power or principle by which the future course of events is predetermined, or 'mapped out' in advance, has exercised a lasting hold on the human imagination. Often personified as some kind of divine or supernatural agency, fate or destiny is usually seen as an inexorable and inevitable force: 'Fate leads the willing, but drags the unwilling', according to the Greek Stoic philosopher Cleanthes. At the same time, it is a force that is indiscriminate and shows no respect for rank or position: 'when fate summons,' wrote the English poet John Dryden, 'monarchs must obey'.

Although deeply ingrained in popular belief, the notion that our future is fixed on a predestined path from which there is no escape sits awkwardly with certain other presumptions of our everyday thought. We normally think that when we do something, we do it freely; my decision to do one thing rather than another is a real choice between genuinely available options. But if the course of my life is mapped out from birth, perhaps even from the beginning of time, how can anything I do be truly free? And if all my future choices are already set in stone, how can I be held accountable for them? If free will is an illusion, my status as a morally responsible agent seems to be in doubt. Credit and blame seem to have no place in a world governed by the iron hand of fate.

Greeks and Romans on fate From earliest times the idea that an individual's destiny was determined at birth figured prominently in Greek popular and religious thought. The usual Greek word for fate, *moira*, meaning 'share' or 'lot', referred in particular to the most significant gift to be apportioned, the span of life itself.

timeline

c.700 BC	c.300 BC	c. AD 100
The Greek poet Hesiod describes the three Fates, or Moirai	Zeno, followed by Cleanthes, set up the Stoic school at Athens	Epictetus, the most influential of the later Stoics, is active in Rome

Science: fate's unlikely ally

On the face of it modern science might seem an unlikely ally for an ancient, primitive-looking notion like fate. In fact, though, the clocklike regularity of Newton's mechanistic universe suggests a deterministic understanding of every event in the universe, including those actions and choices which we usually take to be the products of free will. Simply put, the idea of determinism is that every event has a prior cause; every state of the world is necessitated or determined by a previous state which is itself the effect of a sequence of still earlier states. This sequence can be extended backwards to the beginning of time, suggesting that the history of the universe was fixed from the moment of its inception. Scientific determinism, then, appears to support the idea that our destinies are fixed in advance and hence to jeopardize the notion of free will and, with it, our status as morally accountable agents.

Many scientists and philosophers (so-called 'hard' determinists) accept that determinism is true and that it is incompatible with free will. Our actions, they believe, are causally determined and the idea that we are free, in the sense that we could have acted differently, is illusory. Others ('soft' determinists) agree that determinism is true but deny that it is incompatible with free will. In their view, the fact that we could have acted differently *if we had chosen* gives a satisfactory and sufficient notion of freedom of action; the important point is not that a choice is causally determined but that it is not coerced. Finally, there are libertarians, who reject determinism; human free will is real and our choices and actions are not determined. The problem for this view is to explain how an action can occur indeterminately – in particular, how an uncaused event can avoid being random, as randomness will be no less damaging to the idea of moral responsibility than determinism.

The epic poet Hesiod, active around 700 BC, was the first authority known to represent the Fates, or Moirai, as three aged women who determine a person's fate at the time of his or her birth by spinning the thread of life. Clotho (the Spinner) holds the distaff; Lachesis (the Allotter) draws off the thread; and Atropos (the Inflexible) cuts it with her shears to set the moment of death. The Moirai were fully assimilated into Roman mythology as the three Parcae (Nona, Decuma and Morta), who were originally goddesses associated with childbirth. Their alternative name, Fata, derived from a Latin word meaning 'to speak', carried the implication that a person's fate was the inexorable decree or pronouncement of the gods.

Among ancient thinkers the concept of fate was most central to the philosophy of the Stoics, whose founder Zeno established a school in Athens around 300 BC. The basic doctrine around which Stoicism was built is the idea that nature – i.e. the whole universe – is under the control of *logos*, which was variously interpreted as 'god' (in the sense of cosmic force), divine reason, providence or fate. The fundamental task of the wise man is to distinguish what lies within his power, which can therefore be mastered; and what lies beyond it, which must be accepted with fortitude. The latter disposition, known as *amor fati* (literally 'love of fate'), subsequently became the quintessential Stoic virtue. Epictetus, a Greek who came to Rome as a slave towards the end of the first century AD, memorably summed up the Stoic attitude towards fate:

'Remember that you are an actor in a drama, of such a part as it may please the master to assign you, for a long time or for a little as he may choose. And if he will you to take the part of a poor man, or a cripple, or a ruler, or a private citizen, then may you act that part with grace! For to act well the part that is allotted to us, that indeed is ours to do, but to choose it is another's.'

Que sera sera

One response to fate is to suppose that 'whatever will be will be': human action is ineffectual in the face of destiny, so we might as well sit back and let it happen. The flaw with such a fatalistic approach is that doing nothing because 'your number is up anyway' ignores the highly plausible alternative that doing something might prevent your number coming up. The English writer G.K. Chesterton summed up the error precisely in an essay published in 1928: 'I do not believe in a fate that falls on men however they act; but I do believe in a fate that falls on them unless they act.' This is the sense in which we must grasp our destiny, rather than allow ourselves to be blown wherever the winds of fortune carry us.

Free will and predestination The implications of the idea that future events are in some sense predetermined have caused serious controversies within various religions. In Christianity the omniscience that is usually ascribed to God means that he knows everything, including what is going to happen in the future, so from his perspective the history of the universe is set in advance. Yet how can God's foreknowledge of events be reconciled with the free will that is supposedly a divine gift to humans that allows us to live lives of real moral worth? The capacity for moral goodness is the same capacity that opens the door to moral baseness – without free will, the concept of sin would be meaningless. And it is this potential for sin – something that God, being omnipotent, could have eliminated had he wished – that is usually invoked in order to explain the presence of evil in the world.

> **What God writes on your forehead you will become.**
>
> Qur'an, 7th century AD

Some Christian theologians have felt that mere foreknowledge of all that will happen is insufficient for a deity endowed with every perfection. His majesty requires not only that he sees in advance the destiny of all things but that he actually determines that destiny. According to the doctrine of predestination, associated in particular with St Augustine and John Calvin, God determined the fate of the universe, throughout all time and space, at or before the time he created it; and at the same time he decreed that certain souls would be saved, and (more controversially) others damned. This prescription ensures that every action and choice that people make is made according to God's wishes, but it also means that these actions and choices can have no bearing on the destination of individual souls, whose fate has already been decided.

> **Destiny: a tyrant's authority for crime and a fool's excuse for failure.**
>
> Ambrose Bierce, *The Devil's Dictionary*, 1911

the condensed idea
The iron hand of destiny

16 Soul

Today as in the past, hundreds of millions of people believe that there is something called soul or souls. Christians, Jews, Muslims, Hindus, Sikhs, Taoists, Jains – not to mention ancient Egyptians, Greeks, Romans, Chinese and dozens of others, living and dead – profess belief in such things: rational souls, cosmic or universal souls, bipartite or tripartite souls, immortal souls and souls that perish with bodies . . . Yet, for all this vast historical consensus on the bald fact of the existence of these psychic somethings, there is little agreement about what they are, what kind of relationship they have with bodies, and what might count as evidence for their existence.

The soul, affirms the founder of the Bahá'í faith, is 'a sign of God, a heavenly gem whose reality the most learned of men hath failed to grasp, and whose mystery no mind, however acute, can ever hope to unravel'. 'Dwelling in all things,' proclaim the Hindu Upanishads, 'yet other than all things, whom all things do not know, whose body all things are . . .' Something that is essentially mysterious, intangible, unfathomable: such is the thing through which we partake of the nature of God or gods (or don't) and that allows us to live forever (or doesn't).

> **That Soul/Self [*atman*] is not this, it is not that. It is unseizable, for it cannot be seized; it is indestructible, for it cannot be destroyed; unattached, for it does not attach itself; it is unbound, it does not tremble, it is not injured.**
>
> *Brihadāranyaka Upanishad*

timeline

4th century BC	AD 1640s
Plato argues that souls are immortal and transcendent. Notion of soul separate from body is nonsense, according to Aristotle	Descartes makes definitive statement of substance dualism

In spite of the bewildering variety of theories that have been advanced on the nature of souls, there is some common ground. Defined in part in terms of what it is not – i.e. the body, which is material – the soul is the immaterial essence of a human being. It is the vital principle or aspect that animates and controls the body, giving a person their personality and ensuring the continuity of that personality over time. The soul is the conscious part of a person, the seat of human will, rationality and intellect, and hence generally coextensive with the mind and self. In many religious traditions, the soul is able to live apart from the body and to survive the body's death; by extension, it may also be immortal and subject to various kinds of divine reward and punishment.

The elusive self

Focus all your attention inwards and try to detect 'your self'. However hard you look, however much introspection you bring to bear, you can only ever find individual thoughts, memories, experiences, etc., never the self or 'you' that is the supposed subject of these thoughts (etc.). It may be natural to imagine that there is some substantial self of this kind, a self which we take to be our essence, but in the view of the Scottish philosopher David Hume, it is mistaken. There is no 'thing' to find; we are 'nothing but a bundle or collection of different perceptions, which succeed each other with inconceivable rapidity'. It is like looking at a photograph and expecting to see the viewpoint of the photographer. This perspective is essential to make sense of the view shown in the photograph, but can never be seen in the photograph itself. In the same way, the self is no more than the point of view that gives coherence to, or makes sense of, our thoughts and experiences; it can never itself be given in those experiences. The fruitless search for the essential but elusive inner self is one of the key psychological motivations for the perennial human belief in souls.

1674–5
Malebranche argues that appearance of body–soul causation is action of God

1739–40
The self is merely a 'bundle of perceptions', according to Hume

1949
Gilbert Ryle caricatures mind–body dualism as 'the Ghost in the Machine'

The ghost in the machine The idea that body and soul are essentially different, which is common to most traditions and prominent in Christian belief, opens up a deep rift between the two. The divide can be traced back to the Greeks (if not earlier) and especially to Plato, who argued repeatedly that the soul is immortal and proposed a distinct 'realm of being' populated by perfect and immutable entities (Forms) that could be discerned only by the soul. This picture of a divinely inspired soul temporarily imprisoned in an inferior and earth-bound body impressed itself on the early Christian theologians. St Augustine, for instance, saw the soul as 'a special substance, endowed with reason, adapted to rule the body'.

In the Western philosophical tradition, the idea that body and soul are essentially distinct (so-called 'substance dualism') was most influentially advanced by the 17th-century French philosopher René Descartes. Treating mind and soul as virtual synonyms, Descartes conceived mind as mental substance, immaterial 'stuff' whose essential nature is thinking. Everything else is matter, or material substance, whose defining characteristic is spatial extension (i.e. filling physical space). The picture of the immaterial soul somehow living within and pulling the levers of the material body was famously parodied as the 'Ghost in the Machine' by the English philosopher Gilbert Ryle in his book *The Concept of Mind* (1949).

> **If we are guided by me, we shall believe that the soul is immortal and capable of enduring all extremes of good and evil, and so we shall hold ever to the upward way and pursue righteousness with wisdom always and ever.**
>
> Plato, *The Republic*, 4th century BC

An unbridgeable divide? The big problem for Descartes's picture is that by treating body and soul as *essentially* distinct he opens up a rift that looks unbridgeable. The picture assumes (as we would expect) that body and soul interact – the ghost has to work the levers – but if the two types of substance are *utterly* different, how can any such interaction conceivably occur? How can mental phenomena possibly influence or be causally related in any way to physical states and events in the body? Looked at in this way, Cartesian dualism becomes one facet of a more general philosophical conundrum: the mind–body problem. We are all immediately conscious of our consciousness – that we have thoughts and feelings that are subjective and on which we have a unique and personal perspective; science, by contrast, is rigorously objective and open to scrutiny. We may wonder how something as strange as consciousness can exist in the physical world explained by science; just as certainly we will struggle to find a place for the soul, the presumed seat of consciousness.

Aristotle recognized the dangers inherent in Plato's strict division of body and soul. He argued that the soul is the essence of what it is to be human and that it makes no sense to try to separate it from the body: 'We must no more ask whether the soul and body are one than ask whether the wax and the figure impressed on it are one.' Descartes, too, was aware of the problem, conceding that it would take God's direct intervention to effect the necessary causal relationship between body and soul, but he did little himself to resolve the difficulty. It fell to his immediate successors, such as Nicolas Malebranche, to try to account for causation between body and soul, but his proposed solution (occasionalism) did not so much solve the problem as underline its seriousness. Among recent philosophers, the great majority have been content to solve the riddle of Cartesian dualism by denying it – by claiming that there is only one kind of 'stuff' in the world. Generally they have insisted that, since the subject matter of science is exclusively physical, so too the mind and consciousness must be amenable to scientific explanation, in physical terms. And in such a picture there is little room for souls.

the condensed idea
A mystery no mind can hope to unravel

17 Faith

**'It is the heart which perceives God and not the reason.
That is what faith is: God perceived by the heart, not by the
reason.' Thus in his *Pensées* (1670), Blaise Pascal – both a
pioneering scientist and a devout Christian – captures the
perplexing relationship between faith and reason. For Pascal,
the power of faith is not opposed to that of reason; they are
different in kind and have distinct objects: 'Faith certainly
tells us what the senses do not, but not the contrary of what
they see; it is above, not against them.'**

For believers, religious conviction does not depend on rational argument,
nor is it undermined by it. It is presumptuous, they would claim, to suppose
that our intellectual efforts could make God's purposes transparent or
comprehensible to us. Those who elevate faith above reason – so-called
'fideists' – hold that faith is an alternative path to truth and that, in the
case of religious belief, it is the right route. A state of conviction, achieved
ultimately through God's action on the soul, demands a voluntary and
deliberate act of will on the part of the faithful; faith requires a leap, but it
is not a leap in the dark. 'Faith is to believe what we do not see,' St
Augustine explains, 'and the reward of this faith is to see what we believe.'

Once convinced of the antagonism between faith and reason, both
opponents of faith and its supporters can take up extreme positions.
Martin Luther, the father of Protestantism, insisted that faith must 'trample
underfoot all reason, sense and understanding'; reason, for him, was the

**‘Reason is our soul's left hand, Faith her right,
By these we reach divinity.’**

John Donne, 1633

timeline

early 5th century	1540s	1670
St Augustine elucidates the nature of faith	Martin Luther praises faith over reason, the 'devil's greatest whore'	Blaise Pascal speculates on faith in his posthumously published *Pensées*

'greatest enemy' of faith, the 'damned whore' that must be obliterated in all Christians. In contrast, rationalists and sceptics are unwilling to exempt religious belief from the reasoned, empirically based assessment they would apply to any other area of claimed knowledge; they insist on considering the evidence and reaching a conclusion on that basis. And the enemies of religion are no more temperate in expressing their views: 'Faith is one of the world's great evils,' fulminates Richard Dawkins, leading spokesman of the anti-God squad, 'comparable to the smallpox virus but harder to eradicate.'

> ❝We do not speak of faith that two and two are four . . . We only speak of faith when we wish to substitute emotion for evidence. The substitution of emotion for evidence is apt to lead to strife, since different groups substitute different emotions.❞
>
> **Bertrand Russell, 1958**

Abraham and Isaac

The unbridgeable gap between faith and reason is well illustrated by the biblical story of Abraham and Isaac. Abraham is held up as the archetypal and paradigmatic example of religious faith, for his unquestioning willingness to obey God's command and sacrifice his son Isaac. But isolated from its religious context, Abraham's behaviour appears psychotic and deranged. In comparison to the understanding of the situation he blithely accepts, *any* other interpretation would seem preferable and more plausible: am I mad? is God testing me? is that the devil pretending to be God? In any other situation, Abraham would be regarded as an unhinged (potential) child murderer; his behaviour utterly bizarre.

1748	**1859**	**1997**
David Hume argues that belief in miracles is irrational	In *On Liberty* J.S. Mill extols freedom of thought	Richard Dawkins compares faith to the smallpox virus

The balance sheet of faith In fideistic hands, the fact that religious belief cannot be adequately defended on rational grounds is turned into a positive recommendation. If a (fully) rational route were open, faith would not be needed, but as reason fails to provide a justification, faith steps in to fill the gap. The act of will necessary on the part of the believer adds moral merit to the acquisition of faith; and a devotion that does not question its object is revered, at least by those who share it, as simple and honest piety. Some of the attractions of faith are obvious enough: life has a clear-cut meaning, there is some solace for life's tribulations and the consolation of knowing that something better awaits after death, and so on. Religious belief clearly answers many basic, primordial needs and concerns in humans, and many people are undeniably improved, even transformed by adopting a religious way of life. At the same time the symbols and embellishments of religion have provided almost limitless artistic inspiration and cultural enrichment.

> **Faith consists in believing when it is beyond the power of reason to believe.**
>
> Voltaire, 1764

Many of the points that the fideist would put on the credit side for faith are set down as debits by its opponents. Amongst the most precious principles of secular liberalism, championed by J.S. Mill and others, is freedom of thought and expression, which sits very uneasily with the habit of uncritical assent extolled in the pious believer. The unquestioning devotion valued by the fideist can easily look to the non-believer like credulity and superstition. Ready acceptance of authority can lead people to fall under the influence of unscrupulous sects and cults, and this can sometimes tip over into fanaticism and zealotry. Placing one's faith in others is clearly not admirable unless the others concerned are themselves admirable. When reason is shut out, all manner of excesses may rush in to take its place; and it is hard to deny that at certain times in certain religions, sense and sympathy have flown out of the window to be replaced by intolerance, bigotry, sexism and worse.

So the balance sheet is drawn up, with debits and credits on each side – and often the assets on one side appear as liabilities on the other. To the extent that different accounting methods are used, the accounts themselves are meaningless, and this is often the abiding impression left when believers and non-believers start talking. They generally speak at cross-purposes, fail to establish any common ground, and succeed in moving each other not one inch. Opponents prove to their own satisfaction that faith is irrational; the faithful regard such supposed proof as irrelevant and beside the point. In the end faith is irrational or non-rational; it defiantly sets itself in opposition to reason, and in a sense that is precisely its point.

Hume on miracles

One sure sign of faith is a willingness to believe that God is able to do, and has actually done, things that defy the laws of nature – that he has performed miracles. Miracles are happenings that confound rational expectation and so have always been at the centre of the battle between reason and faith. The essential irrationality of belief in miracles was suggested in a famous argument proposed by the 18th-century Scottish philosopher David Hume. Any such belief must be based on some sort of authority, whether it is the evidence of one's own senses or testimony provided by someone else. But, as Hume points out, 'no testimony is sufficient to establish a miracle, unless the testimony be of such a kind that its falsehood would be more miraculous than the fact which it endeavours to establish.' In other words, it is always more reasonable to reject the 'greater miracle' (a violation of a law of nature) and to suppose that the testimony is false (as a result of deception, delusion, etc.). 'The Christian religion not only was at first attended with miracles,' Hume wryly concludes, 'but even at this day cannot be believed by any reasonable person without one.' As we have seen, however, the faithful do not always regard it as appropriate to be reasonable.

the condensed idea
Belief that is blind to reason

18 Fundamentalism

In the wake of the 9/11 attacks on New York and Washington, an unprecedented wave of Islamophobia swept over the USA. Reflecting the growing mood of fear and suspicion, in which 'fundamentalist' and 'terrorist' became all but interchangeable, President George W. Bush declared a 'war on terror' which would not end 'until every terrorist group of global reach has been found, stopped and defeated'. New only in its intensity, uninhibited demonization of Islamic fundamentalism had begun; the word 'fundamentalist' had become a term of abuse.

In the ensuing conflict, the world's one surviving superpower, self-professed guardian of freedom and democracy, was pitted against an enemy that was widely perceived to be fanatical and alien. Yet, ironically, this same president who was commander-in-chief of civilization's war on fundamentalism was chief executive of a country with the most powerful fundamentalist lobby on earth. Indeed, Bush was, in most significant respects, a fundamentalist himself.

'Heave an egg out of a Pullman window, and you will hit a Fundamentalist almost anywhere in the United States today.' What was true of 1920s America, as recorded by the humorist H.L. Mencken at the birth of Protestant fundamentalism, was no less true in the first decade of the 21st century. In 1990 the Reverend Pat Robertson, multimillionaire televangelist and founder of the far-right Christian Coalition, had announced, 'We have enough votes to run this country'; it was no empty boast, and certainly no presidential candidate could afford to alienate the religious right or to disregard its deeply conservative agenda. So in

timeline

early 20th century	1920	1960s
Protestant fundamentalism emerges in the USA	C.L. Laws coins term 'fundamentalist'	Evangelical radio spreads across the USA

September 2001 a superpower in thrall to Christian fundamentalism went to war on the elusive forces of Muslim fundamentalism.

The battle royal for religion   Today the name 'fundamentalist' is applied to such a disparate array of ideologies and orthodoxies, religious and other, that it is hard to pin down its defining characteristics. Nevertheless, American Christian fundamentalism – the movement for which the term was originally coined – remains one of the least compromising and most ideologically driven manifestations of the phenomenon.

The reactionary movement that sprang up among evangelical Protestants in the USA in the early years of the 20th century was driven initially by alarm and disgust at the reforming tendencies of 'liberal' theologians. These modernizers sought to interpret the bible and the gospel miracles symbolically or metaphorically, in ways that would sit more comfortably with recent social, cultural and scientific trends. In reaction to such doctrinal

The devil's good work

Fundamentalist movements have often shown an ambivalence when faced with modernity, uncertain whether to withdraw from its iniquities or to engage in order to eradicate them. Nowhere has this ambivalence been clearer than in fundamentalism's tortured relationship with modern technology. American Christian fundamentalists denounce many aspects of science and technology as the devil's work, but they have nevertheless displayed remarkable resourcefulness in harnessing the products of technology for their own purposes, reaching vast audiences and amassing huge funds through extensive evangelical programming on radio and television. From the mid-1990s, during their period of massively repressive rule in Afghanistan, there was the bizarre sight of the extreme Islamist Taliban coordinating their project of driving Afghan society back to the stone age by means of mobile phones. And from late 2001, after the Taliban had fallen and al-Qaeda had been ousted from its Afghan strongholds, the terrorist group made a highly effective transition to cyberspace. Suddenly the soldiers of Islam were armed with laptop as well as Kalashnikov, and internet cafés became the logistical and planning centres of the anti-Western jihad.

early 1990s	mid 1990s	Sept. 2001
Start of violent pro-life (anti-abortion) activism in US	Taliban seize control of Afghanistan	9/11 attacks and start of 'war on terror'

> **The true scientist, however passionately he may "believe" ... knows exactly what would change his mind: evidence! The fundamentalist knows that nothing will.**
>
> **Richard Dawkins, 2007**

compromise, which seemed to threaten the centrality of divine revelation, leading conservative theologians asserted the primacy of certain 'fundamentals' of their faith, including the virgin birth and physical resurrection of Jesus, the strict veracity of the miracles, and the literal truth (inerrancy) of the bible. In 1920 the editor of a Baptist journal, Curtis Lee Laws, applied the name 'fundamentalist' for the first time to those 'who still cling to the great fundamentals and who mean to do battle royal' for their faith.

Heaven or hell on earth A unifying theme of different religious fundamentalisms is the conviction that there is a single, authoritative set of teachings that contain the essential and fundamental truth about God (or gods) and his (or their) relationship to mankind. The sacred text is the literal word of the deity and emphatically not open to interpretation and criticism. In the same way, the moral injunctions and codes contained within the text are to be followed to the letter. Hence, for instance, in the view of Christian fundamentalists, the Genesis account of the creation of the world is literally true and anything that conflicts with it, such as Darwinian evolution, is utterly rejected.

Trouble in your own backyard

The West has tended to display a very partial, one-eyed attitude to fundamentalism. Sensationalist reports of how Islamist suicide bombers could be motivated by the promised reward of 72 virgins in heaven are met with slack-jawed disbelief, but equally staggering excesses at home elicit much less horror and sometimes a degree of sympathy. On the face of it, there is little to choose between the motivation of a virgin-inspired suicide bomber and a fundamentalist fanatic such as Paul Hill, an affiliate of the extreme pro-life Army of God, who shot dead an abortion doctor and a clinic escort in Florida in 1994. 'I expect a great reward in heaven ... I look forward to glory,' he announced in a statement before his execution in 2003. Indeed, research suggests that most suicide bombers are motivated less by religious dogma than by very down-to-earth economic, social and political grievances, so in terms of pure, religiously inspired fanaticism US fundamentalists may sometimes have the edge.

The will of God as revealed in sacred texts is, of course, timeless and unchanging, so a natural concomitant to fundamentalism is extreme conservatism. Unquestioning commitment to established traditions often merges with a desire to revive a supposedly superior former state – usually an imagined and idealized past. In all kinds of fundamentalism, such utopian traditionalism leads to a rejection of the forces of change, especially the process of secularization that has shaped the Western world since the Enlightenment.

Hand in hand with religious conservatism goes social and moral conservatism, and most of the civil and political rights that have been hard won in the West over the last three centuries are categorically rejected by fundamentalists of all hues. Belief in absolute scriptural authority implies complete doctrinal dogmatism, so from a fundamentalist's perspective, views and opinions different from their own are simply wrong, and cherished notions of Western liberalism such as cultural and religious tolerance and pluralism are anathema. Free speech, gender equality, gay rights, abortion – all are roundly condemned. The depth of such convictions was amply demonstrated by fulminating US fundamentalist and founder of the Moral Majority, Jerry Falwell, whose immediate response after 9/11 was to blame the attacks on 'the pagans, and the abortionists, and the feminists, and the gays and the lesbians . . . all of them who have tried to secularize America'.

> **Fundamentalists are not friends of democracy . . . Every fundamentalist movement I've studied in Judaism, Christianity and Islam is convinced at some gut, visceral level that secular liberal society wants to wipe out religion.**
>
> **Karen Armstrong,** 2002

Religious fundamentalisms are often messianic or apocalyptic, anticipating the coming of a saviour and/or the end of the world. Such views often lead followers to believe that they enjoy a special and privileged relationship with God, and they may withdraw from society, where non-believers and non-fundamentalists are seen to temporarily hold sway. Others, however, have aspired to political domination, with the aim of imposing a system of government informed by their own views. They reject the separation of state and religion promoted by Western secularism and attempt instead to re-sacralize the political sphere. Elitist and authoritarian, fundamentalists typically wish to topple democratic institutions and to establish theocratic rule in their stead.

the condensed idea
When faith becomes fanatic

19 Atheism

'Whenever I go into a foreign country . . . they always ask me what is my religion. I never know whether I should say "Agnostic" or whether I should say "Atheist" . . . As a philosopher, if I were speaking to a purely philosophic audience I should say that I ought to describe myself as an Agnostic, because I do not think that there is a conclusive argument by which one can prove that there is not a God. On the other hand, if I am to convey the right impression to the ordinary man in the street I think I ought to say that I am an Atheist, because when I say that I cannot prove that there is not a God, I ought to add equally that I cannot prove that there are not the Homeric gods.'

The kind of uncertainty that Bertrand Russell expressed in 1947 has dissipated little in the decades since. In the matter of popular usage, things have changed somewhat from the situation suggested by Russell, but it is hardly in the direction of greater precision or clarity. Today, the word 'atheist' is often applied by the 'man in the street' to those who take a positive position, hostile to religion, in which the existence of a god or gods is explicitly denied. 'Agnostic', on the other hand, is generally reserved for those who sit on the fence – those who adopt a neutral, non-committal stance on religious matters because they are unwilling or unable to decide one way or another. However, these popular usages – the first too narrow, the second too loose – do scant justice to the depth and subtlety of the concepts involved.

Is man only a blunder of God, or God only a blunder of man?

Friedrich Nietzsche, 1888

timeline

399 BC

Socrates executed by Athenian state on charge of impiety

AD 1670

Religious belief as best bet proposed by Pascal in posthumously published *Pensées*

Of gods and teapots Derived from the Greek *atheos*, meaning 'godless', the term 'atheism', in its broadest significance, means rejection of theism, or belief in one or more gods. Such rejection can take several forms, ranging from disbelief to positive denial, and it is this fact that explains the ambiguity surrounding the definition. There are some atheists (certainly a minority) who explicitly deny the existence of a god or gods. Such explicit denial – in effect, a positive doctrine asserting the non-existence of gods, sometimes referred to as 'strong' atheism – requires support in the form of proofs that gods do not exist. The usual strategy, in

Pascal's wager

Suppose we feel that the evidence for God's existence is simply inconclusive. What should we do? We can either believe in God or not. If we choose to believe and are right (i.e. God does exist), we win eternal bliss; and if we are wrong, we lose little. On the other hand, if we choose not to believe and are right (i.e. God doesn't exist), we don't lose anything but don't gain much either; but if we are wrong, our loss is colossal – at best we miss out on eternal bliss, at worst we suffer everlasting damnation. So much to gain, so little to lose: you'd be a fool not to bet on God existing.

This ingenious argument for believing in God, known as Pascal's wager, was set forth by the French mathematician and philosopher Blaise Pascal in his *Pensées* of 1670: ingenious, perhaps, but flawed. The biggest problem concerns what the argument implies about the character of God. In a spirit similar to Nietzsche, who commented that 'I cannot believe in a God who wants to be praised all the time', we might question the worthiness of a god who is impressed by the worship of those who coolly calculate and gamble on the basis of their own self-interest. A god truly worthy of our praise would, we feel, be more along the lines of the one Thomas Jefferson had in mind when he enjoined us to 'question with boldness even the existence of a god; because, if there be one, he must more approve the homage of reason, than that of blindfolded fear'.

1843
Marx denounces religion as the 'opium of the people'

1869
Biologist T.H. Huxley coins the word 'agnosticism'

1947
Bertrand Russell asks, 'Am I an Atheist or an Agnostic?'

such proofs, is to attempt to show that the very notion of a transcendent god – an essentially and ultimately mysterious being, the self-causing first cause that created the universe out of nothing and yet which lies outside it – is literally incoherent or incomprehensible. Such a being is, by definition, beyond our experience and beyond any experience we might conceivably have, and talk of it is literally nonsense.

Many atheists would probably be sympathetic to arguments of this kind, but most are metaphysically less ambitious. While strong atheists propose that there is no evidence for the existence of gods and that there never could be, even in principle, the majority make the more modest claim that there is simply no evidence. In a later article, from 1952, Russell used a memorable analogy, arguing that while it may be impossible to disprove the assertion that there is a china teapot in orbit between the earth and Mars, it is nonetheless eccentric (to put it mildly) to believe that there *is* any such thing in the absence of any evidence to prove it. In the same way, proponents of the weaker form of atheism maintain that the burden of

Atheistic and agnostic origins

Although the word 'atheism' is not attested in English until the 16th century, philosophical ideas that would be described today as atheistic have been circulating since antiquity. In 5th-century Greece several of Socrates' interlocutors in the Platonic dialogues express views that are critical of orthodox religion, while Socrates himself was executed in 399 BC on a charge of 'impiety'. Essentially agnostic views are similarly ancient, although the word itself is relatively recent. The term 'agnostic', formed from the Greek a ('not' or 'without') and *gnosis* ('knowledge'), was first used by the English biologist T.H. Huxley, probably in 1869. His views on the matter had begun to crystallize considerably earlier, however, as

is shown by his comments on the matter of personal immortality in a letter from 1860: 'I neither affirm nor deny the immortality of man. I see no reason for believing it, but, on the other hand, I have no means of disproving it.'

Karl Marx, a famous atheist, believed that religion was a sop to the masses – a conservative force that capitalists exploited to keep the working classes enslaved; a painkiller – hence 'opium' – to relieve the symptoms of social repression. 'Religion is the sigh of the oppressed creature,' he complained, 'the feelings of a heartless world, just as it is the spirit of unspiritual conditions. It is the opium of the people.'

proof lies firmly with those who claim that there is a god and insist, with the Victorian philosopher W.K. Clifford, that 'it is wrong always, everywhere, and for anyone to believe anything upon insufficient evidence'. They point out that even theists are atheistic about every god except their own and that they are merely taking the process one step further.

For weak or empirical atheists, 'weaker' certainly does not mean 'less passionate'. While conceding that there could, in principle at least, be evidence that would change their minds, they insist that all the available evidence is heavily stacked against the supposition that there are gods. On the one hand, there is no longer any need for a 'god of the gaps', as the progress of science, from Newtonian mechanics and geology to Darwinian evolution, has filled out our understanding, systematically plugging the gaps in our knowledge of the world around us that were formerly given a divine explanation. On the other hand, the arguments that have long been advanced as proofs of God's existence – the argument from design, the ontological argument, etc. – are generally regarded as unconvincing and flawed; they compare unfavourably with arguments on the other side, such as the one premised on the problem of evil, that offer a serious challenge to belief in an all-powerful, all-knowing god.

> 'My atheism . . . is true piety towards the universe and denies only gods fashioned by men in their own image to be servants of their human interests.'
>
> **George Santayana, 1922**

the condensed idea
Beyond belief

20 Secularism

'Religious freedom is literally our first freedom. It is the first thing mentioned in the Bill of Rights, which opens by saying that Congress cannot make a law that either establishes a religion or restricts the free exercise of religion. Now, as with every provision of our Constitution, that law has had to be interpreted over the years, and it has been in various ways that some of us agree with and some of us disagree with. But one thing is indisputable: the First Amendment has protected our freedom to be religious or not religious, as we choose, with the consequence that in this highly secular age the United States is clearly the most conventionally religious country in the entire world, at least the entire industrialized world.'

Addressing an audience of students in July 1995 on the topic of 'Religious Liberty in America', President Bill Clinton neatly captures a central paradox of the USA: the fact that one of the most religious countries on earth can simultaneously be one of the most secular. As it turns out, this apparently surprising fact says less about the nature of America than about the diverse meanings of secularism. For while the concept is often associated (and sometimes confused) with ideas such as atheism and humanism, it is not identical with any of them. And in the meaning which Clinton has in mind, secularism is not hostile or opposed to religion at all but refers instead to a particular understanding of the proper place of religion in the constitution and operation of a state.

The wall of separation The First Amendment to the US Constitution, adopted together with the rest of the Bill of Rights in 1791, states that 'Congress shall make no law respecting an establishment of

timeline

14th–15th century	early 1700s	1789–90
Beginnings of humanist movement in Renaissance Europe	Europe devastated by wars of religion	*Laïcité* (secularist state) established in France

religion, or prohibiting the free exercise thereof.' By forbidding the state from declaring an official religion and by guaranteeing freedom of religious expression, the Founding Fathers of the USA laid the foundations of the 'wall of separation' (in Thomas Jefferson's phrase) that divides the proper spheres of faith and politics. These 16 words of the Amendment have been subjected to over 200 years of detailed interpretation by the Supreme Court, and to this day interested groups hotly dispute their precise meaning. Yet it is agreed, minimally, that the provision prevents religion and the state from interfering with one another and ensures that individuals are free in the choice and practice of any religion, or none.

> **Despotism may govern without faith, but liberty cannot. How is it possible that society should escape destruction if the moral tie is not strengthened in proportion as the political tie is relaxed?**
>
> **Alexis De Tocqueville, 1835**

> **When the government puts its imprimatur on a particular religion, it conveys a message of exclusion to all those who do not adhere to the favoured beliefs.**
>
> **US Supreme Court Justice Harry A. Blackmun, 1997**

Profoundly secular in the sense that it has moved the management of worldly affairs from divine to human hands, the Amendment has nevertheless been instrumental in fashioning one of the most vibrantly and variously religious societies on earth. There is no shortage of moral issues that divide Americans deeply and which have the potential to inflame passions and tear communities apart: abortion, euthanasia, stem-cell research, prayer in school, censorship, among many others. Yet powerful constitutional safeguards – and above all the strictly observed separation of church and state – have ensured that such matters have, for the most part, been resolved peacefully and within the confines of the law.

Europe's troubled identity What is most striking about the American experience is that it is quite exceptional. While Europe is and

1791	**1802**	**1990s**	**July 1995**
US First Amendment requires separation of state and religion	President Thomas Jefferson makes first reference to 'wall of separation'	Yugoslav Wars in Balkans fuelled by religious and ethnic tensions	Bill Clinton speaks on 'Religious Liberty in America'

was accepted, not least by those who framed the US Constitution, as the birthplace of secularism, the reality today is that European countries are both less religious and less secular than the USA. This reality is not often fully acknowledged within Europe itself, however. Modern, self-styled 'secular' Europeans typically look uncomprehendingly to the east, where they see the dangerous fundamentalisms of Asia; and superciliously to the west, where they detect the bland fervour of American religiosity. With zealots on each side, the temptation from the superior middle ground is to see secularism as the crowning achievement of European, rather than Western, civilization. But the picture is misleading.

Euro angst

Nowhere has Europe's angst over its secularist identity been clearer than in the recent manoeuvrings of the European Union (EU). The EU – a project originally sponsored by Christian Democrats and sanctioned by the Vatican – came to bitter blows in the early 2000s over the preamble to the constitutional treaty. In its original draft the preamble made mention of both God and Europe's Christian values, but anxieties over what such references said about Europe's shared identity and values finally led to a compromise wording that mentioned 'inspiration from the cultural, religious and humanist inheritance of Europe'. Further soul-searching was occasioned by the eastward expansion of the EU, which first incorporated assertively Catholic Poland and then faced the challenge of accommodating Turkey – a country where, alarmingly from a secularist perspective, greater democratic freedom had been accompanied by an increasingly public demonstration of its Muslim culture and religion.

The European self-image is based on a semi-mythical narrative of secularization that had its origins in the Renaissance, when man first usurped God's place at the centre of the stage of human interest and when distinctively scientific explanations of man's place in the world began to displace theologically inspired accounts. This process reached its crisis, according to the usual story, in the religious wars that reached their bloody climax in the 17th century. At this time the destructive sectarian passions released by the Protestant Reformation were eventually calmed by a secular transformation that was inspired by Enlightenment thinkers such as Hobbes and Locke and swept along on the tide of scientific progress. The cumulative effect of these processes was that political theology based on divine revelation was replaced by political philosophy based on human reason; and that religion was removed to its own protected and private sphere, while an open and liberal public sphere was created in which freedom of expression and toleration of difference prevailed. And it was, furthermore, on this rich secular compost that democracy blossomed and thrived.

Unfortunately, this comforting tale, cherished as both the genealogy and the justification of modern European secular identity, is flawed in crucial respects. With the notable exception of France (where a revolution saw secularism, or *laïcité*, paid for in the blood of its citizens), no European country has been entirely or consistently secular. Indeed, the immediate product of the 17th-century religious wars was not a Europe of modern secular states but a patchwork of confessional, territorial ones; the only freedom (if any) generally allowed to religious minorities who found themselves in the wrong confessional territory was the 'freedom' to go elsewhere. Much of this situation has persisted to this day. The United Kingdom, for example, has an established church, as do the Lutheran countries of Scandinavia, while other nations, such as Poland, Ireland and Italy, remain essentially Catholic. Where strict secularism has prevailed for a time, as for instance in the Soviet Union and eastern Europe, there has often been violence, repression, intolerance and profoundly illiberal government. There is no clearer indication of the equivocal nature of European secularism than the fact that in the last decade of the 20th century the Balkans could be ravaged by wars that were motivated as much by religious differences as ethnic ones.

'We don't do God'

The contrasting experience of Britain and the USA suggests that secularism can be the most effective means of promoting religion. In an interview in 2003 Alastair Campbell, British prime minister Tony Blair's master of spin, shot down a journalist asking about Blair's religious beliefs: 'We don't do God.' Public displays of religiosity are known to be vote losers in the UK – in spite of the fact that the country has an established church (the Church of England) and its monarch is not only head of state but also 'Defender of the Faith'. In contrast, in the USA, where the Constitution requires strict secularity, it is virtually obligatory for aspiring politicians to play the 'religion card' and it is a political platitude that no atheist could ever be elected president.

the condensed idea
Not doing God

21 Creationism

In August 2008, governor of Alaska and self-styled hockey mom Sarah Palin became running mate of the Republican presidential candidate, John McCain. Given the would-be president's relatively advanced age, media attention inevitably focused on the credentials of the 44-year-old 'pit bull in lipstick' who might, in a matter of months, be a heartbeat from occupying the most powerful office on earth. Some of the most heated debate raged around the implications of Palin's commitment to creationism: the belief (minimally) that the world and the life it contains are the work of a divine creator.

> **'Intelligent design is not a genuine scientific theory and, therefore, has no place in the curriculum of our nation's public school science classes.'**
>
> **Senator Edward Kennedy, 2002**

Liberal commentators speculated that Palin's behaviour as president would be significantly influenced by her religious convictions. Just weeks before her nomination, she had announced to a congregation of fellow evangelicals that the bitterly divisive war in Iraq was 'a task from God' and had then requested their prayers for a controversial and environmentally sensitive natural-gas pipeline in Alaska. During her career she had also embraced a tranche of socially conservative views that were closely associated with the creationist lobby, including opposition to abortion, stem-cell research and the extension of gay rights. In her creationist views Palin was certainly in good company. Recent surveys suggest that around two-thirds of adults in the USA accept the central tenets of full-blown 'young-earth' creationism, believing that humans were definitely or probably created in their present form within the last 10,000 years.

timeline

21 Sept. 4004 BC	AD 1802	1925
Date of the creation according to Archbishop James Ussher	William Paley makes classic statement of argument from design	Creationist cause set back by the Scopes 'Monkey Trial'

Just 4,499,993,988 years apart In public discourse today the term 'creationist' is generally used in a narrow sense referring mainly to evangelical Protestant fundamentalists in the USA. Such people believe that the bible is the directly inspired word of God and hence must be interpreted literally as gospel truth. Most contentiously, the early chapters of Genesis are held to give true and accurate accounts of the creation of the world and all the plants and animals that inhabit it (perplexingly, the bible contains two different accounts), a process of manufacture that was supposedly completed in six days at a date within the last 10,000 years. (The year 4004 BC, the creation date calculated by Archbishop James Ussher in the 17th century, is generally regarded as a fair estimate.) Such accounts are in clear and direct conflict with many aspects of the orthodox scientific understanding of how things are. According to the standard geologically established chronology, the earth is approximately 4.5 billion years old, while the vast diversity of species (including humans) to be seen in the world today is the product of evolutionary processes that have taken place gradually over the course of hundreds of millions of years.

Most religious doctrines, Christian and other, have sought to prevent unbridgeable gulfs opening up between science and religion by recognizing a division between the physical and spiritual realms. Thus, for example, according to the Roman Catholic view expressed by Pope John Paul II in 1981, the purpose of the creation stories in the bible is not to offer a scientific treatise but to explain the correct relationship between God and man; understood allegorically or symbolically, rather than literally, these accounts aim to tell us not 'how the heavens were made but how one goes to heaven'. This kind of accommodation, however, is closed off to strict, young-earth creationists by their insistence that the bible is (in the words of the Creation Research Society) the 'Written Word of God and . . . all of its assertions are historically and scientifically true'.

'Teach the Controversy' Creationism in the US has always had a strong political dimension, and over the last century this has expressed itself in a concerted opposition to the teaching of evolutionary theory in public schools. The literal truth of the biblical accounts of creation entails

1960s	**1981**	**1990s**	**2005**
Creation science begins to argue for a young earth (etc.)	Arkansas law requiring 'balanced treatment' ruled unconstitutional	Intelligent Design highlights irreducible complexity	Federal court rules that ID not clearly distinct from creationism

the falsity of evolution, so it is little surprise that the creationists' initial attempts were explicitly anti-evolutionary, aimed at having the study of Darwinism (as they usually called it) removed from public-school curricula. However, much of the momentum behind the call for an outright ban was lost after the notorious Scopes 'Monkey Trial' of 1925.

The Monkey Trial

A watershed in the history of creationism came in 1925 in Dayton, Tennessee, where anti-evolutionist politician William Jennings Bryan sought to fulfil his ambition to 'drive Darwinism from our schools' by leading the prosecution of John Scopes, a young biology teacher who had dared to teach the 'untested hypothesis' of evolution in contravention of a Tennessee state ban. Unfortunately for Bryan, in what soon became known as the 'Monkey Trial' he ran up against a formidable adversary in defending counsel Clarence Darrow. In the farcical climax, Darrow forced Bryan to take the stand as an expert witness on evolutionary theory. The only proof Bryan managed was his own defective understanding of the theory; he was finally obliged to concede that he did not think about things he did not think about, whereupon Darrow caustically enquired: 'And do you think about things that you *do* think about?' The result for the anti-evolutionists was a decidedly Pyrrhic victory, in which Scopes was convicted but cleared on appeal. Bryan himself died just five days after the trial, and popular derision was mercilessly heaped on the 'gaping primates from the upland valleys', as Tennessee's benighted folk were sarcastically called by the journalist H.L. Mencken. But the well of opposition to evolutionary theory ran deep, and as Mencken warned, creationism's 'fire is still burning on many a far-flung hill, and it may begin to roar at any moment'. The fire is now a conflagration and shows no sign of abating.

Since the 1960s creationist energies have increasingly been directed towards the goal of 'balanced treatment'. Marching under the banner 'Teach the Controversy', activists set out to show that scientific arguments could be marshalled in support of the creationist understanding of the world – arguments that were at least as strong as those for evolution – and therefore that the two views should be allowed equal time in science classrooms. A new discipline – 'creation science' – was born, whose main aim was to provide alternative, allegedly scientific explanations for the vast body of evidence (geological, palaeontological, biological, molecular) that massively corroborated orthodox science's account and chronology of the earth and the life it contains.

Warmed-up watchmakers In accordance with the US Constitution's insistence on the separation of state and religion, a number of landmark legal rulings continued to thwart the creation scientists' efforts to redefine what counted as science and so to insinuate their rival theories into US public schools. In the closing years of the 20th century a new strategy was adopted. Disavowing any connection with creationism (tactically, in the opinion of their opponents) and hence with religion, a new generation of 'Intelligent Design' (ID) theorists began to present what was in essence a resuscitated version of the argument from design – an argument that goes back at least to Thomas Aquinas and was most memorably expounded by the English philosopher William Paley in the early 19th century.

If you happened to find a watch on a heath, Paley argued, you would inevitably infer from the complexity and precision of its construction that it must have been the work of a watchmaker; in the same way, when you observe the wondrous contrivances of nature, you are obliged to conclude that they, too, must have a maker – God. In its new ID incarnation, the buzzword was now 'irreducible complexity': the idea that certain functional features in living systems are organized in ways that cannot be explained by the usual evolutionary mechanisms. From this it is inferred that such features, and the living organisms that exhibit them, are better explained as the work of an intelligent designer. Evolutionary biologists, of course, simply deny the premise that there are any such irreducibly complex features. As the British biologist Richard Dawkins memorably put it, in allusion to Paley's famous image, evolution's chief mechanism, natural selection, is a 'blind watchmaker' that fashions the complex structures of nature without any foresight or purpose.

> **'All the ills from which America suffers can be traced back to the teachings of evolution. It would be better to destroy every book ever written, and save just the first three verses of Genesis.'**
>
> **William Jennings Bryan, 1924**

the condensed idea
When world-views collide

22 War

'The most persistent sound which reverberates through man's history is the beating of war drums. Tribal wars, religious wars, civil wars, dynastic wars, national wars, revolutionary wars, colonial wars, wars of conquest and of liberation, wars to prevent and to end all wars, follow each other in a chain of compulsive repetitiveness as far as man can remember his past, and there is every reason to believe that the chain will extend into the future.'

It would take a supreme optimist, blind to mankind's history, to seriously question the Hungarian-born British polymath Arthur Koestler's views on the perennial nature of war. Warfare's persistence and ubiquity have led many to suppose that it must be an ingrained and chronic feature of human nature, while others have clung to the hope that it may be in some way cultural, a consequence of social practices that could in principle be reformed or removed. For an answer we need look no further than the Prussian military theorist Karl von Clausewitz, who famously remarked that 'War is the continuation of politics by other means'. So long as humans remain political animals hungry for land and other resources, there will be disputes about which group lives where and which group tells others what to do. And very often these disputes will be beyond resolution by other, peaceful means, and violent conflict will be the inevitable consequence.

Not all disputes are equally bad, however, nor is the violence used to end them. The debate over the morality of war, as much a live issue today as ever, has a long history. In the 5th century AD, St Augustine attempted to create an accommodation between the pacifist leanings of the early Church fathers and the military needs of imperial rulers. This was the seed

timeline

4th century BC	5th century AD
Sun-tzu writes *The Art of War*, the world's first work of military theory	St Augustine develops Christian doctrine of just war

of the long-standing Christian doctrine of just war, which is founded on the moral obligations to seek justice and to defend the innocent. Just war theory is probably the area of most active debate amongst today's philosophers, but it is not the only perspective. Two extreme views are realism and pacifism. Realists are sceptical about the whole project of applying ethical concepts to war; for them, international influence, national security and self-interest are the key concerns. Pacifists, in contrast, ardently believe that morality must hold sway in international affairs; military action, in their view, is never the right solution – there is always a better way of resolving a problem.

Just war 'War is an ugly thing, but not the ugliest of things: the decayed and degraded state of moral and patriotic feeling which thinks that nothing is *worth* a war, is much worse.' The most humane and least bellicose of men, the Victorian philosopher J.S. Mill nevertheless saw that sometimes it is necessary to fight the good fight. On occasion the motive may be so compelling, the cause so important that recourse to arms is morally justified. In these special circumstances, war may be the lesser of two evils: war may be just war.

The blessings of war

In modern times, no less than in earlier history, war has not lacked its enthusiasts. Writing in 1911, three years before the outbreak of the 'war to end all wars', the Prussian military historian Friedrich von Bernhardi could write glowingly of 'the inevitableness, the idealism, and the blessing of war'. In an essay written at the start of the same ghastly conflict, the English poet and critic Edmund Gosse extolled war as 'the sovereign disinfectant' whose 'red stream of blood . . . cleans out the stagnant pools and clotted channels of the intellect'. Less surprisingly, we find war eulogized by fascists such as Mussolini, who salivates over war that 'imposes the stamp of nobility upon the peoples who have the courage to make it'. It is noteworthy that it is most often war's veterans, such as Dwight D. Eisenhower, who understand its true nature: 'I hate war as only a soldier who has lived it can, only as one who has seen its brutality, its futility, its stupidity.'

13th century	1832	1862	1978
Aquinas refines principles of just war	Publication of Clausewitz's highly influential *On War*	American Civil War prompts J.S. Mill to extol principle of just war	Arthur Koestler remarks on the perennial nature of war

Bismarck fought "necessary" wars and killed thousands; the idealists of the 20th century fight "just" wars and kill millions.

A.J.P. Taylor, 1952

Augustine's ideas on just war were refined in the 13th century by Thomas Aquinas, who was responsible for the now-canonical distinction between *jus ad bellum* ('justice in the move to war', the conditions under which it is morally right to take up arms) and *jus in bello* ('justice in war', rules of conduct once fighting is underway). Much of the current debate over the ethics of war is structured around these two ideas.

Jus ad bellum It is generally agreed that there are a number of conditions all of which must be met to justify a move to war. The most important of these, **just cause**, is also the most disputed. In earlier times this was often some form of religious cause, which would now generally be discounted (in the secular West at least) as ideologically motivated. Modern theorists tend to limit the scope of just cause to defence against aggression. Least controversially, this would include self-defence against a violation of a country's basic rights – its political sovereignty and territorial integrity (e.g. Kuwait against Iraq in 1990/1); and most people would extend it to cover assistance given to a third party suffering such aggression (e.g. the coalition forces liberating Kuwait in 1991). However, it is not enough merely to have just cause; it is also necessary to have **right intention**. The sole motivation must be to right the wrong caused by the aggression that provided just cause. The latter cannot be a fig leaf for ulterior motives, such as national interest, territorial expansion or aggrandisement.

A decision to take up arms should only be taken by the **proper authority**. 'War is the trade of kings', Dryden wrote at the end of the 17th century, but the French Revolution a century later ensured that the right to declare war resided thenceforth with whatever body or institution of the state held sovereign power. The concept of proper authority raises, of course, tricky questions about legitimate government and the appropriate relationship between decision-makers and people. Most would argue, for instance, that the Nazi governors of 1930s Germany lacked not only just cause but also basic legitimacy to declare and wage war.

A country should only resort to war, even a just one, if it has a 'reasonable' **prospect of success**: there is generally no point in sacrificing lives and resources in vain. Others, though, would argue that it is right (and certainly not wrong) to resist an aggressor, however futile the gesture may be. Furthermore, a sense of **proportionality** must be observed. There must be a balance between the desired end and the likely consequences of getting there: the expected good, in terms of righting the wrong that constitutes the just cause, must be weighed against the anticipated damage, in terms of casualties, human suffering, etc.

'To subdue the enemy without a fight is the supreme excellence', according to the Chinese general Sun-tzu, the world's first great military theorist. Military action must always be the last resort and is only ever justified if every other peaceful, non-military option has failed. As the British politician Tony Benn pointed out, in some sense 'all war represents a failure of diplomacy'.

Jus in bello The other aspect of just war theory, *jus in bello*, attempts to define what counts as morally acceptable and proper conduct once the fighting has started. This has a wide scope, extending from the behaviour of individual soldiers in their relation both to the enemy and to civilians, all the way up to major strategic questions, such as use of weapons (nuclear, chemical, mines, scatter bombs, etc.).

> **Mankind must put an end to war, or war will put an end to mankind.**
>
> **John F. Kennedy, 1961**

In this area, two considerations are usually taken as paramount. **Proportionality** requires that means and ends are well matched; thus, to take the extreme case, almost everyone accepts that nuclear attack cannot be justified, however successful it might be in bringing about some military objective. **Discrimination** requires that combatants and non-combatants are strictly distinguished; thus, for instance, it is not considered permissible to target civilians even if it might prove effective in eroding military morale. Many aspects of *jus in bello* overlap with the issue of war crimes and the subject matter of international law, such as the Hague rules and Geneva conventions.

the condensed idea
Politics by other means

23 Duty

You are a member of the Resistance in occupied France and have just been captured by the Gestapo. The officer interrogating you rounds up ten children from your village and threatens to shoot them unless you agree to find and then shoot two of your fellows in the Resistance. You have no doubt that the officer will carry out his threat if you do not comply.

Put in such a ghastly situation, what should you do? In broad terms, moral theorists have tended to take two distinct views on such dilemmas. Some think that we should look at the different outcomes produced by the available courses of action: if you comply, there are two dead Resistance members; if you don't, there are ten dead children. The consequences of your action are what really matter, so the right thing to do (other things being equal) is to obey the officer. Others feel that it matters a lot that it is *you* who is doing the shooting: you have a duty – it is a moral requirement – not to kill people, so you should refuse, however grim the consequences.

In real life, things are rarely, if ever, as simple or stark as this. Things are never truly equal, and there are almost always other and perhaps better options (if the Gestapo officer really gave you a gun, it might be preferable to turn it on yourself – or even better on him). Still, the scenario described may be extreme but it is not fantastic, and it brings into sharp focus some critical features that are also found in more mundane settings. In particular in such situations it is natural to ask where your duty lies. Clearly, some people's rights are going to be seriously infringed, you hold various responsibilities towards the people involved, and you are inevitably faced with conflicting duties. How do you decide what to do?

God-given duty A duty is a responsibility or obligation that is required of you, either by virtue of some position you hold or in

timeline

14th–13th century BC	AD 1688
According to scriptures, God delivers Ten Commandments to Moses on Mount Sinai	Absolute duty to English monarch ended by Glorious Revolution

> **Duty, then, is the sublimest word in our language. Do your duty in all things. You cannot do more. You should never wish to do less.**
>
> Robert E. Lee (attributed), **19th century**

accordance with some custom, law or authority that you more or less willingly accept. For most of humanity, for most of its history, the ultimate authority has been divine. Usually passed down through some kind of scripture and often mediated by some kind of priesthood, the wishes and commands of a god or gods impose obligations on humans, whose duty it is to meet these obligations, by adopting certain codes of conduct, for instance, and performing various services and sacrifices in honour of the deity/deities. In the Judaeo-Christian tradition, the most familiar example is the Ten Commandments, a set of divine prescriptions that impose a number of duties on mankind: a duty not to kill, another not to covet your neighbour's wife, and so on.

Often in human history, the divine authority that has been the principal source of duty has been vested in proxies on earth, giving the latter an absolute right to rule without reference to the will of their subjects. An example is the divine right claimed by the Stuart kings in England and the Bourbon kings of France, which gave them a right and duty to defend Christendom on earth and imposed on their subjects a duty of unquestioning loyalty and obedience. Such absolutism was largely undermined by the revolutions of the 17th and 18th centuries, which introduced constitutional arrangements that imposed mutual rights and duties between monarch and subject.

Kant on duty Philosophically, by far the most influential contribution to the discussion of duty was made by the 18th-century German theorist Immanuel Kant. In Kant's austere conception, actions do not have moral worth if they are motivated by sympathy, friendship or the

1775–83	1785	1789
System of rights and duties established in USA by American Revolution	Kant analyses duty in *Groundwork of the Metaphysics of Morals*	Declaration of the Rights of Man defines citizen rights and duties in France

desire to achieve some particular end; it is only actions that are prompted by a sense of duty alone – a duty to obey moral laws that are determined by reason – that are distinctively moral. The non-moral promptings of desire he calls 'hypothetical imperatives', because if you do not desire the end, you are under no obligation to obey the command. A moral law, in contrast, has the form of a 'categorical imperative': a command that is absolute, unconditional and universal, in the sense that it applies equally to all rational beings.

Acts, omissions and double effect

Take a case like the Gestapo officer and the French Resistance. Suppose you think that it is an absolute moral duty not to kill people, even if the consequence is that more people end up dead. In such a case you are duty-bound to explain why it is so significant, morally, that it is *you* who is or is not doing the killing. It is often suggested that it is worse to act in a way that *causes* people's death than to allow them to die through your inaction. But a decision *not* to act is just as much a decision as a decision to act, so it is far from clear that 'doing nothing' is, in a moral sense, equivalent to 'doing nothing wrong'. Letting your children starve to death may be as morally objectionable as drowning them in the bath. Likewise, in the debate over euthanasia, it may be hard to prove the morally relevant distinction people try to draw between administering death-inducing drugs (a deliberate doing) and withholding life-prolonging drugs (a deliberate not doing).

To bolster the rather rickety act–omission doctrine, another idea that is frequently invoked is the principle of double effect, which depends on separating the consequences of an action that were intended from those that were merely foreseen. An action that has both good and bad results may then be morally justified if it was performed with the intention of bringing about the good results, while the bad results were foreseen but not intended. For instance, it may be known that giving pain-killing drugs to a terminally ill patient will hasten his death. But so long as this consequence is unintended – the *intention* is merely to relieve pain – the action may yet be morally defensible. Whether the distinction between intention and foresight can bear the weight that the double effect principle puts upon it has been much debated.

The genius of Kant's ethical system is how he moves from the purely rational structure imposed by the categorical imperative to actual moral content – to explain how 'pure reason', stripped of inclination or desire, can inform and direct the will of a moral agent. He finds the answer in the inherent value of moral agency itself – value based on the 'single supreme principle of morality', the freedom or autonomy of a will that obeys laws that it imposes on itself. The overriding importance attached to autonomous, free-willed agents is mirrored in perhaps the most famous formulation of the categorical imperative:

> 'Act in such a way that you always treat humanity, whether in your own person or in the person of any other, never simply as a means, but always at the same time as an end.'

Once the inestimable value of one's own moral agency is recognized, it is necessary to extend that respect to the agency of others. To treat others merely as a means to promote one's own interests is to undermine or destroy their agency, so principles (maxims) that are self-serving or damaging to others contravene this formulation of the categorical imperative and so do not qualify as moral laws. In essence, there is a recognition here that there are basic rights that belong to people by virtue of their humanity and that may not be overridden; and hence that there are duties that must be obeyed, come what may.

'Duty cannot exist without faith.'
Benjamin Disraeli, 1847

the condensed idea
Thou shalt not . . .
come what may?

24 Utopia

The Austrian-born philosopher Karl Popper once remarked: 'Those who promise us paradise on earth never produced anything but a hell.' Since the time of Plato at least, there has been no shortage of visionaries, mystics and cranks who have conjured up brave new worlds that have encouraged hope and exhibited folly in more or less equal measure. Most of these earthly paradises never had much prospect of existing outside the minds of their creators, but the few that have been realized in fact have tended to confirm Popper's confidence in mankind's capacity to turn dreams into nightmares.

Today, calling something 'utopian' generally carries the implication that the scheme in question is both idealistic and unattainable. This subtlety of meaning was intended by the man who originally coined the term 'utopia', the English scholar and statesman Sir Thomas More. At the beginning of his *Utopia*, written in Latin and published in 1516, More includes a short prefatory verse which explains that the ideal state he describes, which is called 'Utopia' (from the Greek meaning 'no place'), might also warrant the name 'Eutopia' (meaning 'good place'). More's imaginary island is a humanist paradise, a proto-communist society in which everything is held in common and men and women live together harmoniously as equals; religious intolerance has been banished and education is provided by the state; and gold is valueless and used to make chamber pots.

Marginal voices By deliberating on the best form of government, More was drawing a clear though oblique contrast with the politics of his day, in his own country and in Christian Europe as a whole, which at that time were driven by greed and divided by self-interest. Following More's example, many later writers used the utopian romance as a literary vehicle

timeline

c.375 BC	AD 1516	1649	1868
Plato describes his ideal state (the Republic)	Thomas More coins the name 'utopia'	Communist Diggers active in wake of English Civil War	J.S. Mill coins the term 'dystopia'

that allowed them to criticize the evils of contemporary society without overtly antagonizing dangerous men in high places.

In his post-Marxist *Ideology and Utopia* (1929) the Hungarian-born sociologist Karl Mannheim claims that utopian ideas appeal in particular to subordinate social groups and classes, who are attracted to the potential they offer for change, while dominant groups typically adhere to ideologies that tend to promote continuity and to preserve the status quo. In other words, those who suffer most from society's existing defects stand to gain most from social reform; and turkeys do not vote for Christmas.

Essay into a better future

Amongst today's intellectuals, utopianism is not much in vogue. One criticism of utopias, literary and other, is that they are static and lifeless. Unlike the real world (and unlike their dark cousins, dystopias), they lack the passion and drama of conflict; too often, they are dead structures dreamed up by politicians and economists. In short, utopias offer the dullness of perfection – worlds without the flaws and foibles that generate human interest. But a very different view was common in the 19th century, the heyday of utopian optimism, when the quest for utopias was seen as the key to progress.

Oscar Wilde articulates this buoyant confidence in *The Soul of Man under Socialism* (1891), an essay in which he argues for a socialist world where the drudgery of work has been removed by the benign application of technology. 'A map of the world that does not include Utopia is not worth even glancing at,' he protests, 'for it leaves out the one country at which Humanity is always landing. And when Humanity lands there, it looks out, and seeing a better country, sets sail. Progress is the realisation of Utopias.'

❝Without the Utopias of other times, men would still live in caves, miserable and naked . . . Out of generous dreams come beneficial realities. Utopia is the principle of all progress, and the essay into a better future.❞

Anatole France, *c.*1900

1880	1890	1932	1949
Bellamy's *Looking Backward* published	Publication of William Morris's *News from Nowhere*	Aldous Huxley's *Brave New World*	George Orwell's *Nineteen Eighty-Four*

Accordingly, it is often fringe political figures, lacking a voice within established power structures, who have been most strident in pushing forward utopian schemes. Many utopians have traced society's ills to inequalities in wealth, which are presumed to have spawned greed, envy and social unrest. And hence, like More, they see a remedy in removing such differences and implementing some kind of egalitarian, communist system in their place.

From hope to fear The 19th century saw a great enthusiasm for utopian ideas that was fuelled by the stunning progress of science. While the tone was generally optimistic and the usual panacea was socialism, there was nevertheless a wide spectrum of views expressed. At one extreme, the US novelist Edward Bellamy's *Looking Backward* (1888) has its hero wake up in the year 2000 to discover a world which is classless and egalitarian, yet heavily industrialized and bureaucratic. Horrified by Bellamy's technocratic vision, the English socialist artist and author William Morris provided an antidote in his *News from Nowhere* (1890), which offers a pastoral idyll in which industrial grime has been scrubbed from a land where men and women are free and equal.

Plato's iron fist

Utopias had existed, in conception if not in name, long before Thomas More's day. The earliest and most influential of these is Plato's Republic, which also, ominously, sets an early benchmark for nastiness in imagined societies. The ideal state envisaged by Plato is extremely authoritarian, with a philosophically trained elite known as the 'guardians', who alone have true knowledge and who exercise absolute control over the unenlightened majority. Strict censorship is used to prevent wrong ideas getting about, and a eugenic policy is implemented to ensure that only the right people get to breed.

The signs of anxiety at the remorseless advance of science that begin to surface in Morris's work intensified in the early decades of the 20th century. Where the Victorians were hopeful and dreamed up utopias that were egalitarian and inclusive, the Edwardians were fearful and devised utopias that were elitist and exclusive. For futurists such as novelist and science-fiction writer H.G. Wells, the aim now was not so much to make the world a better place for people to live in, but to make a people more worthy to live in the world. Fears that decent folk would be overwhelmed by the 'people of the abyss' – the ever-growing working poor – coincided with the emergence of new 'sciences' that   seemed to promise ready solutions. Social Darwinism (a cruel distortion of Darwin's ideas) suggested that society's weak and vulnerable could and should be winnowed out by a natural process of selection; in other words, they could be left to fend for themselves while those more fortunate looked on. At the same time, eugenics promised a proactive way of improving and purifying the human stock by any means, including compulsory sterilization.

'The trouble with kingdoms of heaven on earth is that they're liable to come to pass, and then their fraudulence is apparent for all to see.' The horrible truth of British journalist Malcolm Muggeridge's words was evident in the decades following the First World War. The ghastliness of twisted eugenics and social planning was witnessed in the Teutonic nightmare of Nazi Germany, a bucolic monstrosity of blond pigtails and jack boots; and the communist utopia of Marx and Engels was brought to horrifying life in the gulags of Stalin's Russia and in the Cultural Revolution of Mao's China. One positive legacy of these totalitarian perversions was the two great dystopian classics of the 20th century. In Aldous Huxley's *Brave New World* (1932), social stability is gained at the cost of an anodyne existence induced by drugs and brainwashing within a eugenically manipulated caste system. George Orwell's *Nineteen Eighty-Four* (1949) is a totalitarian nightmare in which the abiding image is 'a boot stamping on a human face – forever'.

> **❛The human mind is inspired enough when it comes to inventing horrors; it is when it tries to invent a Heaven that it shows itself cloddish.❜**
>
> **Evelyn Waugh, 1942**

The Diggers

Times of extreme social turmoil are fruitful for utopian reformers, and one such was the period of the English Civil War and its immediate aftermath. Among several radical groups to emerge, one of the more eccentric was the Diggers, or True Levellers, whose visionary leader, Gerrard Winstanley, insisted that God's earth was a treasury common to all and that the institution of property was a consequence of the Fall, and so proposed what was in effect a communist utopia. Intent on restoring the people's right to common land, in April 1649 a party of Diggers started digging the commons at St George's Hill, Surrey. A number of other colonies sprang up, but all were short-lived, roughly handled by the authorities and irate locals alike.

the condensed idea
Heaven or hell on earth

25 Liberalism

'If we were back in the days of the Revolution, so-called conservatives today would be the Liberals and the liberals would be the Tories.' If any 20th-century US president could be expected to blanch at being labelled a liberal, that president would be Ronald Reagan. Yet it was he, in an interview published in 1975, who made this perceptive comment on the complex and entwined histories of two of the world's most influential political ideologies: conservatism and liberalism.

The definition Reagan proceeds to give – 'a desire for less government interference or less centralized authority or more individual freedom' – looks like a textbook summary of classical liberalism, but in his view it was also the 'basis of conservatism'. How can two ideologies, today regarded (especially in the USA) as polar opposites, be mentioned in the same breath by a man who is now revered as a demigod by the conservative Right?

The solution to this conundrum lies principally in the curious history of liberalism. Liberalism, in both its classical and its modern incarnations, has focused consistently on a single, if complex, idea: the importance of individuals as rational agents and of defending their liberty and liberties against abuses of power. In the course of pursuing this end, however, liberals performed a dramatic U-turn in their choice of means. Initially, liberalism's doubts about the state's ability to use its powers responsibly led

> **As Mankind becomes more liberal, they will be more apt to allow that all those who conduct themselves as worthy members of the community are equally entitled to the protections of civil government.**
>
> **George Washington, 1790**

timeline

1651	1688	1690	1775–83	1776
Hobbes's *Leviathan* argues that a sovereign rules only with popular consent	Glorious Revolution brings constitutional monarchy to England	John Locke's *Two Treatises of Government* published	American Revolution fought for 'Life, Liberty and the pursuit of Happiness'	Adam Smith's *The Wealth of Nations* argues the case for free trade

to a call for the scope of government to be strictly limited, especially in the area of commerce. Later, when it became clear that unfettered economic activity produced inequalities in the distribution of wealth that were no less threatening to civil liberties, liberals became more interventionist, looking to expand the state and harness its power to correct these inequalities. It was the adoption by conservatives of the means (but not the end) espoused by earlier, classical liberals, including free trade and minimal state intervention, that provides the context for Reagan's unexpected comments.

Classical liberalism The emergence of liberalism as a political doctrine is generally seen as a response to the horrors of the religious conflicts culminating in the Thirty Years' War that raged in Europe during the first half of the 17th century. Shocked by the massive social turmoil and human suffering caused by decades of religiously and dynastically inspired fighting, the English philosophers Thomas Hobbes and John Locke began to speculate on the basis and justification of government. Both agreed that the sovereign's power was justified only by the consent of the governed, as expressed in a notional social contract between ruler and ruled, and that the latter's freedom should not be limited without good

A temperamental divide

A key distinction between conservatism and liberalism, at least as it seemed to Victorian commentators, was their different outlook on human nature. The conservative assumed that people were basically weak and selfish and life's object was to maintain social order and stability; the liberal assumed that people were basically good and rational and life's object was to extend human happiness. Liberalism's essentially optimistic view of human nature meant that its proponents were typically socially progressive and enthusiastic about social reform and improvement. The contrast was memorably encapsulated by Victorian Britain's greatest liberal prime minister, William Gladstone: 'Liberalism is trust of the people tempered by prudence. Conservatism is distrust of the people tempered by fear.'

1789–99	1859	1933	1979–80
French Revolution fought for 'liberty, equality, fraternity'	John Stuart Mill's *On Liberty* published	Franklin D. Roosevelt launches New Deal to counter effects of Great Depression	Elections of Margaret Thatcher (1979) and of Ronald Reagan (1980) bring New Right 'neo-liberal' policies to Britain and the USA

cause and without consent. Locke's *Two Treatises of Government* were published in 1690, just two years after the Glorious Revolution had established a constitutionally constrained monarch on the English throne; these two works provided much of the theoretical inspiration for the great transformative upheavals of the following century: the American and French revolutions. In the crucible of these epoch-making events, a sense of the importance of human individuality was forged as never before. The individual now emerged from centuries of subservience to king, lord or priest, liberated from the grip of ancient custom and authority.

Insistence on limiting the role of the state and faith in the rationality of the individual combined to produce one of the most distinctive features of classical liberalism: its association with capitalism and free trade. The rationale behind this association was elaborated chiefly by the Scottish economist Adam Smith in *The Wealth of Nations* (1776). Smith opposed government interference, arguing that the energies of an individual acting in a free market in rational pursuit of his own interest would inevitably tend to the common good, since the very fact of serving himself in an exchange economy required that he also serve others. A system in which buyers and sellers act freely and competitively would, Smith argued, be self-regulating and hence as efficient as possible and optimally adjusted to produce wealth for all.

Classical liberalism reached its highest point in the course of the 19th century, when the great utilitarian philosophers Jeremy Bentham and John Stuart Mill applied the lessons learned from Smith's free-market economics – especially the role of free choice and enlightened self-interest – more broadly to the political domain. They developed an elaborate system of individual rights that still lies at the core of modern liberal thinking. By the end of the century liberalism had transformed the political climate of Europe, where limited and constitutional government now largely held sway and industrialization and free trade were generating enormous wealth.

New liberalism Adam Smith himself had foreseen that unrestrained free enterprise could lead to excesses, while Mill had argued that economic inequalities generated by the operation of capitalism would require some form of moderation. A common criticism of liberals had always been that their fixation with limiting public power made them blind to the effects of private power, and by the end of the 19th century it had become clear that the lives of ordinary people were being downtrodden by industrialists and financiers who exercised vast economic and political power. It was in opposition to this new tyranny of a reactionary plutocracy that a generation of 'new' ('social' or 'welfare') liberals emerged. They were ready to expand the power of government to correct economic inequalities, by regulating industry and introducing economic and fiscal reforms. Among the most notable achievements of new liberal thinking was the sweeping welfare and social security initiatives introduced by Roosevelt's New Deal in the 1930s.

> **'Liberalism is the supreme form of generosity; it is the right which the majority concedes to minorities and hence it is the noblest cry that has ever resounded on this planet.'**
>
> **José Ortega y Gasset, 1930**

The new liberal approach flourished in the decades of unprecedented growth and prosperity following the Second World War. From the 1970s, however, confidence in continued progress faltered and then crashed as economic stagnation, high inflation and growing national debt took hold. In the wake of these economic woes, the 'New Right' came to power in both the US and Britain, where Ronald Reagan and Margaret Thatcher (sometimes termed 'neo-liberals') eagerly embraced – in theory if not always in practice – central dogmas of classical liberalism: contraction of the state and free trade. In the war of words waged by the New Right, liberalism was ruthlessly parodied as uncontrolled big-state, tax-and-spend, 'politically correct' mumbo-jumbo and the word 'liberal' became, in US politics, virtually a term of abuse. Such a situation, in a country that is constitutionally and historically the most liberal (in all its senses) that has ever existed, is extraordinary. Nevertheless, the flame of enlightened and progressive liberalism still burns, as the Democratic presidential nominee John F. Kennedy eloquently protested half a century ago:

'What do our opponents mean when they apply to us the label "Liberal"? If by "Liberal" they mean . . . someone who is soft in his policies abroad, who is against local government, and who is unconcerned with the taxpayer's dollar, then the record of this party and its members demonstrate that we are not that kind of "Liberal". But, if by a "Liberal" they mean someone who looks ahead and not behind, someone who welcomes new ideas without rigid reactions, someone who cares about the welfare of the people . . . then I'm proud to say that I'm a "Liberal".'

the condensed idea
Social progress and individual freedom

26 Democracy

Today, over the full spectrum of political views from left to right, there is an extraordinary and unprecedented consensus that democracy is preferable to any other form of governance. Such is the level of agreement on this point that 'democratic' has become all but synonymous with 'legitimate' in many political contexts. One curious consequence of this is that many regimes that would clearly fail on any normal reckoning to qualify as democratic have nevertheless chosen to style themselves as such. So, for instance, the former East Germany – a repressive and authoritarian one-party state – was officially known as the 'German Democratic Republic'.

Even if we discount bogus claims of this kind, the process of democratization across the globe over the last century has been impressive. Broad estimates given by various independent observers agree that in the year 2000 roughly half the world's population enjoyed political institutions that provided historically high levels of democratic government.

The rapid expansion of democracy during the 20th century is explained in part by the spectacular failure of the alternatives. Speaking before the House of Commons in 1947, shortly after the total defeat of fascism, Winston Churchill famously observed that 'Democracy is the worst form of government except all those other forms that have been tried from time to time.' Within half a century democracy's chief rival as the basis of political organization, communism, had come messily unstuck in Russia and Eastern Europe.

Such is the world's current obsession with democracy that it is easy to forget quite how recent a phenomenon it is. For over the last two-and-a-half millennia almost every political theorist has been energetically opposed to democracy, in principle and in practice. The most general charge is simply

timeline

507 BC	AD 1651	1690
Cleisthenes introduces democratic reforms in Athens	Hobbes discusses balance between state power and individual liberty	Locke identifies popular consent as the basis of state authority

that democracy is anarchic and little better than mob rule, while specific criticisms have focused on the competence of the people (however that is defined) to participate in the process of government. Even a critic as generally sympathetic to democratic principles as J.S. Mill was nevertheless deeply concerned at the 'collective mediocrity' of the masses, who no longer 'take their opinions from dignitaries of Church or State, from ostensible leaders, or from books'. H.L. Mencken, an American humorist, put it more pithily in the 1920s when he characterized democracy as 'a pathetic belief in the collective wisdom of individual ignorance'.

> **Democracy means simply the bludgeoning of the people by the people for the people.**
>
> **Oscar Wilde, 1891**

Greece and direct democracy Fierce criticism of democratic government dates back to its infancy in Athens, the Greek city state that is generally credited with being the 'cradle of democracy'. (The word itself is derived from the Greek meaning 'rule by the people'.) The system of popular government that was progressively put in place by the Athenian people was probably the purest form of direct democracy that has ever been realized. At the heart of the system introduced by the popular leader Cleisthenes in 507 BC was the ecclesia, or 'assembly', which was open to all eligible citizens (Athenian males over the age of 18). The ecclesia met regularly to debate important state business and would reach decisions by show of hands on the basis of a majority of those present. The virtues of democratic Athens were most forcefully proclaimed (at least as recorded by the historian Thucydides) in a funeral oration delivered in 430 BC by the Athenian leader Pericles. He praises the constitution, which 'favours the many, not the few', and stresses the significance of liberty, equality before the law and political preferment gained on the basis of merit, not wealth or class.

Such enthusiasm was emphatically not shared by Greece's two most influential philosophers, Plato and Aristotle. Both were writing in the following century, in the wake of Athens's disastrous defeat in 404 BC by deeply authoritarian Sparta, a calamity that coloured their shared view that democracy was chronically unruly, corrupt and unstable. 'Democracy is a charming form of government,' commented Plato acidly, 'which is full of variety and disorder and which dispenses equality to equals and unequals

1787	**1789–99**	**1945**	**1989**
The Constitution defines the mechanisms of US democratic government	Radical democracy seen for the first time during French Revolution	End of Second World War marks defeat of fascism	Communism regimes collapse in Soviet Union and Eastern Europe

Some more equal than others . . .

Few regimes in place before the 20th century, whatever name they chose to give themselves, would today qualify as full democracies simply because their franchises were so risibly small. In Athens, where women, resident foreigners and slaves were excluded from the enfranchised *demos* ('people'), some scholarly estimates – admittedly rather speculative – suggest that perhaps as few as one in ten of the total population was eligible to vote. The situation was even more restricted in 19th-century Britain, where stern property requirements meant that even after the Great Reform Act of 1832, only about seven percent of the adult population were able to vote; universal suffrage was not achieved until 1928, when the vote was finally extended to all adult women. In the US many African Americans were effectively (though not legally) disenfranchised until the Civil Rights Act of 1964.

alike.' According to Aristotle's lastingly influential classification of political constitutions, democracy is the corrupt or perverted form of 'polity', an ideal constitution in which the many govern in pursuit of the common good. In a democracy, by contrast, those in control – the lower strata of society – rule in their own interest and can therefore be expected to appropriate the wealth and property of the better-off citizens.

Representative democracy Another point on which Plato and Aristotle agreed was that the Greek model of direct democracy, involving continuous and face-to-face participation on the part of citizens, was practicable only in small states such as Athens. This basic difficulty – the apparent impossibility of incorporating such a system in a state or nation with a relatively large territory and population – remained unresolved into the modern era. It was not until the 17th and 18th centuries that serious discussion of democracy and popular sovereignty resurfaced, stirred up in the welter of ideas generated by Enlightenment thinkers.

In 1651, in the immediate aftermath of the English Civil War, Thomas Hobbes posed the question that lay at the heart of much subsequent theorizing on democracy: how should the sovereign power of the state, justified by the need to protect (among other things) the rights of individuals, be constrained in order to prevent its misuse to curtail those same rights? John Locke, writing four decades later, argued that the bestowal of such authority on the government by the governed, and the concomitant limitation of their own liberties, must only be done with the consent of the governed. Debate on the proper relationship between people and state thus resolved itself into an argument on the appropriate balance between might and right; between the claims of the state on one side and the rights of the individual on the other.

The fruit of this endeavour, hard and bloodily won in the course of two revolutions, first in America and then in France, was the liberal notion of constitutionally based representative democracy. Much refined and elaborated over the years, this theory – the 'grand discovery of modern times', according to James Mill, father of J.S. Mill – stipulated a range of political mechanisms, including regular elections and competition between parties and candidates, that would ensure that governors remained accountable to governed and hence that the latter retained ultimate authority and control over the political process.

'The most tyrannical of all governments'

Even among the most enlightened of early-modern theorists, the consuming concern was that majority rule would lead to the rights of minorities being trampled underfoot. Writing in 1787, John Adams, future second president of the USA, reflected the deep concerns of the Founding Fathers at the prospect of all branches of government coming under the control of the majority: 'Debts would be abolished first; taxes laid heavy on the rich, and not at all on others; and at last a downright equal division of everything be demanded and voted.' The fourth president, James Madison, wrote disapprovingly in 1833 of 'the sweeping denunciation of majority governments as the most tyrannical and intolerable of all governments', but limiting the powers of majorities was a prime motivation behind the separation of powers and the elaborate system of checks and balances that are so prominent in the constitution for which he was largely responsible.

the condensed idea
Bludgeoning of the people by the people?

27 Conservatism

'The science of government being ... so practical in itself and intended for such practical purposes – a matter which requires experience, and even more experience than any person can gain in his whole life, however sagacious and observing he may be – it is with infinite caution that any man ought to venture upon pulling down an edifice which has answered in any tolerable degree for ages the common purposes of society, or on building it up again without having models and patterns of approved utility before his eyes.'

In his *Reflections on the Revolution in France* of 1790, the Irish-born politician and writer Edmund Burke champions a political outlook that values above all (as Wordsworth later put it) 'institutes and laws hallowed by time' and 'the vital power of social ties Endeared by custom'. A preference for practice grounded in experience over abstract theory; an aversion to change for change's sake; an unwillingness to risk what serves its purpose for what might, speculatively, serve it better: over the succeeding two centuries these and other ideas would come to define one of the chief polarities of modern political thought – conservatism.

If it ain't bust ... The basic and very human instinct from which conservative thought emerged is neatly captured in a maxim first credited to the 17th-century English statesman Viscount Falkland: 'If it is not necessary to change, it is necessary not to change.' The particular change that so much offended Burke was the French Revolution. Writing in 1790, before the revolution had descended into bloody mayhem, Burke observed the ideological fervour that drove the revolutionaries – a passion partly inspired by the abstract speculations of the Enlightenment *philosophes* – and correctly predicted the horrors that lay ahead. Idealistic, ideological,

timeline

1651	1762	1789–99
Thomas Hobbes argues that self-interest is primary motive for human action	Publication of Jean-Jacques Rousseau's *Social Contract*	French Revolution prompts reactionary fears across Europe

A disposition to preserve

Probably the most common criticism of conservatism is that it is merely reactionary: stuck in an idealized past and unwilling to adapt to present and future needs. Thus the Victorian moralist Matthew Arnold, for instance, complained that 'the principle of Conservatism . . . destroys what it loves, because it will not mend it'. It is true that some conservatives have not helped themselves in this respect, inviting ridicule as they indulge in flights of nostalgic whimsy. A recent example was the Conservative prime minister John Major, who in 1993 delivered a panegyric to Britain as a land of 'warm beer, invincible green suburbs, dog lovers, and . . . old maids bicycling to Holy Communion through the morning mist'. However, true conservatism is far from being resistant to reform, as Burke makes perfectly clear: 'There is something else than the mere alternative of absolute destruction or unreformed existence . . . A disposition to preserve and an ability to improve, taken together, would be my standard of a statesman. Everything else is vulgar in the conception, perilous in the execution.'

scornful of all that had gone before – everything about the French Revolution revolted Burke's conservative instincts.

Just as Burke's diatribe is essentially reactive, so too is conservatism in general. The political attitude that Burke espoused inspired later conservatives who stood in opposition to social and political developments that threatened the status quo in their own day. Throughout much of the 19th century, successive waves of liberal reform and social disruption caused by the processes of industrialization provided the greatest provocations to conservatives. Some of these issues, such as universal suffrage, carried over into the 20th century, but increasingly conservative energies became focused on resisting the perceived threat of socialism and communism.

The democracy of the dead Tradition, wrote G.K. Chesterton with gentle mockery, is the 'democracy of the dead', which involves 'giving votes to the most obscure of all classes, our ancestors'. For conservative traditionalists, however, 'being disqualified by the accident of death' is no disqualification at all. Burke sees the accumulated wisdom of tradition,

1790	**1832**	**1861**	**1980s**
Burke makes the first great statement of conservative values	In *The Prelude* Wordsworth hails 'the Genius of Burke'	Publication of Mill's *Considerations on Representative Government*	Reaganomics and Thatcherism set neo-liberal agenda in US and Europe

broadly interpreted to include the sum of the customs and practices that together form our culture, as a trust to be reverently passed from generation to generation. He agrees with Hobbes and Rousseau that society is a contract, but in his view the agreement is honoured not through fear of the state's absolute power but because it is in essence a harmonious 'partnership not only between those who are living, but between those who are living, those who are dead, and those who are to be born'. The steady progress of society is guided by this collective wisdom, which inevitably exceeds the intelligence of any individual and which invariably counsels restraint when it comes to social change. As Gladstone later noted, conservatives (unlike liberals) share a basic 'distrust of the people tempered by fear'. They are inclined to believe that humans are naturally selfish and base; and hence that political and social practices and institutions that have stood the test of time – 'the pleasing illusions which make power gentle and obedience liberal' – are required to curb these destructive instincts.

The wisdom of ignorance Writing in 1861, the liberal J.S. Mill asserted that the Conservatives were 'by the law of their existence the stupidest party'. The comment was somewhat unjust, in that he was referring to their tendency to be untrue to their own principles, a habit they shared with other political parties. There is a sense, however, in which conservatives are unashamedly ignorant. Just as Socrates' wisdom lay in his awareness of how little he knew, conservatives are typically sceptical about the extent of human knowledge, and this scepticism colours many of their other views.

Most generally, reliance on the wisdom of the past – belief in the value of experience and of the tried and tested – follows naturally from doubts over the ability of present-day policy-makers to know the true consequences of their initiatives. If the state cannot be trusted to strike out in new directions without bringing on a host of unforeseen problems, the best policy, as a rule, will be to stick to the empirically proven and to limit the scope of government as far as possible. The small-state and limited-government policies favoured by generations of conservatives flow readily from a

❝Conservative ideal of freedom and progress: everyone to have an unfettered opportunity of remaining exactly where they are.❞

Geoffrey Madan, (1895–1947)

A political chameleon

As conservatism is an essentially reactive position, its policies are inevitably determined, to some degree, by what it is reacting against. For this reason the range of ideas associated with conservatism has been enormously variable over time. The recent obsession with free-market economics has puzzled some commentators, but the strongly neo-liberal agenda of the Reagan–Thatcher era of the 1980s, in which the priorities were free markets, deregulation and minimizing the size of the state, was in many respects a classic conservative response to the lavish and costly welfarist policies that had gone before. In the same way, the apparently odd coupling of Reaganomics (economically very hands-off) with extreme social conservatism (morally very hands-on) was a typical reaction to the youth counterculture that took hold in the 1960s.

conviction that private individuals and local, autonomous institutions are in the best position to make decisions in their own interests. On this view, the task of central government – the servant of the people, not their master – is merely to provide the framework of law and security that gives individuals and local bodies the liberty and space to make choices for themselves.

Perhaps the most obvious difference between conservatives on the one hand and socialists and liberals on the other is the faith that they put in the feasibility of social improvement. Grand schemes designed to cure the ills of society are 'floating fancies' (Burke's phrase) dreamed up by utopian rationalists who cast aside the lessons of history in the excitement of their own abstractions. Conservatives are deeply suspicious of such social panaceas, which they believe are founded on an unwarranted assumption of the perfectibility of mankind. This attitude – cynical and defeatist, as it appears to opponents – has prompted the criticism that conservatives show contempt for human endeavour and aspiration. In response, the conservative is likely to note how frequently, as a matter of historical record, hell has been reached by roads paved with good intentions; or, as Ambrose Bierce noted in his *Cynic's Word Book* (1906), a Conservative is 'a statesman enamoured of existing evils, as distinguished from the Liberal, who wishes to replace them with others'.

the condensed idea
Adherence to the old and tried

28 Imperialism

Although the word itself is of relatively recent coinage, imperialism – the practice of stronger states gaining control over and exploiting weaker ones – is as old as history itself. A narrative of the ancient civilizations of Mesopotamia and the Mediterranean basin reads like a catalogue of imperial domination: the Babylonian and Assyrian empires; the Persian empire of Cyrus the Great; the vast Macedonian empire of Alexander the Great ... In time the remnants of these mighty empires mostly succumbed to what would become in due course one of the greatest and longest-lasting of all empires – the expansive land empire of the Romans, which at its peak stretched from Britain to northern Africa and the Middle East.

Given the lasting significance of the Roman empire, it is appropriate that both 'empire' and 'imperialism' are derived from a Latin word – *imperium*. The most basic meaning of *imperium* is 'power to command' and can refer to the authority either of a civilian magistrate or of a military commander. This, too, is apt, for the essence of imperialism in all its forms is power: power wielded in an unequal relationship in which one state exercises control or influence, directly or indirectly, over another. Again and again, history has shown that peoples that enjoy some kind of military or other superiority over their neighbours look to exploit it to further their own interests. And most perniciously, such physical superiority is often projected through a lens of racial and cultural 'otherness', to produce a sense of moral superiority that can serve to justify the most shameless brutality and exploitation.

timeline

mid-6th century BC	478–404 BC	336–323 BC	From 3rd century BC
Persian empire established in the Middle East by Cyrus the Great	Alliance of Greek states against Persia is transformed into Athenian empire	Alexander the Great of Macedon conquers a vast empire extending to India	Beginnings of Roman empire as Rome's power expands beyond Italy

Of slaves and poodles

Chastened by the final withdrawal of US forces form Vietnam in 1975, successive administrations relied on a range of less formal means to ensure that American influence continued to be felt around the world. Most effective of these was the huge clout delivered by the US's powerful economy, which allowed Washington policy-makers to spread the message of freedom (and free trade) and democracy (and anti-communism) by dangling vast carrots in the form of American investment and loans. The visible symptoms of global US economic and cultural penetration were signs and billboards that sprouted all around the world, courtesy of the McDonald brothers and the Coca-Cola Company.

For critics of US foreign policy, such informal methods were quite sufficient to sustain a charge of American imperialism (or neo-imperialism). But it was not until 2001, in the wake of the 9/11 terrorist attacks, that the dustsheets were finally pulled off to reveal the full majesty of the American imperial machinery. Official denials were of course forthcoming from the Washington neo-conservative hawks ('We don't do empire,' claimed Secretary of Defense Donald Rumsfeld), but the truth was plain to see – for George W. Bush's enemies and allies alike – as the 'war on terror' was waged first in Afghanistan and then in Iraq. With impressive prescience, during the Second World War, the future British prime minister Harold Macmillan had foreseen the way things were heading: 'We . . . are Greeks in this American empire . . . We must run [things] as the Greek slaves ran the operations of the Emperor Claudius.' In the early years of the 21st century the full import of these words and the highly asymmetrical 'special relationship' they portended became apparent to British mandarins and above all to Bush's much-pilloried 'poodle', prime minister Tony Blair.

Naked and unapologetic Today the word 'imperialism' is used almost exclusively in a negative sense, usually by oppressed peoples or states to denounce the policies of their oppressors. However, before the 20th century, imperialist activity was almost always a cause of national pride, not of embarrassment or shame.

15th–19th century AD	1880s–1914	1920s–1945	From 2001
European colonization of the Americas, India, etc.	Scramble for Africa sees European powers race to acquire African territories	Fascist dictators initiate new phase of aggressive imperialism	'War on terror' introduces new phase of American imperialism

It may be no surprise to hear fascist leaders such as Hitler and Mussolini triumphantly trumpeting the glories of imperialist aggrandizement. For them, imperial domination was part of the natural order; it was human destiny that the strong would prevail over the weak. It is more shocking, however, to find that these monsters of modernity were in fact parroting a line that can be traced back through such revered figures as de Tocqueville, Francis Bacon and Machiavelli to the 'cradle of civilization' itself. In 432 BC, just before the outbreak of the Peloponnesian War, the Greek historian Thucydides tells how a delegation of Athenians addressed the Spartan assembly in an effort to avert war. In justification of their imperial rule over other Greeks, they insist that they are only doing what anyone else would do in their place: 'it has always been the way that the weaker should be subject to the stronger'. Justice, in their view, 'never deterred anyone from taking by force as much as he could'; the only relevant considerations are political expedience and power.

Not much seemed to change over the succeeding 2500 years. From the 1880s to 1914, Britain, Germany and other European powers looked to extend their imperial possessions as they engaged in a frantic 'scramble for Africa'. The First World War messily snuffed out these jingoistic ambitions. This scramble was pursued with such vigour that by 1914 roughly four-fifths of the earth's land surface was under the dominion of a handful of colonial powers, which by this date had been joined by Japan and the USA. Throughout this period the tone adopted by the imperialists was magnificently

The highest stage of capitalism

The assumptions of imperialism took a ferocious battering in the course of the First World War, and in its immediate aftermath they were hit by a fierce barrage of communist rhetoric. In a pamphlet written in 1917, Lenin finessed the Marxist interpretation of imperialism, arguing that it was the inevitable 'highest stage' of capitalism that could only be defeated by revolution. This stage marked the crisis point at which declining domestic profit rates forced fully industrialized capitalist economies to pursue, in competition with other capitalist states, new overseas markets for their overproduction. Partly as a result of the Marxist critique, 'imperialism' is now fixed as a term of disapprobation not only in communist propaganda but also in the mouths of aggrieved politicians in post-colonial states.

unapologetic, Athenian in all but its lack of candour. Speaking in 1899, Lord Rosebery, former British prime minister and champion of so-called 'Liberal imperialism', argued that colonial activity was a natural extension of popular nationalism: 'sane Imperialism,' he declared, 'as distinguished from what I may call wild-cat imperialism, is nothing but this – a larger patriotism.' Writing in the *Contemporary Review* of the same year, J.L. Walton precisely captured the unqualified triumphalism of the age: 'The Imperialist feels a profound pride in the magnificent heritage of empire won by the courage and energies of his ancestry, and bequeathed to him subject to the burden of many sacred trusts.'

The White Man's burden Walton's reference to the burden of empire evokes an imperialist attitude, dimly represented since the start of the modern era of European colonization in the 15th century, which had become more or less orthodox by the middle of the 1800s. The supposed 'virtues of empire' were notoriously set forth in a poem by Rudyard Kipling, which caused an immediate controversy when published in 1899. In urging the reader to 'Take up the White Man's burden . . . To serve your captives' need', Kipling suggested both that the business of imperialism was a vocation dutifully accepted by the colonial powers and that its effects were basically beneficial to the subject peoples, who were characterized, with haughty condescension, as 'Half devil and half child'. This was the myth of the 'civilizing mission'; the idea that the nations of the West took it as their task, as another British statesman, Lord Palmerston, airily put it, 'not to enslave but to set free'. The view that the blessings of civilization and culture that were bestowed (imposed) on subject peoples could serve as a justification (pretext) for imperialist policies was shared by many of Britain's political and intellectual elite, including such liberal luminaries as J.S. Mill.

> **Take up the White Man's burden –**
> **Send forth the best ye breed –**
> **Go bind your sons to exile**
> **To serve your captives' need;**
> **To wait in heavy harness,**
> **On fluttered folk and wild –**
> **Your new-caught, sullen peoples,**
> **Half devil and half child.**
>
> Rudyard Kipling, *The White Man's Burden,* 1899

the condensed idea
To enslave or to set free?

29 Nationalism

'Our Country! In her intercourse with foreign nations, may she always be in the right; but right or wrong, our country!' This famous toast was reputedly given at a banquet in 1816 by the US naval hero Stephen Decatur. Usually shortened (with some distortion) to 'Our country, right or wrong!', the phrase is still used to this day, generally without the least consideration of its full implications. The point was not lost on Mark Twain, however. By adopting it 'with all its servility,' he said, we 'have thrown away the most valuable asset we had: the individual's right to oppose both flag and country when he . . . believed them to be in the wrong.'

Patriotism, suggests Decatur's toast, should blind us to the fact that something is wrong purely because it is done by, or in the name of, our country. On the face of it, this is an extraordinary, not to say immoral, view. The notions on which it is based – patriotism and, more particularly, its close cousin nationalism – have stirred such passions and incited such violence over the last two centuries that they must bear much of the responsibility for the dire conflict and strife that have scarred the world during those years. An 'infantile sickness . . . the measles of the human race', in Einstein's opinion, nationalism was the principal cause of two world wars in the 20th century and has recently been deeply implicated in horrendous violence and grotesque 'ethnic cleansing' in places as far apart as Rwanda and the Balkans. It is not all negative, however. Nationalist feeling can also elicit astonishing loyalty and create deep social cohesion, for instance among oppressed minorities, and has been the mainspring of heroic sacrifice and selfless resistance to tyranny.

timeline

1775–83	1789–99	c.1870
The USA, forged in the American Revolution, inspires liberal nationalism	French Revolution fought for 'Liberty, Equality, Fraternity'	Italian state created after half-century of nationalist endeavour

> ❝**Patriotism is a lively sense of collective responsibility. Nationalism is a silly cock crowing on its own dunghill.**❞
>
> **Richard Aldington, English novelist and poet, 1931**

The genius of a nation While patriotism may mean no more than love of one's country and a general concern for its welfare, nationalism is more focused, usually combining patriotic feeling with some kind of active political programme. Typically, the central aim of such a programme is to win statehood, implying independence and sovereignty, for a community whose members meet certain criteria by virtue of which they constitute a 'nation'. Once such an autonomous state has been formed, the secondary aims are to promote and perpetuate its well-being and to defend those qualities and characteristics which together form its identity and sense of nationhood. Nationalists insist that the state so formed – the nation-state – can claim the loyalties of its members above all other loyalties and that its interests have precedence over all other interests.

What, then, is a nation, and what are the attributes that constitute its identity? Most nationalists would broadly sympathize with the view expressed by the poet Samuel Taylor Coleridge in his *Table Talk* of 1830: 'I, for one, do not call the sod under my feet my country. But language, religion, laws, government, blood – identity in these makes men of one country.' Giuseppe Mazzini, one of the architects of Italian unification, made essentially the same point 30 years later, when he insisted that a particular territory is only a foundation: 'The country is the idea which rises upon that foundation; it is the sentiment of love, the sense of fellowship which binds together all the sons of that territory.' Both authorities agree that it is not (primarily) a matter of land – although a recognized territory with strong borders will almost invariably be a necessary condition for the long-term survival of a nation-state.

The essential point about the nation cherished by the nationalist is that it always has some special character or identity that is all its own. There is, as Ralph Waldo Emerson suggested in 1844, a 'genius of a nation which is not

1871	**1922–45**	**1991–2001**	**1994**
Germany formed into nation-state under leadership of Bismarck	Fascist dictators pursue extreme nationalist policies in Europe	Nationalist hatreds fuel war in Balkans	Nationalist-inspired genocide in Rwanda

to be found in the numerical citizens, but which characterizes the society'. Jules Michelet, author of a vast and intensely nationalist 19th-century history of his country, famously declared that 'France is a person' and insisted that the nation was an organic unit, an eternal being whose essence was a distillation of its buried past – the diverse relics and traditions drawn from the '*silences de l'histoire*'. This distinctive national character is the unique and ineffable product of various historical, geographical and cultural factors: common origin and ethnicity; a single language; a shared fund of myths and memories; traditional values and customs. These are the factors, some or all of which are assumed by the nationalist to define membership of the nation.

A modern phenomenon According to the nationalist conception, then, the world is a patchwork of unique communities, each bound together by a complex web of historical, cultural and other factors.

The two faces of nationalism

From early in its development, nationalism moved in two very different directions: one liberal and progressive, the other authoritarian and backward-looking. This parting of the ways helps to explain the ugly role that nationalist-fuelled extremism was to play in the 20th century.

The Founding Fathers of the USA were profoundly patriotic, but the nationalist feeling they shared was essentially liberal and forward-looking, based on reason and universal in outlook; they saw themselves blazing a trail for mankind as a whole in its march towards greater liberty and equality. The vision of the new American nation was a direct inspiration, just a few years later, for the nationalism of the French revolutionaries, who expressed their universal aspirations in their famous slogan: 'Liberty, Equality,

Fraternity'. In both America and France the formation of the new nation was an act of self-determination willingly undertaken by its members. Partly as a reaction to the excesses of the French and the depredations of their leader Napoleon, the German nationalism that evolved in the first half of the 19th century took on a very different complexion. Romantic and inward-looking, it favoured instinct over reason; tradition over progress; authority over freedom. Rejecting universalism and the idea of the brotherhood of nations, this version of nationalism was at once self-absorbed and exclusive, fabricating a national history that emphasized difference and superiority. It was this conception of the nation and the kind of nationalism it inspired that were exploited by the fascist dictators of the 20th century.

The difficulty with this picture is that in certain respects it is rather distant from reality. Ethnic groups have been intermingling for thousands of years, so no present-day population of any size is ethnically homogeneous; and in any case common ethnicity tends to have less to do with community bonding than factors such as shared language and religion.

> **'Nations do not think, they only feel. They get their feelings at second hand through their temperaments, not their brains.'**
>
> **Mark Twain, 1906**

The nation-state is now firmly established as the normal unit of political organization, while nationalism and national self-determination are widely accepted as legitimate political aspirations. It is indeed a central part of nationalist folklore that the cherished nation is of great antiquity, with historical and cultural roots stretching back into the immemorial past. The consensus of recent scholarship, however, is that such a picture is seriously misleading – that nation-states are in most respects modern constructions and that the idea of their continuity since antiquity is basically a product of 'retrospective nationalism'. This is not to say that people throughout history have not always been attached to the land of their birth and to customs and traditions handed down by their ancestors. But the patterns of allegiance in the pre-modern world were essentially different. The primary loyalty was not to the state as such but to a divinely sanctioned monarch; and beneath the monarch there was a complex hierarchy of localized loyalties that were owed to feudal lords or aristocratic elites. And at the base of all other beliefs was the notion that every human belonged to an overarching religious community that aspired, ultimately, to encompass all mankind. Only when these ancient ties began to loosen, in a process that began with the turmoil of the American and French revolutions, was it possible for the forces of modernity – secularization, popular sovereignty, the concept of human rights, the scientific revolution, industrialization – to shape the nation-state and the nationalist sentiment that it inspired.

the condensed idea
The measles of the human race

30 Multiculturalism

In 1903 a bronze plaque was mounted inside the pedestal of New York's Statue of Liberty. Engraved upon it was Emma Lazarus's sonnet 'The New Colossus', which includes what is probably history's most famous invitation: 'Give me your tired, your poor,/ Your huddled masses yearning to breathe free,/ The wretched refuse of your teeming shore.' The expected treatment of those entrusted to Liberty's care was explained in a hit play, _The Melting Pot_, premiered in Washington just five years later: 'America is God's Crucible, the great Melting Pot where all the races of Europe are melting and re-forming! . . . Here shall they all unite to build the Republic of Man and the Kingdom of God.'

The millions of immigrants who flooded into the USA in the early decades of the 20th century were given little choice but to submerge themselves in the melting pot triumphantly proclaimed by the play's author, Israel Zangwill. At this time it was generally taken for granted that the various incoming ethnic groups would undergo a process of integration – 'Americanization' – in which their diverse customs and identities would be absorbed into the existing and dominant American culture. At the same time, however, a radically different attitude to the issue was being articulated by an immigrant university lecturer and philosopher, Horace Kallen. He argued that an America in which ethnic, cultural and religious diversity was retained and celebrated would thereby be both enriched and strengthened.

> **_E pluribus unum_**
> **"Out of many [comes] one"**
> **Motto on the Seal of the United States**

Initially a minority view, what Kallen called 'cultural pluralism' gathered support as the

timeline

476	630s	1903	1908
Roman empire falls – or dissolves?	Arab conquests of Syria and Egypt	'Give me your tired, your poor' poem mounted in Statue of Liberty	Israel Zangwill's _The Melting Pot_ premiered in Washington

> **‘Understand that America is God's Crucible, the great Melting Pot where all the races of Europe are melting and re-forming! A fig for your feuds and vendettas! Germans and Frenchmen, Irishmen and Englishmen, Jews and Russians – into the Crucible with you all! God is making the American.’**

Israel Zangwill, *The Melting Pot*, 1908

century wore on, and by the 1960s his approach had become established as the orthodox position within the USA. The image of the melting pot was increasingly replaced by other metaphors, such as a mosaic or (humorously) a salad bowl, in which the overall effect is achieved by parts or ingredients that retain their original character or flavour. The debate over the scope and desirability of cultural pluralism – or 'multiculturalism', as it is now generally known – has since developed into one of the most pressing issues of our age.

Imperial imperatives Today, the social challenges which multiculturalism is supposed to address are due mainly to human migration, often economically motivated, but throughout history essentially the same issues have been raised by conquest and the needs of imperial control. Pioneers and unrivalled masters of the assimilationist approach were the Romans, who would move swiftly from a phase of military oppression to the process of Romanization: urban settlements, fitted out with baths and the other trappings of the Roman way of life, were built so that the conquered peoples could live and grow accustomed both to the joys of *pax Romana* and to its less palatable aspects, such as imperial taxes. The process of assimilation was so successful that, famously, the provincials tended to become more Roman than the Romans themselves – to such an extent that some have argued that the Roman empire did not so much fall as dissolve. A rather different approach, in which different cultures were tolerated and allowed to persist alongside the dominant (conquerors') culture, was seen in the seventh-century Arab conquests of Syria and Egypt, where the victors did not require the

1915	**1990**	**11 Sept. 2001**	**2007**
Horace Kallen's *Democracy Versus the Melting Pot* published	Norman Tebbit proposes cricket test of immigrant loyalties	Islamist terrorists launch attacks against USA	Election of Nicolas Sarkozy as president of France

conquered peoples to convert to Islam but allowed both Christians and Jews to retain their faiths – provided they paid a special discriminatory tax.

Out of the melting pot . . . Both assimilation and multiculturalism, as responses to ethnic diversity, are based on theoretically liberal principles but differ in their interpretation of equality and how it can and should be realized. Assimilation, as its name suggests, is founded on the notion of equality as sameness. Social justice demands that everyone enjoys the same rights and opportunities; no discrimination on the basis of ethnic origin or culture should be allowed; and so the means by which rights are conferred and protected – citizenship – should be the same for all. This model has been most exhaustively elaborated in France, where the ideal of universal citizenship has been taken to imply that manifestations of ethnic (and other) differences should be suppressed, at least in the public domain. A frequent criticism of the French model is that it assumes that ethnicity and culture are contingent and detachable aspects of a person's or group's identity, and that political concepts such as citizenship can somehow remain neutral in the matter of colour and culture. Some object that such a neutral political domain is a myth, and that immigrants are being asked in effect to suppress their own culture and to conform to the dominant values of the host nation. The criticism is given weight by the depth and persistence of social discord among France's ethnic minorities and by the rhetoric of the French political right (echoed by Nicolas Sarkozy, the president elected in 2007), which habitually invites immigrants 'to love France or leave it'.

> **When you live in France, you respect the rules. You don't have lots of wives, you don't circumcise your daughters, and you don't use your bath to slaughter sheep in.**
>
> Nicolas Sarkozy, 2006

Multiculturalism, too, has grown from liberal roots: it maintains that a plurality of different ways of life should be tolerated or even encouraged, provided they do not adversely affect or interfere with other people. But it has decisively rejected the assimilationist view of equality as sameness. Instead, multiculturalism has taken its lead from the so-called 'identity politics' that have transformed other areas of political activism. Just as gays and feminists, for instance, no longer see equality with (respectively) heterosexuals and men as the criterion of success, in a similar way ethnic minorities, including immigrants, are now demanding that their native cultures and values are given equal recognition and allowed to express themselves in their own right and in their own terms. Again, however, this

Beyond the Tebbit test

In a 1990 interview with the *Los Angeles Times* the British Conservative politician Norman Tebbit posed a question that has caused reverberations ever since: 'A large proportion of Britain's Asian population fail to pass the cricket test. Which side do they cheer for? It's an interesting test. Are you still harking back to where you came from or where you are?' The so-called Tebbit test, much criticized at the time, is obviously flawed: by its reckoning the great majority of Scots, for instance, would not qualify as British. Nevertheless, Tebbit's comments evidently struck a chord with many in the white population. It is easy to dismiss the fears that the test was tapping into as racist, but the truth is that they are as much alive today as ever.

Subsequent surveys have shown that a clear majority of black and Asian people living in Britain – some immigrant, others born in the country – think of themselves as British. As a matter of empirical fact, a wide variety of groups of different ethnic origins can and do live together in peace and as functional communities while retaining many of their native ways and customs – including their sporting allegiances. But equally clearly there has to be *some* common ground. With a plurality of groups comes a plurality of loyalties, and such loyalties are always divided to some degree. What happens when such allegiances pull in different directions? At what point does such division become incompatible with common citizenship? What amount of common culture, identity or history is sufficient to provide the 'glue' that holds a multicultural society together? Such questions have become increasingly urgent in the wake of the Islamist attacks in the US and Europe, as evidence of radicalization, especially among Muslim youths, has grown. Sadly, at a time when tolerance and restraint are needed more than ever, many people are beginning to ask questions a great deal more sinister than the Tebbit test.

raises doubts over the liberal host society's role as a neutral matrix into which alien mores can be embedded. At the very least the host must display a degree of toleration that some of the newcomers might wish to deny. And if multiculturalism implies a level of cultural relativism that precludes judgement of minority practices, the liberal host may find itself called upon to protect a range of customs, illiberal by its own lights, such as forced marriage and female genital mutilation. Such tensions at the heart of liberalism are certain to generate alarms and anxieties between the elements that make up a modern multicultural society.

the condensed idea
Melting pot or salad bowl?

31 The social contract

Why do people enter into legal contracts? Provided that the contract is fair, the parties involved generally feel that their interests are better served if they are bound by the terms of the agreement than if they are not. You might not otherwise choose to present yourself at a particular location at 9.00 from Monday to Friday, but you are prepared to place yourself under an obligation to do so on condition that someone else is obliged to pay an agreed amount of money into your bank account every month. In general, it is worth agreeing to restrict your freedom in some ways in order to gain some greater good.

Several philosophers, including Hobbes, Locke, Rousseau and (nearer our own time) John Rawls, have developed political theories in which the state's legitimacy is based on an implicit agreement, or social contract. Broadly speaking, the citizens of the state agree to relinquish some of their rights, or transfer some of their powers, to a governing authority in return for the latter's protection and preservation of life, property and social order.

Hobbes's *Leviathan* Rational consent to a contract must involve consideration of how matters would stand if the terms of the contract were not in force. In the same way, it is a common feature of social-contract theories to start with an evocation of the 'state of nature': a hypothetical pre-social condition of mankind in which the laws and constraints imposed by the state are absent. The state of nature imagined by the English political philosopher Thomas Hobbes is unremittingly bleak and

timeline

1651

Thomas Hobbes's *Leviathan* argues
the case for absolute sovereignty

1690

John Locke's *Two Treatises
of Government* published

pessimistic. People's prime motivation, he assumes, is 'a perpetual and restless desire of power after power, that ceaseth only in death'. Acting in isolation, humans are concerned only with their own pleasure, interest and preservation. Constantly in competition and at war with one another, there is no possibility of trust and cooperation; and with no basis of trust, there is no prospect of creating prosperity or enjoying the fruits of civilization – 'no arts; no letters; no society; and which is worst of all, continual fear, and danger of violent death'. And hence, he famously concludes, in the state of nature 'the life of man [is] solitary, poor, nasty, brutish, and short'.

> **By art is created that great Leviathan, called a commonwealth or state, which is but an artificial man . . . and in which, the sovereignty is an artificial soul.**
>
> **Thomas Hobbes, 1651**

It is in everyone's interest to work together in order to escape this hellish condition, so why do people in the state of nature not agree to cooperate? Because there is always a cost to pay in complying with an agreement and always a gain to be had from not doing so. If self-interest is the only moral compass, you can be sure that someone else will always be ready to seek an advantage by non-compliance, so the best you can do is to break the contract first. And of course everyone else reasons in the same way, so there is no trust and no agreement: long-term interest is always sure to give way to short-term gain, apparently leaving no way out of the cycle of distrust and violence.

The question then is how individuals mired in such wretched discord can ever reach an accommodation with one another and so extricate themselves. The crux of the problem, for Hobbes, is that 'covenants, without the sword, are but words'. What is needed is an external power or sanction that *forces* all people to abide by the terms of a contract that benefits them all. People must willingly restrict their liberties for the sake of cooperation and peace, on condition that everyone else does likewise; they must 'confer all their power and strength upon one man, or upon one assembly of men, that may reduce all their wills, by plurality of voices, unto one will'. The solution, then, is joint submission to the absolute authority of the state (what Hobbes calls 'Leviathan') – 'a common power to keep them all in awe'.

1762	**1971**	**1979–80**
The 'noble savage' appears in Jean-Jacques Rousseau's *The Social Contract*	John Rawls develops idea of justice as fairness in *A Theory of Justice*	New Right administrations in Britain and the USA champion 'trickle-down economics

Rawls and justice as fairness   Notable among modern social-contract theorists is the US political philosopher John Rawls, whose *A Theory of Justice* (1971) was arguably the most influential contribution to the debate over justice and equality made in the second half of the 20th century. Any conception of social justice, Rawls argues, comprises the notion of impartiality. Any suggestion that the principles and structures on which a social system is based are skewed towards a particular group (a social class, for instance, or a political party) automatically renders that system unjust. So how should the burdens and benefits of a society be distributed amongst its members in such a way as to make it just?

To capture the idea of impartiality, Rawls introduces a thought experiment which is basically a modern reworking of the state of nature. In what he calls the 'original position', all personal interests and allegiances are forgotten: 'no one knows his place in society, his class position or social status, nor does anyone know his fortune in the distribution of natural assets and abilities, his intelligence, strength, and the like.' Placed behind this 'veil of ignorance' and ignorant of what role in society we will be given, we are obliged to play safe and to ensure that no one group is given an advantage at the expense of another. As in Hobbes, it is purely rational self-interest that drives decision-making behind the veil; and it is the fact that we, when placed in this position, contract into certain social and economic structures and arrangements that makes them distinctively just.

Locke on consensual government

Writing nearly half a century after Hobbes, another great English philosopher to use the idea of the social contract to explore the basis of government was John Locke. Hobbes refers to Leviathan (his symbolic name for the power of the state) as 'that mortal God', indicating that sovereignty is ceded to the state by human convention, not by divine dispensation (the orthodox view at the time). In this regard Locke agrees with Hobbes, but his conception of the state of nature – the pre-social condition of mankind without government or law – is considerably less bleak than Hobbes's, so the contract formed between people and sovereign is consequently less draconian. Whereas Hobbes requires the state's power to be unlimited and absolute in order to stave off the horrors of the 'war of all against all', Locke makes the case for what is essentially constitutional monarchy: the people consent to make over their power to the sovereign on condition that he uses it for the common good, and they reserve the right to withdraw that power (by rebellion if necessary) if the sovereign fails in his contractual duties.

Rawls's substantive thesis is that the most prudent thing that we, as rational decision-makers placed in the original position, can do to safeguard our own future (unknown) interests is to embrace what he calls the 'difference principle'. According to this, inequalities in society are justified only if they result in its worst-off members being better off than they would otherwise have been. This idea has generated a vast amount of criticism, positive and negative, and it has been invoked in support of ideological positions across the political spectrum, some of them far from Rawls's own essentially egalitarian, left-wing position. To take an extreme example, the principle does not preclude a huge windfall for those who already enjoy the lion's share of society's goods, provided that it is accompanied by an improvement (however small) for the worst-off. So Rawlsian corroboration could be sought for the so-called 'trickle-down economics' pursued by the New Right administrations of Reagan and Thatcher in the 1980s, in which tax cuts for the wealthiest were justified by an (allegedly) consequent improvement in the fortunes of the less advantaged. This claim was disdainfully dismissed by the economist J.K. Galbraith as 'horse-and-sparrow economics' – the theory that 'if you feed enough oats to the horse, some will pass through to feed the sparrows'.

> **The principles of justice are chosen behind a veil of ignorance.**
>
> **John Rawls, 1971**

The sleep of reason

The French philosopher Jean-Jacques Rousseau was much influenced by Hobbes's ideas, but his best-known work, *The Social Contract* (1762), shares none of the bleakness seen in the Englishman's conception of humans in the state of nature. Whereas Hobbes sees the power of the state as a necessary means of taming people's bestial nature, Rousseau considers that human vice and other ills are the *product* of society – that the 'noble savage', naturally innocent and content in the 'sleep of reason' and living in sympathy with his fellow men, is corrupted by education and other social influences. This vision of lost innocence and non-intellectualized sentiment proved inspirational for the Romantic movement that swept Europe towards the end of the 18th century.

the condensed idea
Society by consent

32 Republicanism

'In America the law is king. For as in absolute governments the King is law, so in free countries the law ought to be King; and there ought to be no other.' The radical Thomas Paine made this famous claim in his revolutionary pamphlet *Common Sense*, in which he argued that republicanism and a complete break from the British Crown were the only solution to the American colonists' grievances. On 4 July 1776, just six months after Paine's pamphlet was published, the Second Continental Congress convened in Philadelphia, where they formally adopted the text of the Declaration of Independence. Thus they took a decisive step towards creating what would become the most complete and powerful republic of modern times.

A decade later, in 1787, John Adams, the future second president, echoed Paine's insistence on the importance of the rule of law. Giving what he believed to be 'the true and only true definition' of the word, he characterized a republic as 'a government, in which all men, rich and poor, magistrates and subjects, officers and people, masters and servants, the first citizens and the last, are equally subject to the laws'. Another of the Founding Fathers, Alexander Hamilton, in a letter from 1780, sheds further light on the central role of law in the republican concept of government, when he favourably contrasts 'the obedience of a free people to general laws' with 'that of slaves to the arbitrary will of a prince'.

> **The obedience of a free people to general laws, however hard they bear, is ever more perfect than that of slaves to the arbitrary will of a prince.**
>
> **Alexander Hamilton, 1780**

timeline

510 BC	27 BC	AD 1688
Expulsion of Etruscan kings marks creation of the Roman republic	Roman republic comes to formal end as Augustus becomes emperor	Glorious Revolution brings constitutional monarchy to England against the sceptics

The predominant modern meaning of the word 'republic' is so loose that it has been casually appropriated for virtually every state in the world that does not have a monarch. But the remarks of Paine, Adams and Hamilton, three giants of the American Revolution, point to a rarer and richer meaning of the word. In this conception, which has its roots in the ancient world, the rule of law, amongst other constitutional safeguards, acts as a bulwark against arbitrariness in the conduct of government. Republicanism, understood as the philosophy and creed of those who support such political systems, goes far beyond bland opposition to monarchical systems.

The Roman model According to the classic republican paradigm, the chief culprit and agent of arbitrary rule is an overbearing monarch (a 'royal brute', in Paine's phrase) whose overthrow, putting sovereignty in the hands of the people, becomes part of the foundation myth of the new regime. This classic (and classical) scheme was initially seen in a political system that would become, in due course, the greatest source of inspiration for later republican thinkers: the Roman republic. (Appropriately, the word 'republic' is derived from the Latin word for 'state' or 'public affairs', *res publica*.)

According to Roman tradition, the republic was established in 510 BC, following the expulsion of the Etruscan kings in a revolt led by the republican hero Lucius Brutus. The immediate cause of the insurrection was the rape of a Roman matron called Lucretia by Sextus Tarquinius, obnoxious son of the equally obnoxious last king, Tarquin the Proud. The constitution introduced after the fall of the kings was nominally a democratic republic, in that sovereign power rested with the people and all adult male citizens were allowed to take part in political life, but in practice power was largely in the hands of a broad-based oligarchy of 50 or so noble families, who reserved for themselves the main magistracies (political offices). The real nexus of power was the Senate, where the affairs of state were debated and decided by former magistrates, all of whom were members for life.

> **The republican is the only form of government which is not eternally at open or secret war with the rights of mankind.**
>
> **Thomas Jefferson, 1790**

1775–1883
American Revolution leads to birth of USA

1776
Thomas Paine's *Common Sense* calls for republicanism and break from British

1787
John Adams stresses importance of rule of law in concept of republic

There were, however, numerous constitutional safeguards to prevent abuses of power. For instance, all offices were fixed-term (mostly annual), and even the highest offices, the two consulships, were strictly circumscribed by law and subject to veto by the ten tribunes, who were elected solely by the common people (plebeians) in order to protect their interests.

From Rome to Washington In spite of the many constitutional safeguards that evolved over the course of nearly four centuries, the Roman republican system was far from perfect. In the end it collapsed under the accumulated weight of corruption and abuse and was bloodily replaced by the highly autocratic imperial regime initiated by Augustus in 27 BC. The fascination that Rome's republic held for later theorists, including many of those involved in framing the US Constitution, lay as much in the indomitable spirit of its great figures as in the detail of its constitutional arrangements. The cardinal virtue of the heroes of the republic, lovingly recalled by late-republican nostalgists such as Cicero,

> **Wickedness is the root of despotism as virtue is the essence of the Republic.**
>
> Maximilien Robespierre, 1794

was *pietas* or dutifulness: the kind of unstinting and selfless devotion to the public interest displayed by the tyrant-slaying Brutuses; the Scipios, destroyers of Carthage; and the older and younger Cato – the austere Censor and his great-grandson, who committed suicide in 46 BC rather than compromise his Stoic principles.

This Roman *pietas* was an important inspiration for the civic virtue that became the hallmark of American republicanism. According to republican thinking as it developed in 1770s America, the essential quality in the upstanding citizen was a willingness to step forward in the service of the state and to place the common good before any selfish or partisan interests. Generally this meant having a significant stake in society and a degree of education that would allow reasoned deliberation among independent-minded and intellectual equals. One consequence, following the assumptions of the time, was that women and unpropertied workers (and of course slaves) had to rely on the virtuous (male, white) elite for their

> **The chief objection to one-person rule is the frequent descents of autocrats into megalomania, to which is added, when the post is hereditary, incompetent heirs.**
>
> Anthony Quinton, 1995

The crowned republic

In 1775, the year before the American colonies declared their independence from Britain, the despotic motherland received an unexpected compliment: 'the British constitution is . . . nothing more or less than a republic, in which the king is first magistrate. This office being hereditary . . . is no objection to the government's being a republic, as long as it is bound by fixed laws, which the people have a voice in making, and a right to defend.' This observation was made by the future second president, John Adams, whose objection to the British was not that their system of government was inherently unjust but that they chose to deny to their American cousins 'the basic rights guaranteed to all Englishmen, and which all free men deserved'. Since the final overthrow of Stuart absolutism in the Glorious Revolution of 1688, England (Britain from 1707) had been, in Adams's much-quoted phrase, 'an empire of laws, and not of men', or what H.G. Wells described in 1920 as a 'crowned republic'. The secret of attaining popular government without overthrowing the monarchy had been to introduce a constitutional arrangement that conformed to the 'English formula', as Trotsky called it: a government in which the monarch 'reigns but does not rule'. Some degree of republican sentiment has always been present in Britain, especially at times of royal unpopularity, but it has rarely been an issue of practical politics.

protection. While the Founding Fathers tended to regard themselves as liberal *and* republican, the kind of public-spirited republicanism that they promoted was at odds with liberalism to the extent that the latter was concerned with protecting the (selfish) rights of individuals against the (reasonable) demands of the state. At the same time social conservatism and austerity, both bolstered by deep religiosity, were far removed from classical liberalism's fondness for wealth creation and economic individualism. These underlying tensions, republican and liberal, were destined to shape the psyche and culture of the USA over the next two centuries.

the condensed idea
Government of laws, not of men

33 Communism

**'The Communists disdain to conceal their views and aims.
They openly declare that their ends can be attained only
by the forcible overthrow of all existing social conditions.
Let the ruling classes tremble at a Communistic revolution.
The proletarians have nothing to lose but their chains.
They have a world to win. WORKING MEN OF ALL
COUNTRIES, UNITE!'**

With this strident call to arms, Karl Marx concludes *The Communist Manifesto*, a pamphlet of fewer than 12,000 words, written in collaboration with Friedrich Engels and published in 1848 as a platform for the largely ineffective, quarrelsome and short-lived Communist League. Although its immediate impact was limited, this brief text has arguably done more than any other comparable document to shape the modern world. Three years before the *Manifesto* was published, Marx had written disdainfully of philosophers who were content merely to interpret the world. 'The point,' he declared, 'is to change it.' Radical and revolutionary that he was, he can scarcely have dreamed the extent to which his wish would be realized.

In the century after his death in 1883, the 'spectre of communism' that Marx had conjured up in the opening words of the *Manifesto* came to unquiet life in the form of a wave of communist regimes in which his ideas – or what passed for his ideas – were tested literally to destruction. In the end what transpired in the real world under his name, especially in Stalin's Russia and Mao's China, was to leave an indelible stain on his reputation. As the statues of Lenin came crashing down in clouds of dust in the years after 1991, Marx's notion of revolutionary struggle culminating in a classless socialist society seemed as bankrupt as the Soviet system itself; it appeared that communism had indeed been consigned to the 'ash-heap of

timeline

1818	1844	1848	1867–94	1883
Karl Marx born in Trier in the Rhineland	Marx meets lifelong collaborator Friedrich Engels in Paris	*The Communist Manifesto* published on behalf of the Communist League	*Das Kapital* (in three volumes) sets out Marx's theory of capitalist system	Marx dies in London

history', just as US president Ronald Reagan had predicted in 1982. Yet in the years since, as the dust has settled, a more measured view has become possible. In a world where the forces of global capitalism have brought stupendous inequalities, you do not have to be a die-hard socialist to appreciate the fundamental human decency of Marx's vision of a society in which each gives according to his ability and takes according to his need.

Impetus to change The *Manifesto*'s spectre of communism was not originally of Marx's making. The first half of the 19th century had seen European society transformed by an unprecedented technological and industrial revolution. This transformation had caused an astonishing increase in economic productivity and had brought extraordinary gains in the overall wealth of industrializing countries, but these newly created riches had largely been funnelled into the pockets of the capitalist elite. Thus the further enrichment of the already well-to-do had been achieved, at least in the eyes of critics, at the expense of working people, whose condition in the same period had grown steadily more wretched.

Such massive (and, as it seemed, massively unfair) social change inevitably provoked a political reaction. For a decade or more before the *Manifesto*'s publication in 1848 the 'powers of old Europe' had been growing increasingly alarmed at the stirrings of communist radicals – agents of an extreme socialist movement, mobilized on behalf of the working people, that was committed to the violent overthrow of capitalist society and the abolition of private property. It was against this background, in response to the perceived injustices of contemporary society, that Marx began to elaborate his communist ideas both as a political doctrine and as a practical programme for action.

> **It is as wholly wrong to blame Marx for what was done in his name, as it is to blame Jesus for what was done in his.**
>
> Tony Benn, British socialist, 1982

1917	**1922–53**	**1949**	**1991**
Russian revolutionary Lenin begins first attempt to realize Marxist principles	Stalin exercises tyrannical power in Soviet Union	Mao Zedong oversees foundation of People's Republic of China	Soviet Union collapses

Heaven can wait

'The ruling ideas of every epoch,' wrote Marx in 1845, 'are the ideas of the ruling class.' In other words, the prevailing 'ideology' – the sum of orthodox views expressed in the media, in education, etc. – always reflects the views of the dominant class and so serves to justify the unequal economic and political power they enjoy. In 1902, 15 years before the Russian Revolution, the future first leader of the Soviet Union, Vladimir Ilich Lenin, accepted Marx's analysis of ideology but thought that he had not properly understood its implications in the motivation towards revolution. Marx had assumed that the proletariat would rise up spontaneously to overthrow their oppressors, but Lenin realized that the dominant ideology would induce a 'false consciousness' that would blind the workers to their own interests and induce them in effect to connive in their own oppression. What was needed, in Lenin's view, was a vanguard to lead the workers to the light – an elite vanguard selected from radicalized intellectuals like . . . himself. The vanguard would lead the way in setting up the 'dictatorship of the proletariat', the transitional and temporary phase (according to Marx) that would finally culminate in the establishment of full-blown communism. The problem for communism in its many 20th-century manifestations is that it never progressed beyond the transitional phase: political power was concentrated in the vanguard and stayed there; the dictatorship was not of the proletariat but of the increasingly centralized communist party. Communist heaven and the end of history would have to wait.

History as class struggle The twin pillars of Marx's thought are a distinctive economic theory allied to an equally distinctive understanding of historical progress. According to Marx, the force that drives history inexorably forwards is economic development. For any society, the first priority is always to produce whatever is required to ensure its own survival. Such production can only be achieved with the 'mode of production' characteristic of the age: that is, the combination of raw materials that are on hand; the tools and techniques that are available to process them; and the human resources that can be brought to bear in various capacities. The underlying structure imposed by these economic factors will determine the pattern of social organization within the society as a whole, and in particular, the relations between the various social elements, or 'classes'.

At each historical stage one class is dominant and controls the means of production, exploiting the labour of the working class in order to further its own interests. The modes of production characteristic of past and present ages are inherently unstable, however. 'Contradictions' in the relations between the various social elements lead inevitably to tensions and upheavals, and eventually to conflict and revolution in which the dominant class is overthrown and replaced. Hence the observation in the *Manifesto*: 'The history of all hitherto existing society is the history of class struggles.'

Industrial capitalism, the mode of production in Marx's day, was in his view a necessary stage of economic development, which had brought a huge increase in industrial output. However, the bourgeoisie, the dominant capitalist class who owned the means of production, had used their economic power to generate vast wealth for themselves by buying and selling commodities at a profit that was due – entirely, in Marx's view – to the labour of the working class (the proletariat). According to the scientific laws (as Marx saw them) controlling the capitalist system, the process of industrialization would lead inevitably to ever greater impoverishment of the proletariat. Eventually a crisis would come when it would be clear to the working class that the gap between their interests and those of the bourgeoisie was unbridgeable. At that point the workers would rise up and overthrow the bourgeois ruling class, take control of the means of production and abolish private property. They would then establish 'a dictatorship of the proletariat', to defend their interests against a bourgeois counter-revolution. The power of this transitional state, however, would gradually 'wither away', to be replaced – at the 'end of history' – by fully realized communism: a stable, classless society in which there is freedom for all and the means of production are held in common and operated for the benefit of all.

> **The theory of the Communists may be summed up in the single sentence: Abolition of private property.**
>
> **Karl Marx, 1848**

the condensed idea
'Workers of the world, unite!'

34 Fascism

'The foundation of Fascism is the conception of the State, its character, its duty, and its aim. Fascism conceives of the State as an absolute, in comparison with which all individuals or groups are relative, only to be conceived of in their relation to the State. The conception of the Liberal State is not that of a directing force, guiding the play and development, both material and spiritual, of a collective body . . . On the other hand, the Fascist State is itself conscious and has itself a will and a personality . . .'

The first fascist dictator to consolidate his rule in Europe, Benito Mussolini had been a journalist before he became *il Duce* (leader) of the Italian Fascist Party. Mussolini was always ready to expatiate on the principles of the political system that he had done more than anyone to develop. In 1932 he put his name to an essay entitled 'The Doctrine of Fascism', which appeared as part of the entry on Fascism in the *Enciclopedia Italiana*. While much of the piece is believed to be the work of Giovanni Gentile, the self-proclaimed 'philosopher of Fascism', it remains one of the seminal documents on an ideology that was destined to bring untold suffering and death to tens of millions of people in the most vicious conflagration in human history. A model of articulate fanaticism, the essay precisely records the most salient features of fascist thinking, amongst which the role of the overarching and sanctified state (as in the passage cited above) is rightly given prominence. The cherished state, object of obsessive and extreme 'blood-and-soil' nationalist sentiment, remained for all fascist regimes the symbolic totem that was the ultimate justification for the appalling atrocities that were carried out in its name.

> **'Fascism is not a new social order in the strict sense of the term. It is the future refusing to be born.'**
>
> **Aneurin Bevan, British politician, 1952**

timeline

1917	1919	1922
Russian Revolution spreads fear of communism through Europe	Discontent caused by Treaty of Versailles lays seeds of future fascist regimes	Mussolini becomes prime minister following March on Rome (dictator from 1925)

A deadly cocktail

One of the ironies of the rise of fascism in Europe in the 1920s and 1930s is the extent to which it was driven by fear of events rather than events themselves; fascism was, as the Italian writer Ignazio Silone once observed, 'a counter-revolution against a revolution that never took place'. In the wake of the Russian Revolution of 1917, the threat of international socialism was felt widely across Europe, and this fear was exploited incessantly by fascist leaders, whose rhetoric and propaganda painted the most lurid picture of the Red Peril looming in the East. The orthodox Marxist view was indeed no more favourable towards fascism, which was interpreted as the last, desperate throw of the dice by authoritarian capitalists; 'fascism in power,' declared Communist International secretary Georgi Dimitrov in 1935, 'is the open, terroristic dictatorship of the most reactionary, the most chauvinistic, the most imperialistic elements of finance capitalism.' In fact, though, the real conundrum was the extent to which fascism was indebted to, or derivative of, communism, not only in its totalitarian conception of state control but also in matters of ideology. As no less a figure than Hermann Göring, future head of Hitler's Luftwaffe, observed in a speech in 1933: 'Our movement took a grip on cowardly Marxism and from it extracted the meaning of socialism; it also took from the cowardly middle-class parties their nationalism. Throwing both into the cauldron of our way of life there emerged, as clear as a crystal, the synthesis – German National Socialism.' Nazism as a cocktail of Marxism and bourgeois nationalism: a toxic brew indeed.

A mongrel creed The view of fascism as spiritual nationalism was echoed a year later, in 1933, by the founder of the Spanish fascist Falange, José Antonio Primo de Rivera:

'Fascism was born to inspire a faith not of the Right (which at bottom aspires to conserve everything, even the unjust) or of the Left (which at bottom aspires to destroy everything, even the good), but a collective integral, national faith . . . '

What Primo de Rivera also reveals here is the extent to which fascism was ideologically heterogeneous, borrowing from ideologies that it viscerally

1933	1945	1975
Adolf Hitler appointed Chancellor of Germany. Fascist Falange founded in Spain (part of Franco's ruling party from 1937)	Deaths of Mussolini and Hitler bring 'era of fascism' to an end	Last of fascist dictators, Francisco Franco, dies in Madrid

detested, including Marxism and democratic liberalism. The various fascist parties and regimes that sprang up across Europe between the world wars were highly diverse in their political programmes, which were typically opportunistic and tailored to local requirements, and there was rarely much appearance of ideological soul-mates embarked on a common political project. Essentially mongrel in its principles, fascism was distinguished from the start less by any shared philosophical underpinning than by its ruthless organization and style, marked by strict authoritarian control, extreme violence and a fetishistic attention to tribal mythology and symbolism.

Cometh the moment . . . While the contradictions of fascist ideology put it beyond easy analysis, what is generally agreed is that the so-called 'era of fascism' – the period between 1922 and 1945 – was essentially a product of the First World War and its tragically inadequate dénouement at Versailles. In Italy, where fascism had its first success in 1922 with Mussolini's March on Rome, the rise of one-party dictatorship was in part a response to popular discontent with the country's liberal

The stamp of nobility

The essence of fascist rule was unbridled power. Even the name signifies as much, derived from the Latin *fasces*, the bundle of rods and an axe carried before Roman magistrates to symbolize their power. The totalitarian system was inegalitarian – Mussolini wrote of the 'immutable, beneficial and fruitful inequality of mankind'; anti-democratic – elections were disallowed (or rigged) and only a single political party was tolerated; and illiberal – complete subordination of the individual to the state was demanded. Militarism and imperialism were the expression of the state's vitality: 'War alone brings up to its highest tension all human energy,' asserted Mussolini, 'and puts the stamp of nobility upon the peoples who have courage to meet it.' The terrible scope of the fascist experiment was conveyed by the English diarist Harold Nicolson, writing in Rome in January 1932: 'They certainly have turned the whole country into an army. From cradle to grave one is cast in the mould of *fascismo* and there can be no escape . . . It is certainly a socialist experiment in that it destroys individuality. It also destroys liberty.'

democratic institutions and in particular to the government's failure to secure expected territorial gains in the postwar negotiations. In Germany the humiliation of defeat and grievances over confiscated territories were exacerbated by an economic crisis brought on by crippling war reparations and hyperinflation that rapidly ruined the livelihoods of ordinary people.

In both Italy and Germany, the many bitterly felt slights to the nation's pride were deftly manipulated by fascist propagandists and transformed, over time, into a full-blown myth of national decline and humiliation. Thus Mussolini, for instance, could fancifully portray the Italian people as a race that had laboured under 'many centuries of abasement and foreign servitude'. Part of the myth, especially prevalent in Germany, focused on the blood purity of the national stock, an idea that was supported by much bogus scientific theory and which led eventually to nightmarish racial and eugenic policies of compulsory 'euthanasia' and mass extermination.

> **Fascism is not defined by the number of its victims but by its way of killing them.**
>
> **Jean-Paul Sartre,** 1953

The countries that fell prey to fascist regimes saw themselves as victims: victims of weak and incompetent government at home and of a malevolent conspiracy of forces abroad. The allure of ultra-nationalist fascist rule was that it promised to wipe away the stain of shame. Pride would be restored through national rebirth, a regeneration achieved by the people united in a common struggle. Enemies within and without, such as socialists, liberals and Jews, would be eliminated, and this called for iron discipline and popular sacrifice under a strong and resolute leader: a man, indeed, such as a Mussolini or a Hitler.

the condensed idea
A toxic synthesis of
left and right

35 Racism

It is one of the more extraordinary facts in history that the United States of America – self-proclaimed 'home of the free' and bastion of liberty, equality and human rights – should have been, for the first 89 years of its existence, a society whose economy and general prosperity depended on slave labour. Indeed, slavery had been legalized in the American colonies for over a century before the birth of the USA in 1776, and many aspects of the discriminatory treatment that it entailed lasted for a hundred years after its formal abolition in 1865. This shameful fact at the heart of American history – this contradiction between the most elevated principle and the most debased practice – played a central role in establishing the idea that humankind could be divided into natural, biologically determined groups known as 'races'.

The first English colonists, settling in North America at the beginning of the 17th century, doubtless entertained notions of their own cultural and moral superiority over the native Americans with whom they came into contact and over the black Africans who arrived shortly afterwards. It was not until the end of the 17th century, however, that such thinking – the idea that these non-Europeans were both different and inferior because they belonged to distinct races – began to coalesce into a rationalization of what had initially been justified (if at all) by economic necessity alone: the institution of slavery.

Throughout the 18th and 19th centuries the sense of racial 'otherness', at first largely intuitive and barely conceptualized, was amplified and reinforced both by the discriminatory legislation of lawmakers and by the theorizing of intellectuals and scientists. Thinkers such as Kant and

timeline

1642
Massachusetts becomes first
state to legalize slavery

1865
Slavery abolished
in the USA

Voltaire explicitly endorsed the view that 'savages' or 'primitives' were racially inferior, while the energies of scientists were channelled into identifying the racial divisions of the human species; some even went so far as to propose that other racial groups constituted different species – in effect, that they were not human, or fully human, at all. At any rate, by the early years of the 20th century, after many decades of habituation, the idea that there were natural differences between human groups that followed racial lines and which justified differential social treatment had become fully ingrained in most societies around the world.

> I refuse to accept the view that mankind is so tragically bound to the starless midnight of racism and war that the bright daybreak of peace and brotherhood can never become a reality.

Martin Luther King Jr, 1964

Racisms Today, the term 'racism' has (at least) two different though related meanings. In popular usage, racists are people who are hostile towards, and contemptuous of, those who are different from themselves in physical appearance, geographical origin, and so on; and this hostility and contempt may be apparent in aggressive or violent behaviour. The target of such behaviour may be more or less precisely defined, but typically racism of this kind is barely intellectualized and is not supported by theoretical justifications.

Second, and distinct from the first meaning, 'racism' may refer to a particular view about how things stand in the world; a systematic set of beliefs and attitudes that form a distinctive worldview or ideology. The central part of this view is the belief that everybody belongs to one, and only one, of several groups, called 'races', each of which is biologically distinct from the others. Members of a particular race share certain markers of their racial identity, especially visible physical characteristics such as common skin colour and distinctive facial features. There are also certain behavioural and psychological qualities, such as temperament and intellectual ability, that are thought to be characteristic of each race. These various physical and behavioural differences are dependent on the unique biology of the race concerned; they are genetically determined and so are hereditary, innate and permanent. The various races are not equal

1933	**1964**	**early 1990s**
First anti-Jewish racial policies implemented in Nazi Germany	Civil Rights Act outlaws racial segregation in the USA	Apartheid system brought to a (legal) end in South Africa

The greater crimes of the white society

One of the more despicable tactics adopted by racists is to exploit sociological data that indicates a disproportionately high level of delinquent or criminal behaviour on the part of a targeted racial group and to suggest that it is evidence of the natural delinquency or criminality of the group concerned. In Britain and the USA, for instance, a relatively high level of criminal activity carried out by black males could be inferred from criminal and penal records. The tactic depends on treating such behaviour as if it were purely a product of biological determination, entirely unaffected by social and other factors. Speaking in January 1968, just months before his assassination, a true understanding of the situation was shown by Martin Luther King Jr: 'It is incontestable and deplorable that Negroes have committed crimes, but these are essentially derivative crimes. They are born of the greater crimes of the white society.'

(in terms of mental capacity, moral worth, etc.), so it is possible in principle to rank them according to their relative superiority.

Racism in this second, ideological sense might explain or even justify the (probably pre-theoretical) behaviour of the racist in the first, popular sense. More significantly, however, the assumptions of the racist worldview can be, and have been, used by politicians and legislators to justify discriminatory policies and institutions in society at large. Most notoriously, in South Africa, until its abolition in the early 1990s, the system of apartheid, or 'separate development', formally sanctioned a range of discriminatory measures against the non-white majority population, who were segregated and cordoned off in certain designated areas, restricted to low-status jobs, and denied access to most political and economic opportunities and privileges.

Science and race Up until the 1970s the view that humankind could be meaningfully divided into racial categories was still held by many scientists; they assumed that such categories were biologically determined and that their task was to study the differences and relationships between them. In essence, they were ploughing the same scientific furrows as their predecessors a hundred and more years previously. By the middle of the 19th century, the task of classifying different races and, in particular, of establishing 'the Negro's place in nature' had spawned various new methods and techniques. The practitioners of one such art, known as craniometry, busied themselves in measuring the internal capacities of skulls. They convinced themselves that the brains of blacks were smaller than those of whites, and on this basis concluded that the latter were endowed with superior innate intelligence. The obsession with relative intelligence was given a boost in the 20th century with the advent of IQ (intelligence quotient) testing. This was adopted with particular alacrity in the USA, as researchers found that blacks performed less well (on average) in such tests than whites and thereby confirmed their prejudices.

The most surprising fact about the scientific consensus surrounding race is that it lasted as long as it did. Broad agreement among scientists about the validity of racial categories was never matched with any agreement about the detail (even, at the most basic level, about how many races there were) – all of which should have been a clue that something was amiss. While there had always been the occasional dissenting voice, there was little in the way of serious challenge to the prevailing orthodoxy until well into the 20th century, by which time the genetic basis of human inheritance had been largely understood. First blood group patterns, and later various other genetic markers, failed to show any correlation with the conventional racial categories. Indeed, it soon became clear that there is much more genetic variation *within* a racially defined group than there is *between* any two such groups. At the same time, others began to look critically at the work of earlier researchers and found that both their methods (for instance, IQ testing) and their interpretations were seriously flawed.

Today, the biological conception of race is almost universally rejected by scientists. It is generally understood that the idea of race is a social construction, of relatively recent origin, that can only be understood in the context of specific historical, cultural and political circumstances. Human physical variations, including those such as skin colour on which racial categories are typically based, are fully explicable, in evolutionary terms, as relatively superficial adaptations to changing environmental conditions. Amongst scientists and intellectuals, the notion of race as a biological category swiftly collapsed under the weight of evidence. Unfortunately if inevitably, it is certain to take much longer to eradicate from the popular imagination an idea that has done so much to blight societies and the lives of individuals.

the condensed idea
The starless midnight of racism

36 Feminism

'From the tyranny of man, I firmly believe, the greater number of female follies proceed ... Asserting the rights which women in common with men ought to contend for, I have not attempted to extenuate their faults; but to prove them to be the natural consequence of their education and station in society. If so, it is reasonable to suppose, that they will change their character, and correct their vices and follies, when they are allowed to be free in a physical, moral, and civil sense ... Let woman share the rights, and she will emulate the virtues of man ...'

This plea for justice and equality for the 'oppressed half of the species' is made in the closing paragraphs of Mary Wollstonecraft's *A Vindication of the Rights of Woman*, published in 1792 to a reception of mixed shock and admiration. The 32-year-old firebrand – a 'hyena in petticoats', in the opinion of a dyspeptic Horace Walpole – railed against a restrictive system of education and upbringing that produced in women a 'slavish dependence', a 'weak elegancy of mind', and no other ambition than to attend to their looks and please men. If only women were allowed the same opportunities as men, she insisted, they would prove to be no less intelligent and no less able. Although there had been isolated female voices in the long-running and often rather genteel 'debate about women', Wollstonecraft injected it with a new passion and urgency: she had given notice that an authentic feminist consciousness was emerging.

It is a testimony to the achievements of the feminist movement that, in Western countries at least, a high degree of equality between the sexes (though not yet complete equality) is generally taken for granted. It is easy to forget that less than a century ago the lives of women were severely restricted,

timeline

1792	1848	1869
Mary Wollstonecraft protests against subordination of women	First US women's rights convention held at Seneca Falls, New York	Publication of J.S. Mill's *The Subjection of Women*

socially, economically and politically. A woman's place truly was in the home – although she would generally have been denied the right to own it.

Votes for women   In the century after Wollstonecraft's death in 1797, the clamour for change grew steadily louder. In the middle years of the 19th century, the movement gained an energetic supporter in John Stuart Mill, who argued in *The Subjection of Women* (1869) that 'the legal subordination of one sex to the other . . . ought to be replaced by a principle of perfect equality, admitting no power or privilege on the one side, nor disability on the other'. In both the USA and Europe the cause of women's emancipation was given impetus by the struggle to abolish slavery, as it brought home to female abolitionists the unpleasant irony that the political status and rights they were demanding for black people were in many respects superior to those they enjoyed themselves.

Over the following half-century feminist energies throughout the Western world were devoted almost exclusively to the business of winning the right to vote. Lobbying that started off polite and ladylike ran up against deeply entrenched establishment opposition and turned more and more militant, as suffragettes on both sides of the Atlantic launched a campaign that included boycotts, demonstrations, arson and hunger strikes. Such tactics – establishing the tradition of political activism that was to become a hallmark of feminism – eventually paid off as laws extending the franchise to women were passed in Britain (1918 and 1928) and the USA (1920).

> **❝I myself have never been able to find out precisely what feminism is: I only know that people call me a feminist whenever I express sentiments that differentiate me from a doormat or a prostitute.❞**
>
> **Rebecca West, English writer, 1913**

The second wave   Victories in winning the vote notwithstanding, Western societies were still riddled with sex-based inequalities in almost every area of life. At the very first women's rights convention in the USA, held at Seneca Falls, New York, in 1848, a resolution was passed demanding that women be granted 'equal participation with men in the various trades, professions and commerce'; more than 70 years later, it was

1918	**1920**	**1960s**	**1990s**
Vote granted to British women over 30 (over 21, as for men, after 1928)	19th Amendment to US Constitution prohibits disenfranchisement on basis of sex	Start of feminism's second wave	Start of feminism's third wave

painfully obvious that little progress had been made towards economic equality. Yet while it was clear that much work still had to be done, the sense of common purpose created by the struggle for women's suffrage quickly dissipated once that objective had been achieved. Loss of focus, worsened by the distractions first of world depression, then of world war, left the women's movement deflated and fragmented for decades.

Just as it had taken the fervour generated by the abolitionist movement to galvanize the so-called 'first wave' of feminism, so now it took a new period of hope and crisis in the 1960s – the era of civil rights, Vietnam, the hippie revolution and student protest – to kick-start the 'second wave'. All at once a thousand new initiatives, aimed at a thousand perceived injustices, sprang up everywhere. But this renewed and widespread activism brought to the surface differences and divisions that had long existed within feminism.

Mainstream, or liberal, feminists tended to take a pragmatic line, aiming for strict equality with men in every area. For them, the primary task was reform that prevented any form of discrimination: removing formal or informal barriers that stopped women breaking through the 'glass ceiling' in the workplace; providing adequate maternity-leave rights and childcare arrangements; ensuring that equal educational and training opportunities were available for women.

There had always been more radical voices within feminism. As early as 1898, the leading US anarchist Emma Goldman had scoffed at the idea that liberation could be won merely by winning the vote; a woman could gain true freedom only 'by refusing the right to anyone over her body; by refusing to bear children, unless she wants them; by refusing to be a servant to God, the state, society, the husband, the family'. Later feminists questioned whether strict equality with men – rather than protective legislation

Hell hath no fury . . .

In a speech made exactly 200 years after the publication of Wollstonecraft's *A Vindication of the Rights of Woman*, the right-wing evangelical minister Pat Robertson described feminism as 'a socialist, anti-family political movement that encourages women to leave their husbands, kill their children, practise witchcraft, destroy capitalism and become lesbians'. While witchcraft and infanticide are less well attested, it is doubtless true that none of the other recommendations has lacked feminist advocacy at some time or another. This is as much a tribute to the sheer breadth and diversity of feminism, however, as it is to its extremism – although there has been no shortage of extremists either.

that explicitly defended women's interests – was what they should really be fighting for. Was it right to measure progress in overturning the historical subordination of women by their success in gaining access to power and privilege in a patriarchally organized world – in a system that was founded on the assumption of male dominance? For many, outdoing men on their own terms, playing them at their own games, was not enough. As the Australian feminist Germaine Greer commented in 1986: 'I didn't fight to get women out from behind vacuum cleaners to get them onto the board of Hoover.'

Underpinning these concerns was an extensive theoretical debate on the nature and origins of women's oppression. Central to this was a distinction between sex and gender that was based on the idea that femininity is a social construction; the notion, prefigured by Simone de Beauvoir in *The Second Sex* (1949), that 'woman is not born but made' and that she is 'the Other' – a person who is defined, asymmetrically, in relation to male norms. In this radical critique the subordinate position of women is so inextricably wound up in the texture of patriarchal society that nothing short of a revolutionary reshaping of that society will suffice.

Towards a global sisterhood

In the 1990s a 'third wave' of feminism emerged, partly as a response to the perceived shortcomings of earlier feminists. To some extent it was a change of style more than substance: savvy, assertive, ironic, playful self-awareness took the place of the boiler-suited earnestness of the second wavers. 'Girl power' (as it was commercially packaged) displaced flower power; a generation brought up on Madonna took over from one raised on Joan Baez. There was substance behind the gloss, however. Perhaps the most persistent failure of the mainly white and relatively well-heeled second wave, in spite of its pretensions to 'global sisterhood', was an inability to fully understand the needs and encompass the aspirations of black and Third World feminists. The third wave achieved a level of inclusivity and pluralism beyond anything that had gone before, thereby holding out the promise of a genuinely global feminism.

the condensed idea
Equal, not the same

37 Islamism

'The ruling to kill the Americans and their allies – civilians and military – is an individual duty for every Muslim who can do it in any country in which it is possible to do it, in order to liberate the al-Aqsa Mosque [in Jerusalem] and the holy mosque [in Mecca] from their grip, and in order for their armies to move out of all the lands of Islam, defeated and unable to threaten any Muslim. This is in accordance with the words of Almighty God, "and fight the pagans all together as they fight you all together", and "fight them until there is no more tumult or oppression, and there prevail justice and faith in God".'

The full horror of this fatwa (religious decree), issued in February 1998, would be realized three and a half years later, when, within the space of 17 minutes, two domestic airliners cut through a brilliant azure sky over the streets of Lower Manhattan and crashed with lethal force into the twin towers of the World Trade Center. The fatwa formed part of a fuller declaration that called for a 'Jihad against the Jews and the Crusaders' and was released by the World Islamic Front, a group of extreme Islamist bodies marshalled by soon-to-be 'world's most wanted man' Osama bin Laden. The declaration may have been the clearest statement of the dire threat posed by radical Islamism to the West and the 9/11 attacks may have been its most devastating expression. But the former was by no means the first warning nor, sadly, was the latter the last attack. The grievances that drove political Islam were long-standing but poorly understood, and this lack of understanding – on both sides – has had the gravest repercussions that continue to shake the world to this day.

timeline

1979–89
US supports Mujahideen in Soviet–Afghan War

1980–8
US supports Saddam Hussein in Iran–Iraq War

The new caliphate The suicide attacks of 11 September 2001 were the fruit of years of planning by agents associated with al-Qaeda, a network of terrorist groups under the leadership of bin Laden. Given the scale and manner of the attacks, it was inevitable that al-Qaeda would become the international face of Islamism, and its extreme agenda was naively assumed in some quarters to reflect the views of Muslims generally. To make matters worse, the portrait of Islamic fanaticism was fleshed out with gruesome details provided by the Taliban, a fundamentalist Muslim regime which harboured al-Qaeda bases in Afghanistan, where it had seized power in 1996 and proceeded to impose highly repressive theocratic rule on the Afghan people. Terrorist atrocities, near-medieval social repression, suicide bombings, televised beheadings – all conspired to paint the most lurid picture of Islamic fundamentalism, and by false implication, of Islam itself.

The overriding aim of most radical Islamists is, in the words of a 2008 al-Qaeda webcast, to 'establish the Shari'a Islamic state that will unite the Muslims of the earth in truth and justice'. The current oppressed state of Muslim countries is seen as the consequence of straying from the true path of Islam, and the remedy involves strict observance of the teachings of the Qu'ran and implementation of Shari'a, Islamic law as revealed by God. Islam is the one true faith and its scope is universal, so the new caliphate will encompass all mankind, everywhere on earth.

Islamists frequently invoke a number of grievances against the West, which are held in part because they are seen as obstacles to their return to the

> **❝Leave us alone to establish the Shari'a Islamic state that will unite the Muslims of the earth in truth and justice. A single word of American protest shall be silenced by a thousand Islamic bombs.❞**
>
> Al-Qaeda webcast, 2008

1990–1	11 Sept. 2001	Oct. 2001	Mar. 2003
US-led coalition defeats Saddam following Iraqi invasion of Kuwait	Terrorist attacks kill close to 3000 in USA	US-led coalition attacks Taliban in Afghanistan	Invasion of Iraq by US and 'coalition of the willing'

true path. First and foremost is the existence of Israel. Support of 'the Jews' petty state' (as the 1998 fatwa put it) is one of the perennial complaints levelled at the USA, and the series of conflicts in Iraq and the alleged destabilization of other Middle Eastern countries are seen as a means of perpetuating the Israeli state. A second major grievance, again articulated in the 1998 fatwa, was US occupation of 'the lands of Islam in the holiest of places, the Arabian Peninsula, plundering its riches, dictating to its rulers, humiliating its people, terrorizing its neighbours'. Particularly humiliating was the presence of US military bases, for over a decade after the 1990–1 Gulf War, in 'the Land of the Two Holy Places', i.e. Saudi Arabia, with its sacred sites at Mecca and Medina.

Jihad

Just as the word 'crusade' has all the wrong connotations for Muslims, so the concept of *jihad* has done more than any other to cement in Western minds the link between Islam and violence. Yet the interpretation of the word is much disputed by Muslims themselves. For the radical Islamist, *jihad* means 'holy war' and is used to justify a range of actions that includes suicide attacks, roadside bombings and targeting of civilians. The literal meaning of *jihad*, however, is 'struggle in the way of God', and moderate Muslims take it to refer primarily to internal spiritual conflict; it may refer to external war, but only in defence of the faith. The 'war on terror' that has raged in Afghanistan and Iraq in the wake of the 9/11 attacks has often been understood on both sides as a battle of 'hearts and minds'. The distaste among ordinary Muslims for indiscriminate killing of civilians, including women and children, is combined with a strong sense that such methods are un-Islamic and contrary to the proper spirit of *jihad*. This *should* mean that the radical Islamists are defeated in the ideological battle and become progressively marginalized. Unfortunately, though, the means chosen by the US and its allies to wage the war on terror have proved just as effective in alienating moderate Muslim opinion. Each side, incapable of comprehending the other, does all it can to lose the battle for hearts and minds.

The 'Islamic threat' In many respects, both before and after 9/11, the response of the Western powers, and of the USA in particular, to the perceived 'Islamic threat' has tended to confirm the suspicions of Muslims, radical and moderate alike. Europe and the US have generally been insensitive to Muslim concerns that stem from centuries of friction and conflict with the West and from a period of colonial occupation that lasted for much of the 20th century. Muslim countries have often been portrayed as backward and opposed to modernity, but the chief focus of their fears is in fact what they see as economic and cultural imperialism. The West readily assumes that 'progress' means movement towards its own liberal, secular values, but to many Muslims Westernization is unwelcome and a mark of post-colonial arrogance.

The US's motives in its interventions in the Middle East are generally questioned by Muslims, and it is hard to fully refute the charge that a primary US objective in the region is 'plundering its riches' (i.e. protecting its oil interests) and its preferred method 'dictating to its rulers' (i.e. exercising control by supporting friendly, if not always savoury, regimes). The fact that US actions have been driven more by self-interest than by principle is borne out by several decades of American foreign policy. For instance – to take merely the most notorious cases – US support for the Afghan Mujahideen during the 1980s Soviet invasion was partly responsible for the emergence of the Taliban, al-Qaeda and bin Laden himself (who fought in an Arab contingent against the Soviets). The other great bogeyman of the Middle East, Saddam Hussein, was likewise supported by the US in the Iran–Iraq War during the 1980s, in the hope that his regime would act as a counterweight to the Islamic state led by the radical Ayatollah Khomeini in neighbouring Iran. Such interventions have rarely worked out as US policy-makers intended and have done nothing to win the 'hearts and minds' of ordinary Muslims.

the condensed idea
A clash of civilizations?

38 Capitalism

In the first decade of the 21st century, the world's economies were buffeted by turbulence of almost unprecedented severity. Plummeting consumer confidence; a collapse in investment and sales; widespread business failures and home repossessions; spiralling unemployment; steep falls in stocks and house prices: the consensus of every financial indicator pointed to a contraction of economies that presaged deep global recession.

At the root of this economic turmoil was a dire 'credit crunch' – a massive squeeze on credit available to businesses and consumers. And this crunch was itself the product of an earlier credit binge, which was principally the handiwork of bloated city bankers, insufficiently regulated and addicted to risk, whose apparently boundless hubris and greed had seen over two trillion dollars of 'toxic' debt accumulate in the arteries of financial systems worldwide. For greed, read 'profit motive'; for lack of regulation, read 'free enterprise': then it becomes clear that the financial crisis of the early 21st century called into question the most basic principles of capitalism, the dominant economic system in most parts of the world for most of the last two centuries.

> **The inherent vice of capitalism is the unequal sharing of blessings; the inherent virtue of socialism is the equal sharing of miseries.**
>
> **Winston Churchill, 1954**

Adam Smith and free trade Although use of the term 'capitalism' is not attested before the 1850s, the essential dynamics of its operation were fully understood and explained by the Scottish economist Adam Smith in *The Wealth of Nations*, published in 1776. At this date many of the conditions in which capitalism could flourish were already in place. The expansion of overseas trade had seen the emergence of a merchant class whose entrepreneurial skills had allowed them to accumulate sufficient wealth to invest in the new industries

timeline

1776	1848	1854	1867–94
Principles of free trade set out in Adam Smith's *The Wealth of Nations*	Overthrow of capitalism predicted in Marx's *The Communist Manifesto*	First attested use of 'capitalism' (in Thackeray's *The Newcomes*)	Marx gives definitive critique of capitalism in *Das Kapital*

spawned by the incipient industrial revolution. At the same time agricultural workers, displaced from a life of subsistence on feudally managed estates, had begun to form a body of free wage labourers. However, commerce was still widely encumbered by monopolies and other protectionist measures imposed by the state, and it was against the background of such constraints that Smith wrote his seminal work.

Keynesians versus Monetarists

The deepest fault line in the theory and practice of capitalism has always been the extent to which scrutiny, regulation and intervention on the part of the state are compatible with the proper operation of the capitalist system. John Maynard Keynes, arguably the most influential economist of the 20th century, wrote damningly of the 'decadent international but individualistic capitalism' that prevailed in the years after the First World War: 'It is not intelligent. It is not beautiful. It is not just. It is not virtuous. And it doesn't deliver the goods.' Insisting that markets were neither perfect nor self-regulating, Keynes advocated state intervention in the form of increased government spending, which would boost demand in the economy, increase employment and so overcome recessionary pressures. Keynesian ideas dominated economic thinking in the USA and Europe in the decades following the Great Depression of the 1930s, but from the 1970s they were largely displaced by monetarism, a doctrine chiefly credited to the US economist Milton

Friedman. Reverting to the classical view of the perfection of the free market, monetarists insisted that Keynesian intervention (interference, in their view) would merely increase inflation and upset the natural balance of markets. The limit of state activity should be to keep inflation down (by limiting the money supply) and to eliminate external constraints on the market.

The opposition between Keynesian and monetarist views came to a head in the grim economic malaise that shattered global finances in the first decade of the 21st century. Attempted cures included colossal bail-outs of financial institutions and multibillion-dollar stimulus plans, all predicated on unprecedented levels of government borrowing and spending. State intervention on such a staggering scale implied the bankruptcy (more or less literally) of the unregulated free market so beloved of monetarists. It remained to be seen whether massive Keynesian intervention would fare any better.

1929	1933	1970s	2007
Stock market crash in USA triggers Great Depression	Keynes criticizes free trade in his essay 'National Self-Sufficiency'	Monetarist policies gain favour in Europe and the USA	Beginning of deep global economic downturn ('credit crunch')

Boom and bust

As Karl Marx observed in 1848, capitalism is habitually plagued by 'commercial crises that by their periodical return put the existence of the entire bourgeois society on its trial, each time more threateningly'. There is no consensus on the reasons for these cycles of growth and recession but they are remarkably persistent. Marx himself believed that instability was endemic to the system and was certain to get worse over time, eventually leading to the overthrow of the bourgeoisie by the working people. However, he underestimated capitalism's ability to adapt to changing circumstances.

Smith claimed that the free market was the most effective mechanism in coordinating economic activity. He recognized that in a free market, where the drive towards personal gain was counterbalanced by the forces of competition, producers would have a natural incentive to provide the goods and services that consumers wished to purchase, at a price that offered a reasonable but not excessive profit on their investment. The market mechanism would thus bring optimal efficiency by closely coordinating supply and demand, and the dynamic relation between these two forces would ensure appropriate levels of cost (in production, wages, distribution, etc.) and profit.

Laissez-faire A crucial aspect of classical capitalism as conceived by Smith and his followers was that it was naturally self-regulating; that is, its proper variables (cost, price, demand, etc.) were determined from within the system, as functions of the system as a whole. For this reason, these variables could be manipulated neither by any single party within the system nor by any party without. The correct price of a product, for instance, was a function of supply and demand within a given market and could not be imposed unilaterally or externally without undermining the system itself. For this reason, probably for the first time in history, the proper realm of economics was conceived as essentially distinct from that of politics.

This division was the theoretical justification for the classical liberal doctrine of laissez-faire – the idea that the state should refrain from attempting to plan or direct the course of the market. Smith allowed that the state had 'the duty of erecting and maintaining certain public works and certain public institutions' – facilities, in other words, that private entrepreneurs would have no interest in supplying – and debate over the public or private provision of society's needs, such as transport and education, would continue till the present day. This aside, the state's role should broadly be restricted to facilitating commerce, for instance by providing a formal legal framework in which contractual obligations could be made and upheld.

> **'Advocates of capitalism are very apt to appeal to the sacred principles of liberty, which are embodied in one maxim: The fortunate must not be restrained in the exercise of tyranny over the unfortunate.'**

Bertrand Russell, 1928

Growing pains Advocates of capitalism stress its unparalleled capacity to generate economic growth. Unquestionably, the period of capitalism's dominance has coincided with a spectacular increase in economic output. Writing in 1848, Karl Marx conceded that in a hundred years of ascendancy the bourgeoisie, or capitalist class, had 'created more massive and more colossal productive forces than have all preceding generations together'. But this was also a period of massive industrialization, and capitalism's critics suggest that the 'subjection of Nature's forces to man', by means of mechanization, steam power, railways and more besides, was the main cause of economic growth, not market forces as such.

Adam Smith noted that the urge to accumulate wealth, the central concern of capitalism, tended to encourage entrepreneurs to expand their businesses. This allowed progressive division of labour (splitting of the manufacturing process into smaller, simpler tasks) and other efficiencies that contributed to economies of scale. While such developments undoubtedly contributed to growth – and helped to line the pockets of capitalist financiers still further – critics such as Marx were quick to denounce the *kind* of growth involved. Smith had suggested that the 'invisible hand' of the market would guide individuals acting in their own interests to promote, unconsciously, a greater, collective good, but experience hardly supported any such hope. In the event, the new wealth was anything but evenly shared and the gap between rich and poor grew wider and wider. At the same time the conditions of the working people deteriorated, as they worked long hours in squalid factories at tasks that became ever more tedious and repetitive.

the condensed idea
The unequal sharing of blessings

39 Globalization

The US economist Joseph Schumpeter once proposed, somewhat archly, that the evolution of capitalist culture could be 'easily – and perhaps most tellingly – described in terms of the genesis of the modern lounge suit'. Such an approach might be extended, with no less profit, to the phenomenon of globalization, where the ubiquitous lounge suit – uniform of business people and politicians alike – has become a symbol of the homogenization of human culture and experience across the planet. For some, the increasingly permeable borders of the world's nations offer an historic opportunity to establish a benign cosmopolitanism; for others, growing conformity to Western norms threatens to smother the rich diversity of the peoples of the earth.

Globalization is nothing new. The imperialists, missionaries and traders of earlier centuries aspired to extend their power, faith and commerce as widely as possible across the globe, and they deposited a great weight of cultural baggage, willy-nilly, wherever they went. What is new today, however, is the astonishing scale and speed of the political, economic and cultural transformation.

The global village The process of globalization is driven by the apparent compression of distance and time, a phenomenon that was memorably explored in the 1960s by the Canadian media theorist Marshall McLuhan:

'Electric circuitry has overthrown the regime of 'time' and 'space' and pours upon us instantly and continuously concerns of all other men. It has reconstituted dialogue on a global scale. Its message is Total

timeline

1962	1971
First use of the term 'global village' in McLuhan's *The Gutenberg Galaxy*	The first Asian McDonald's opens, in Tokyo, Japan

Change, ending psychic, social, economic, and political parochialism . . .
Ours is a brand-new world of allatonceness. 'Time' has ceased, 'space'
has vanished. We now live in a global village.'

The 'electric circuitry' McLuhan had in mind at this date (1967) was
primarily television, but every innovation dreamt up in the information
technology revolution of the following decades served only to confirm his
prescience. Mobile phones, the internet, email, social networking: each
new technology enhanced the reality of rapid global communications. At
the same time, shrinkage of virtual space was matched in real space by the
availability of cheap international flights, which at once brought the most
distant parts of the world within easy and affordable reach of millions of
ordinary people.

As national borders became increasingly porous, the outward flow of both
commodities and ideas was of course strongest from the economically and
politically dominant regions, above all from the USA. Export of and
exposure to Western products and practices inevitably had the effect of
eroding or at least modifying local beliefs and customs. And as the flow
became a torrent, fears and hopes began to grow that, for the first time in
history, some form of global culture might emerge. At issue, for proponents
and opponents alike, was the reality or otherwise of a new world order: a
shared political and economic arena, fashioned by the technology of
worldwide interconnectedness.

All rosy in the village garden McLuhan was enthusiastic about
the prospect of life in the global village and many since have shared his
optimism. A notable, if extreme, example is Francis Fukuyama, American
philosopher and erstwhile neo-conservative, who speculated
in 1992, in an ecstasy of post-Cold War euphoria, that
the collapse of authoritarian rule in the Soviet Union and
elsewhere might mark 'the end point of mankind's ideological
evolution and the universalization of Western liberal
democracy as the final form of human government'. In this
worldwide triumph of liberalism, Fukuyama hazarded, a
'true global culture has emerged, centering around

> **'The new electronic
> interdependence
> recreates the world
> in the image of a
> global village.'**
>
> **Marshall McLuhan, 1962**

1988	2001	2015
Debord ridicules McLuhan in *Comments on the Society of the Spectacle*	9/11 attacks in US demonstrate global reach of terrorism	World population of obese adults set to reach 700 million (according to WHO)

technologically driven economic growth and the capitalist social relations necessary to produce and sustain it'.

It is not necessary to strip much of the varnish from Fukuyama's rosy picture to see whose ideas are likely to dominate the agenda at a meeting of the global village council. In company with many other pro-globalists, Fukuyama bases his argument on a largely unquestioned assumption of the benign impact of liberal market economics of the kind developed in the West over the last two centuries. The swift and unfettered movement of money and goods over the globe, made possible by technological innovation, will bring great efficiencies and benefits for all: more and cheaper commodities to already rich countries; more and better-paid employment to currently impoverished ones. In the case of the latter, growing prosperity will lead in due course to improved education and greater political sophistication; and if history is our guide, this in turn will lead to liberalization and democracy – in short, an advance beyond ancestral parochialisms into a more collaborative and harmonious world order.

Are we what we eat?

Food has always been a powerful vehicle of cultural transmission and transformation. New World plants such as maize, peanuts and sweet potatoes, for instance, were introduced to Europe by returning conquistadors, and from there they proceeded to revolutionize farming practices and diets in Asia and Africa. European diets, tied for thousands of years to local and seasonal crops, now encompass a bewildering array of exotics such as bananas and mangoes, while every kind of fruit and vegetable is expected to be available and affordable at any time of year – whatever the environmental cost.

The gigantic Western fast-food corporations, such as McDonald's and Kentucky Fried Chicken, have long been the bogeymen of anti-globalists. Although much of the evidence is circumstantial, Big Macs and finger-lickin' deep-fried chicken wings are not only held responsible for a dreary homogenization of the world's diets but are also implicated in the creation of a new horror: 'globesity'. As a consequence of deteriorating global food habits (more meat, fat, processed sugars, etc.), the World Health Organization projects that by 2015 some 700 million adults worldwide will be obese. Yet the impact of these supposed giants of cultural imperialism has often been far from predictable, and they have been variously credited with the emergence of polite waiters in Moscow, queuing in Hong Kong, and cleaner public toilets throughout the world.

Rose blight A sample of the kinds of objection raised against globalization was given in 1988 by the French avant-garde thinker Guy Debord, in a scathing attack on McLuhan, the 'most convinced imbecile of the century'. Beguiled by the meretricious freedoms and attractions offered by the global village, the 'sage of Toronto' had failed to appreciate the shallow vulgarity of village life: 'Villages, unlike towns, have always been ruled by conformism, isolation, petty surveillance, boredom and repetitive malicious gossip about the same families.'

Conformism and boredom lie at the heart of the anti-globalist critique. The debased and commoditized popular culture of the USA and other Western countries is seen as swamping local practices and customs. The unstoppable march of this cultural imperialism sees local cuisines rudely snuffed out by Ronald McDonald and Colonel Sanders; the authentic statements of indigenous film-makers drowned out by the shrill din of Hollywood's latest blockbuster; the vibrancy of traditional dress eclipsed by the gaudy colours of Benetton and Abercrombie. And behind the superficial consumerism lies a soulless array of aggressive and cynical multinational corporations: vast businesses that 'swindle the West and exploit the rest', by snatching jobs from Western workers and replacing them with slave labour in Third World sweat shops.

Hybrid culture Predictably, the truth about globalization is neither as grim nor as cheery as its opponents and proponents suggest. The global culture that is welcomed on one side and decried on the other is in fact largely fictitious. Nothing approaching such a culture currently exists, and there is little prospect that it will become a reality in the near future. The most salient fact to emerge from the voluminous research into the effects of globalization is that it is anything but a one-way process. When different cultures meet, it is almost never the case that one simply dominates and displaces the others; rather, there is a subtle and fascinating process of cross-fertilization in which something new and distinct emerges – something that may have an enriching effect on all sides. In the end, the not-so-surprising fact is that humans, being humans, are curious to experience new tastes and sounds as they become available, but they nevertheless retain a strong sense of belonging to a particular locality and of sharing in a complex system of local customs and beliefs.

the condensed idea
Life in the global village

40 Classicism

Writing in the middle years of the 15th century, Leon Battista Alberti defined beauty in architecture as 'the harmony and concord of all the parts achieved by following well-founded rules and resulting in a unity such that nothing could be added or taken away or altered except for the worse'. Italian artist, architect and polymath, Alberti wrote treatises on painting, sculpture and architecture that established him as the foremost theorist of the Renaissance. The 'well-founded rules' Alberti had in mind are the principles and precepts embodied in the great architectural relics of the Greek and Roman world. No less valid for other forms of artistic expression, his characterization of beauty exactly captures the spirit of classicism.

For Alberti and his contemporaries, the buildings, sculptures, plays, poems and theoretical works of antiquity were a direct inspiration: they were 'classic' – from the Latin meaning that they constituted the 'highest class' – and presented a canon of perfection; a set of standards or paradigms to which they could aspire and against which they could measure their own achievement. This reverence for the works of the ancients encompassed, of course, the various qualities that those works were believed to embody: harmony; symmetry and proportionality; clarity of expression; restraint and avoidance of unnecessary detail or adornment.

While the Renaissance was the first great expression of these values since antiquity, it was not the last, and the term 'classicism' was applied to a number of later artistic and aesthetic movements. While the classicist canon in theory comprised solely the works of the ancient Greeks and Romans, in practice it was constantly revised and enhanced by later

timeline

1420–36	c.1450	1501–4	1508–9	1509–10
Filippo Brunelleschi's dome for the cathedral at Florence	Piero della Francesca's *Flagellation of Christ*	Michelangelo's *David*	Donato Bramante's Palazzo Caprini	Raphael's *The School of Athens*

> **Rome's ancient genius o'er its ruins spread**
> **Shakes off the dust, and rears his reverent head**
> **Then sculpture and her sister arts revive,**
> **Stones leaped to form, and rocks began to live . . .**

Alexander Pope, *An Essay on Criticism,* **1711**

works which themselves became canonical. So it was that artists belonging to later traditions of classicism would seek to emulate, instead or as well, the works of the great Renaissance masters such as Michelangelo, Raphael and Bramante. Sometimes, the term 'neoclassical' is used to refer to a revival of interest in classical models that is marked by a particular desire to re-examine or reinterpret the canonical heritage. In practice, however, such motivations are hard to distinguish from those of classicism, and the terms are often used with little or no difference of meaning.

The mathematics of nature In the visual arts, restraint, moderation and the other principles of classicism have been especially valued as an antidote to the perceived licence and excesses of some other aesthetics, such as Gothic, Baroque and Romanticism. In contrast to such extravagances, one of the chief justifications for following classical models is supposedly their sober ability to simulate reality and hence to be 'true to nature'. This is the force of the boast made by the painter and architect Giorgio Vasari, in his *Lives of the Artists* (1550), when he claimed that contemporary Florentine artists, and Michelangelo in particular, had surpassed both nature and the ancients in their art. The strict codes of rules and conventions that are so characteristic of classicism are the rational means by which the artist is assisted in emulating the masters of the past and thus guided towards the goal of realism or naturalism.

Alberti believed that the 'laws by which Nature produced her works' could be applied to the works of architecture, and to this end developed a theory of proportionality that related human and architectural form. In painting, the application of mathematical rules was pursued by Alberti's contemporary Piero della Francesca, whose ordered and harmonious compositions have a unique geometric purity. A similar simplicity is seen in the classically

1640	1648	1677	1711	1793
Pierre Corneille's *Horace*	Nicolas Poussin's *Landscape with the Burial of Phocion*	Jean Racine's *Phèdre*	Alexander Pope's *An Essay on Criticism*	Jacques-Louis David's *Death of Marat*

inspired architecture of Alberti's friend Filippo Brunelleschi, whose works include the magnificent dome of the cathedral in Florence. It was the desire to represent naturalistic space in compositions that led Brunelleschi to develop the system of perspective, the theoretical rules of which were formalized in treatises by both Piero and Alberti. Piero's own *Flagellation of Christ* is one of the most famous and striking demonstrations of the illusion of depth created by the use of perspective.

Later classicisms There was a second flourishing of classicism in the 17th century, most notably in Italy and France. The Frenchman Nicolas Poussin was the dominant figure in a group of artists, active mainly in Rome, who were opposed to the emotional drama and formal licence of the Baroque. Instead, they combined Baroque colour with a revival of antique forms. Poussin was strongly influenced by the Bolognese painter and draughtsman Domenichino, who had created an austere classicism that featured simplified and static compositions, grandiose figures and archaeologically accurate details. At the peak of his powers in the 1640s, Poussin refined the idea of the 'ideal landscape', the natural elements of which were an expression of almost mathematical order and contemplative grandeur.

At home with the ancients

The scope of the term 'classicism' has expanded steadily over the years, to the extent that aesthetic movements so named may now enjoy little or no direct inspiration from the classical world; it may suffice that they are characterized (for example) by a particular purity or clarity of expression. Indeed, the word 'classic' is now applied so promiscuously that it can be used of anything that is considered definitive or perfect of its kind, from the smooth swing of a golfer to an enduring popular song. This attenuated meaning is a far cry from the first revival of classicism in the Renaissance, when classically inspired humanists would not so much pay homage to the ancients as treat them as friends and familiars. In a letter written in 1513 the political theorist Niccolò Machiavelli's account of his reading habits gives an astonishing insight into his capacity to lose himself in the company of his ancient acquaintances:

'Evenings I return home and enter my study; and at its entrance I take off my everyday clothes, full of mud and dust, and don royal and courtly garments; decorously reattired, I enter into the ancient sessions of ancient men. Received amicably by them, I partake of such food as is mine only and for which I was born. There, without shame, I speak with them and ask them about the reason for their actions; and they in their humanity respond to me.'

Poussin himself was an important influence on the French painter and portraitist Jacques-Louis David, who was the greatest exponent of the neoclassicism that flourished in the late 18th and early 19th centuries. Lacking ancient models for his art, David looked reverently to the example of Poussin. In his own severely noble paintings, the forms are more simplified and the details more archaeological, but at his best he can attain great poetic realism, as for example in his *Death of Marat* (1793), without losing any of his classical poise.

Nature to advantage dressed In literature the attractions of ancient authors were essentially the same as in the visual arts: the precedence of reason over emotion; expression of ideas of universal validity; a style marked by clarity, control and dignity. The delight in apparently effortless yet artful expression, with never a word wasted, was captured (precisely, of course) in Alexander Pope's *An Essay on Criticism* (1711), when he famously observed: 'True wit is Nature to advantage dressed,/ What oft was thought, but ne'er so well expressed.' In Pope, too, we find classicism's insistence on truth to nature, achieved through observance of time-honoured rules:

> 'Those rules, of old discovered, not devised,
> Are nature still, but nature methodized;
> Nature, like liberty, is but restrained
> By the same laws which first herself ordained.'

Pope was a leading representative of the Augustan Age in England, so named after the Roman emperor Augustus, whose reign was the golden age of poets such as Horace and Virgil. An even more rigorous form of neoclassicism was seen in the previous century on the French stage. Here, a set of rules known as the 'unities', derived from Aristotle's *Poetics*, came to be rigidly observed. According to these rules, a play's action was limited to a single plot and a single place and was restricted to a span of 24 hours. In the hands of great masters such as Corneille and Racine, the unities could produce drama of concentrated power and psychological depth. In less skilled hands, however, slavish imitation within a rigid framework of rules could result in much clumsiness and contrivance.

the condensed idea
Rome's ancient genius

41 Romanticism

A dashing cavalry officer, brandishing his sabre astride a rearing, mad-eyed stallion, gallops fearlessly, recklessly into a swirling crimson inferno that could be the flames of hell, surely to his certain doom. 'I can make nothing of this brushwork,' commented Jacques-Louis David as he inspected the swirling pigment of 21-year-old Théodore Géricault's *Charging Chasseur* at the Salon de Paris in 1812. David, more than four decades Géricault's senior, was the undisputed leader of France's neoclassical painters; his recent work had included the vast, and static, *Coronation of Napoleon*. David was never likely to make much of the younger man's canvas.

The raw dynamism of Géricault's *chasseur* was a far cry from the austere and studied repose of David's Leonidas, Socrates, Brutus – or Napoleon. The obscure cavalryman riding heroically into an unnamed battle brashly announced the arrival of a new sensibility. The meticulous neoclassical mastery of conventional forms was to be replaced by rougher and ruder accomplishments. 'Genius is the fire of a volcano which must and will burst forth,' proclaimed Géricault, 'because the truly creative artist is constrained by a law of his being to shine, illuminate and amaze the world.' Wayward and impetuous; obsessed with death and the macabre (he painted a series of still lifes of criminals' severed heads and limbs); dead himself after a tempestuous career of just 11 years: Géricault was everything that David was not; he was everything that could be asked of an artist imbued in the new aesthetic that critics later called Romanticism.

The profound shift in attitude and outlook of which Géricault was a pioneer swept across Europe before and after the turn of the 19th century. Rooted in German philosophical speculation, the Romantic world-view

timeline

1774	1789	1800	1800/1802
Johann Wolfgang von Goethe's *The Sorrows of Young Werther*	William Blake's *Songs of Innocence* (*Songs of Experience*, 1794)	Friedrich von Schelling's *System of Transcendental Idealism*	William Wordsworth's preface to *Lyrical Ballads* (1798, with S.T. Coleridge)

represented a profound cultural transformation, by no means restricted to painting or indeed to the arts alone. As John Stuart Mill observed in 1837, it was an 'era of reaction against the narrownesses of the eighteenth century'; not only an 'insurrection against the old traditions of classicism', but a rebellion against what the new generation saw as the numbing rationality of the Enlightenment. According to this new aesthetic, what mattered was individual self-expression, not selfless labour within an established tradition; instinct and spontaneity, not learning and cultivation; creative (and often rough) genius, not elegant (and always polished) imitation. While the so-called 'Romantic period' is conventionally limited to the first half of the 19th century, in truth its influence – its unremitting emphasis on originality, passion, sincerity of expression, authenticity of voice – has extended undiminished to the present day.

> To see a world in a grain of sand
> And a heaven in a wild flower,
> Hold infinity in the palm of your hand
> And eternity in an hour.

William Blake, 'Auguries of Innocence', *c.*1803

Fatal attraction

The new aesthetes of the Romantic movement were anxious to liberate the energies of the human spirit, to let it rise up and sing of its joy and exaltation; yet their songs of celebration were forever tinged with melancholy and overshadowed by death. This conflict is well illustrated in the long life of the greatest German poet, Johann Wolfgang von Goethe. In his younger days Goethe was a leading figure in a rebellious writers' movement known as *Sturm und Drang* ('storm and stress'), a formative influence in shaping the Romantic sensibility. A novel he wrote at this time, *The Sorrows of Young Werther* (1774), the story of an artist's unrequited love and suicide, provides a prototype for the tormented outcast, a part that was later played publicly and to perfection by Romantic heroes such as Shelley and Byron. But Goethe famously turned away from his rebellious youth to a classical maturity, ruefully observing three years before his death in 1832 that 'Classicism is health, Romanticism is disease.' It was a disease that was often fatal and could count Géricault, Shelley, Byron and Keats among its numerous victims.

1812	1814	1819–24	1821	1839
Théodore Géricault's *Charging Chasseur*	Sir Walter Scott's *Waverley*	Lord Byron's *Don Juan*	Percy Bysshe Shelley's *Adonais* (elegy on John Keats's death in that year)	William Hazlitt's *Sketches and Essays* (published posthumously)

A race apart The Romantics' objection to (neo)classicism was fundamental. As the English critic William Hazlitt bluntly put it in his essay 'On Taste': 'Rules and models destroy genius and art.' They were also opposed to the *ancien régime* with which classicism was inextricably bound up; it was enthusiasm for the republican ideals of the French revolutionaries that prompted the English poet William Wordsworth's famous line: 'Bliss was it in that dawn to be alive, but to be young was very heaven.' Yet at the same time – as befitted a movement that prized individuality and self-expression above all else – Romanticism was both extraordinarily diverse and deeply cut through with contradictions. As a leading light of the new aesthetic and one of its most articulate advocates, Wordsworth wrote a long and passionately argued preface (1800, expanded 1802) to the verse collection *Lyrical Ballads*, which is now seen as a manifesto of the Romantic movement. Even here, at this early date, many of the tensions within the movement are already visible. For instance, in a famous passage he addresses the question 'What is a poet?':

> 'He is a man speaking to men: a man, it is true, endued with more lively sensibility, more enthusiasm and tenderness, who has a greater knowledge of human nature, and a more comprehensive soul, than are supposed to be common among mankind; a man pleased with his own passions and volitions, and who rejoices more than other men in the spirit of life that is in him.'

The poet is a man of the people, who speaks to them in their own language – a person of liberal sympathies, of course, in keeping with the progressive forces of the times. Yet the real poet at once sets the imaginary poet apart, giving him a heightened sensibility and self-consciousness that permanently distances him from the masses. These free spirits of Romanticism, who had triumphantly broken the shackles of aristocratic patronage to make their own mark in the world, nevertheless redefined art as the most rarefied of activities, one that was bound to differentiate them from the ordinary run of mankind.

> **'It is the addition of strangeness to beauty, that constitutes the romantic character in art.'**
>
> **Walter Pater, English critic, 1889**

Glory gone from the earth Friedrich von Schelling, the leading philosopher of German Romanticism, believed that 'the classic temper studies the past, the romantic temper neglects it'. Yet while classicism may

Nature and the mirror of the soul

The philosophical basis of Romanticism was the privileging of nature over civilization (derived from Jean-Jacques Rousseau), coupled with the idea that nature is, ultimately, the mirror of the human soul (derived from Immanuel Kant). In the preface to *Lyrical Ballads* (1800) Wordsworth explains how the poet 'considers man and nature as essentially adapted to each other, and the mind of man as naturally the mirror of the fairest and most interesting qualities of nature'. It is in this subtle nexus of ideas that the Romantic's love affair with himself – with the creative power of his own mind – begins. The Romantic's perception of the divine in nature (what Thomas Carlyle called in 1831 'natural supernaturalism') was thus the direct justification for the elevation of the poet to the status of hero – or god.

have been in thrall to the traditions of the past, Romanticism was shot through with a profound nostalgia, both for the lost innocence of childhood and for the lost nobility of the past. In the works of William Blake and Wordsworth, deeply influenced by Rousseau, the pure imaginative power of the child is extolled over the shameful and corrupted inauthenticity of adulthood. In a similar spirit, the dignity of rural life is elevated far above the cold and soulless existence in the industrializing cities. Yearning for the past, however, is often for an imagined and idealized past, and as Wordsworth suggests in his ode 'Intimations of Immortality' (1807), it is a world that is gone forever, for 'there hath passed away a glory from the earth'. Yet another strand of the Romantic mania for idealized antiquity was the work of Walter Scott, whose historical novels were full of daring deeds and much nostalgic sentiment; taken together, they were, in Hazlitt's view, 'almost like a new edition of human nature'. Such tales of exaggerated chivalry and heroism were, indeed, 'romances' in the old sense, from which Romanticism took its name.

the condensed idea
The addition of strangeness to beauty

42 Modernism

Although sometimes described as a single aesthetic or movement, modernism is far broader than such a description suggests. It is in fact an attitude or set of beliefs; a specific mindset that proposes a particular way of looking at the world and, especially, of responding to or engaging with the very broad concept of modernity. More precise definition depends on the kind of modernity involved, which can range from a relatively narrow artistic or cultural context to the full panoply of changes and developments – cultural, social, political, philosophical, scientific – that characterize the so-called 'modern' period.

Such broad and narrow definitions are not independent. In the context of the West, modernity in the broadest sense is more or less precisely defined by the intellectual, rational and secular forces that have been active since the start of the Enlightenment in the 17th century. In the 19th and early 20th centuries, there was a series of seismic shifts in human understanding of the world and man's position in it, initiated by the momentous achievements of Marx, Darwin, Freud, Einstein and others. It was partly in sympathy with, or reaction to, the new world-view painted by such transformational figures that many dynamic forms of modernism emerged in the early decades of the 20th century. The outbreak in 1914 of the most terrible and traumatic war in history was another vital catalyst in modernist thinking.

In general, the modern phase of history has been regarded as progressive and sporadically revolutionary. Modernists, accordingly, have tended to see themselves, often quite exclusively, as constituting the cultural avant-

timeline

1909	1913	1922
Schoenberg's Piano Pieces, op. 11 (first atonal compositions)	Stravinsky's *The Rite of Spring*	Joyce's *Ulysses* and Eliot's *The Waste Land*

garde; innovative, radical, challenging, experimental. Modernism has also tended to be self-referential and at times introverted, seeing its own efforts and accomplishments as absolutely valuable and worthwhile in their own right, irrespective of broader contexts. In this light, progress could be seen as an end in itself, art as an autonomous domain; and modernists have consequently been interpreted as taking up the rallying cry of 19th-century aestheticians: 'art for art's sake!' Certainly some of the intellectual inspiration for modernism appears to come from the second half of the previous century – from the French poet and critic Charles Baudelaire, for instance, and from his fellow poet Arthur Rimbaud, who wrote in 1873: *il faut être absolument moderne* ('one must be absolutely modern').

In the age of lost innocence

Just as modernism is a reaction to (or expansion of, or conversation with, or critique of, or commentary on) modernity, in the same way postmodernism is a reaction to (or expansion of, or conversation with . . .) modernism. And for the same reasons, it is a very slippery idea to catch hold of. The one thing that postmodernism cannot do, of course, is pretend that modernism didn't happen; and just as modernism at the beginning of the 20th century was marked by a certain earnestness of purpose, so postmodernism at the end of the century was infused with a large measure of knowingness and, above all, irony. The prevailing mood was explained – with a delightfully postmodern lightness of touch – by the Italian writer Umberto Eco in his *Postscript to the Name of the Rose* (1983):

'The postmodern reply to the modern consists of recognizing that the past, since it cannot really be destroyed, because its destruction leads to silence, must be revisited: but with irony, not innocently. I think of the postmodern attitude as that of a man who loves a very cultivated woman and knows he cannot say to her 'I love you madly,' because he knows that she knows (and that she knows that he knows) that these words have already been written by Barbara Cartland. Still, there is a solution. He can say, 'As Barbara Cartland would put it, I love you madly.' At this point, having avoided false innocence, having said clearly that it is no longer possible to speak innocently, he will nevertheless have said what he wanted to say to the woman: that he loves her, but he loves her in an age of lost innocence.'

1925–6	1927	1930	1939
Gropius's Bauhaus in Dessau, Germany	Mies van der Rohe's Weissenhof Estate in Stuttgart, Germany	Le Corbusier's Pavilion Suisse in Paris	Joyce's *Finnegans Wake*

Towards abstraction In the visual arts, the forces of modernism spawned a bewildering array of avant-garde styles and movements before and after the start of the 20th century, including Post-Impressionism, Expressionism, Cubism, Symbolism, Vorticism, Dadaism, Futurism and Surrealism. The inspiration behind these groups was so diverse and the direction they took so various that it is hardly illuminating to lump them together as modernists. All modernist artists, to a greater or lesser extent, were bent on subverting or abandoning the norms and conventions of the past. With this came a new perception of the function of art, one that presented a radical challenge to the view going back to Aristotle and the ancients that beauty and aesthetic value resided in imitation and representation (*mimesis*), an ideal that encouraged realism and a belief that the task of the artist was to hold up a mirror to nature. Rejection of this tenet, which had been central to the understanding of art for thousands of years, initiated a march (far from smooth) towards abstraction, which was to characterize much of the development of art during the 20th century.

> ❝**Modernity is the transient, the fleeting, the contingent; it is one half of art, the other being the eternal and the immovable.**❞
>
> **Charles Baudelaire, 1869**

'Make It New' 'We have to drop our manner of on-and-on-and-on, from a start to a finish, and allow the mind to move in cycles, or to flit here and there over a cluster of images.' D.H. Lawrence's plea that writers should abandon tired Victorian conventions of narrative and chronology had already been significantly answered by the time he made it in 1932. A decade earlier, in 1922, modernist literature had had its *annus mirabilis* in the publication of (arguably) its greatest prose and poetic masterpieces: James Joyce's *Ulysses* and T.S. Eliot's *The Waste Land*. Eliot's despairing yet darkly humorous poem is a collage of fragmentary images and complex allusions, presented in a kaleidoscope of shifting perspectives and points of view. Joyce's novel, meanwhile, uses interior monologue and stream-of-consciousness techniques to conduct an unprecedented exploration of his characters' inner thoughts, memories and perceptions. Later, in *Finnegans Wake* (1939), Joyce would combine stream of consciousness with multilingual punning and a baffling 'dream language', thus extending the limits of complexity and difficulty for which much modernist literature has been criticized.

Beyond tonality Among composers, as among painters, the forces of modernism were felt but provided no sure direction or unanimity of outlook. The single most significant development, in retrospect at least, occurred in the first decade of the 20th century, when Arnold Schoenberg's experimentation with atonality signified an epochal break with the notions of consonance and dissonance that for centuries had been the accepted basis of music. The greatest success in creating the 'shock of the new', however, was achieved on 29 May 1913, when Igor Stravinsky's ballet *The Rite of Spring* was premiered in Paris. So violent was the reaction to the raw primitiveness of the music, with its driving rhythms and clamorous orchestration, that a riot ensued. The conflict between modernist innovation and popular taste that remains unresolved to this day was underway.

‘Make It New.’

Ezra Pound, 1934

Without lies and games In 20th-century architecture, the concept of modernism was more unitary and coherent than in other areas, becoming especially identified with the movement known as 'International Modern' (or 'International Style'). Purportedly rational and functional design, combined with a dogmatic rejection of all adornment, superfluity and historical reference, typically resulted in clean, white, box-like buildings, with flat roofs and strip windows. The most innovatory and progressive architects of the period, including Le Corbusier, Walter Gropius and Mies van der Rohe, preached an ethos of 'New Objectivity', in which subjectively human elements – and aesthetic style as such – were firmly suppressed. Gropius called for buildings that were 'shaped by internal laws without lies and games; all that is unnecessary, that veils the absolute design, must be shed'. The result was functional, logical, objective design that exploited industrialized construction, modern materials and mass-produced components. International Modern, already dominant among progressive architects in the 1920s and 1930s, became orthodox in the period of postwar reconstruction. Conformist and homogenized in unimaginative hands, modernist architecture became increasingly detached from and unresponsive to actual human needs. The number of key modernist buildings that were demolished in the second half of the century is a reflection of the extent to which the movement failed to live up to the promises of its prophets.

the condensed idea
The shock of the new

43 Surrealism

In the years 1868 and 1869 a dark and darkly comic prose poem called *Les Chants de Maldoror* was published in Paris under the name of the enigmatic Comte de Lautréamont. The hero – an anti-hero indeed – of this collage of sadistic torture and misanthropy is the deranged Maldoror, who rails against God and utterly despises all social convention. Towards the end of the book, this hideous force of twisted nature, lusting after a 16-year-old flaxen-haired innocent, lasciviously compares his beauty to 'the chance encounter of a sewing machine and an umbrella on a dissection table'.

'Lautréamont' was in fact the pseudonym of Isidore Ducasse, an obscure French writer, who died in 1870, aged just 24, during the Siege of Paris which hastened the end of the Franco-Prussian war. Largely forgotten for nearly half a century, Ducasse was fortuitously rediscovered by a group of artists and writers who, in the shadow of a far greater conflict in Europe, were attracted both by his utter repudiation of Western society and culture and by his startling and unsettling use of language. Above all, they admired the violence with which he rejected the ordinary notions of rationality and reality that were foisted on an unthinking public by force of habit and convention.

Beyond Dada In 1918 a copy of Ducasse's book fell into the hands of the French poet and critic André Breton, who was impressed, among other things, with the way the author had juxtaposed strange and apparently unrelated images. Soon-to-be founder and leading theorist of Surrealism, Breton was at this time linked with its principal forerunner, Parisian Dada. The Dadaists, too, were motivated by revulsion against the rationalism which they felt had dragged Europe into the horrors of the First World

timeline

1868–9	1915	1917	1920
Lautréamont's *Les Chants de Maldoror*	European Dada founded in Zurich	Guillaume Apollinaire coins the term 'surrealist'	Breton and Soupault's *Les Champs magnétiques*

War; and they too were fascinated by the bizarre and the irrational, wishing to shake and shock society out of its complacency. But while Dada was ultimately subversive and nihilistic – 'essentially anarchic' and marked by a 'certain spirit of negation', as Breton would later say – Surrealism was more positive in its ambitions and aimed to transform society through revolution. (Many Surrealists, including Breton, joined the Communist Party in the 1920s and 1930s, although the association was always strained and did not last.)

From around 1920 a group led by Breton, disillusioned with Dada's essential negativity, began to break away. Already by this date Breton had begun to experiment with 'automatism', a method of writing (later extended to drawing) which attempted to remove movement of the hand from conscious control, so freeing the unconscious mind to take over. The first product of this technique – *Les Champs magnétiques* (Magnetic Fields), co-written with his friend Philippe Soupault – was published in 1920. Automatism remained a fundamental concern for the Surrealists, and it is central to the definition of Surrealism that Breton gives in the first *Surrealist Manifesto*, which was published in 1924 and is usually

The Hallucinogenic Toreador

In 1929 Surrealism gained its most colourful exponent, who in time would become its public face throughout the world: the 25-year-old Spaniard Salvador Dalí. Dalí's 'hand-painted dream photographs', as he called them, were particularly unsettling as the hyper-realism of the depiction clashed so violently with the near-hallucinatory quality of the assembled images. The 'paranoiac-critical' method he developed attempted to reproduce the paranoiac's capacity to interpret the world according to a single obsessional idea. It also featured the famous double images which are such a prominent element of his work – the ambiguous forms that can be simultaneously interpreted in different ways, as part of a landscape, for instance, or as part of a human body. By these means Dalí set out to accomplish his thoroughly Surrealist mission: 'to systematize confusion and thus to help discredit completely the world of reality'.

1924	**1924–5**	**1926**	**1927**	**1931**
The first *Surrealist Manifesto*	Miró's *Harlequin's Carnival*	Magritte's *The Menaced Assassin*	Ernst's *Forest and Dove*	Dalí's *The Persistence of Memory*

considered to mark the official start of the movement. (It is also at this point that Breton lays claim to the name 'Surrealism', which had originally been coined by his friend, the recently dead poet Guillaume Apollinaire.) Surrealism, Breton tells us in the *Manifesto*, is:

> 'Psychic automatism in its pure state, by which it is intended to express, either verbally, or in writing, or in any other way, the true functioning of thought. Thought expressed in the absence of any control exercised by reason, and outside all moral and aesthetic considerations. Surrealism rests on belief in the higher reality of specific forms of association, previously neglected, in the omnipotence of dreams, and in the disinterested play of thought.'

The influence of Freudian psychology, in which supreme significance is accorded to the power of the unconscious, is felt throughout the *Manifesto*. The ultimate goal of Surrealism, in Breton's view, is to transform and merge 'those two seemingly contradictory states, dream and reality, into a sort of absolute reality, of surreality'. It is precisely the purpose of techniques such as automatism to break down the boundaries between dream and reality, reason and madness, objective and subjective experience. As he wrote later, in *Le Surréalisme et la Peinture* (1928), the 'fundamental discovery of Surrealism' is that 'without any preconceived intention, the pen which hastens to write, or the pencil which hastens to draw, produces an infinitely precious substance all of which . . . seems to bear with it everything emotional that the poet harbours within him'.

Furry cups and other objects

One of the most characteristic forms of Surrealist art was the object. Both made or found (*objet trouvé*), these usually small-scale works were so varied as to defy classification – although the Surrealists gleefully tried, producing a list of strange categories that included the 'ready-made', Breton's 'poem-object' and Dalí's 'symbolically functioning object'. Dalí was especially keen to promote the object as a distinctive art form, and in 1931 proposed that its essential characteristics should be that it was 'absolutely useless from the practical and rational point of view, created wholly for the purpose of materializing in a fetishistic way, with the maximum of tangible reality, ideas and fantasies having a delirious character'. Probably the most celebrated of such objects is Meret Oppenheim's *Cup, Saucer and Spoon in Fur* (1936), which is also known simply as *Object*.

Automatic painters Initially Surrealism was concerned predominantly with literary activity and had a somewhat awkward relationship with the visual arts (Breton endorsed painting as a Surrealist activity while also describing it as a 'lamentable expedient'). By the mid-1920s, however, several artists, mainly former members of Dada, were attempting to adapt the techniques of automatic writing to produce works that flowed spontaneously from the subconscious. And like the Surrealist poets (and the Dadaists before them), they were fascinated by the role of chance in the creative process.

In 1925 Max Ernst, earlier an important figure in German Dada, pioneered various techniques that allowed an initial, partial image to be produced by chance, which could then be developed further, either by the artist or in the mind of the spectator. 'Frottage' involved rubbing graphite over grained surfaces such as floor boards, 'upon which a thousand scrubbings had deepened the grooves'. In 'grattage', Ernst would scrape away the upper layers of paint to reveal unexpected patterns in the layers beneath.

> **'The simplest Surrealist act consists of dashing down into the street, pistol in hand, and firing blindly . . . '**
>
> **André Breton, 1930**

Breton described the Spanish artist Joan Miró as 'probably the most Surrealistic of us all', but in fact he never officially joined the group and always clung to his highly distinctive personal vision. *Harlequin's Carnival* (1924–5) was inspired by the author's 'hallucinations brought on by hunger'. The teeming canvas presents a joyous gathering of fantastic creatures resembling bees, cats and shrimps, which make music and frolic playfully around a scattering of abstract and semi-abstract shapes and signs that have surfaced from the artist's subconscious imagination.

Snapshots of the impossible By 1930 many Surrealist artists, feeling the limitations of automatism as a means of exploring the subconscious, had turned to other techniques. An important influence was the Italian Giorgio de Chirico, who, in the decade before the release of the first *Surrealist Manifesto*, had painted stark and depopulated piazzas into which trains, tailor's dummies and other incongruous elements had been eerily introduced. The Belgian artist René Magritte started to paint his distinctive 'snapshots of the impossible': meticulously detailed and apparently naturalistic scenes in which the banal and the bizarre are startlingly and disturbingly juxtaposed.

the condensed idea
The omnipotence of dreams

44 Censorship

In his last great novel, *Lady Chatterley's Lover*, the English novelist D.H. Lawrence makes liberal use of earthy Anglo-Saxon terminology in giving an explicit yet poetic account of an adulterous affair between an aristocratic lady and her husband's gamekeeper. For this reason, for more than three decades after it was written in 1928, the complete novel was considered to be unpublishable in the country of the author's birth.

Then, in 1960, Penguin Books decided to risk prosecution by publishing a full text of the novel in Britain. The trial that followed swiftly turned into a media jamboree. At its comical climax the chief prosecutor, Mervyn Griffith-Jones, solemnly asked the jury: 'Would you approve of your young sons, young daughters – because girls can read as well as boys – reading this book? Is it a book that you would have lying around in your own house? Is it a book that you would even wish your wife or your servants to read?'

Knee-deep in sexual filth   The prosecution, brought under the recently revised Obscene Publications Act (1959), reflected the British establishment's view that such frank material was likely to 'outrage public decency' and to 'deprave and corrupt' the minds of ordinary people. The kind of corruption envisaged in such legislation was made explicit in 1917 by a New Zealand magistrate, who surmised that public distribution of Maupassant's *A Spa Love Affair* would allow the 'literary hogs . . . to wallow knee-deep in sexual filth', so opening up 'that broad highway that leads to the mental hospital, the gaol, and the premature grave'. The jury's verdict in the Chatterley trial in favour of Penguin was an indication that the British public was no longer prepared

> **Whenever books are burned, in the end men too are burned.**
>
> **Heinrich Heine, 1821**

timeline

4th century BC	AD 1232
Plato's *Republic* prescribes strict censorship of the arts	Inquisition set up to snuff out heretical thinking in the Catholic Church

> **If all printers were determined not to print anything till they were sure it would offend nobody, there would be very little printed.**

Benjamin Franklin, 1731

to tolerate such lofty paternalism; it no longer wanted (if it ever had wanted) somebody looking after its moral well-being. People, it seemed, wished to make up their own minds on such matters and gave notice that censorship – official curtailment of free expression in the (supposed) public interest – was no longer, or at least not always, acceptable.

Penguin's main defence in the Chatterley trial was that Lawrence's novel had 'literary merit', a fact that E.M. Forster and a procession of other literary luminaries came before the court to corroborate. The idea that the literary or artistic quality of a book could be taken into account in such a case was new in the 1959 anti-obscenity legislation. However, the underlying principle – that the ethics and the aesthetics of art are two very different things – was a much older idea that also informed Oscar Wilde's comment in his preface to *The Picture of Dorian Gray* (1891): 'There is no such thing as a moral book or an immoral book. Books are well written or badly written. That is all.'

State control Those brought up in the traditions of Western liberalism are inclined to think of freedom of expression as an absolute right and hence of censorship as inherently objectionable. Such a view is naive in failing to recognize the extent to which such freedom is still and always has been significantly circumscribed. Indeed, until the principle of liberty and the rights of the individual came to prominence in the 17th-century Enlightenment, the common view was that society had a right and a duty to control the moral and political behaviour of its citizens by regulating the flow of information and blocking the expression of opinions that it deemed pernicious. In the *Republic*, Plato does not hesitate to recommend strict censorship of all artistic expression, and even in democratic Athens the philosopher Socrates was executed in the 4th century BC on a

1644	**1791**	**1960**
Milton's *Areopagitica* argues against licensing of books	First Amendment of US Constitution guarantees freedom of speech and of the press	Penguin Books cleared of obscenity for publishing *Lady Chatterley's Lover*

charge of not recognizing the city's gods. Throughout history – until the present day in many parts of the world – imposition of religious orthodoxy has been taken to justify the most radical censorship. In the Catholic Church, for instance, the Inquisition was established in the 13th century to eradicate, often terminally, those holding or expressing heretical views. The Catholic *Index Librorum Prohibitorum* ('list of prohibited books') was set up by Pope Paul IV in 1559 and not finally abolished until 1966; its most illustrious victim, in 1633, was Galileo, 'a prisoner to the Inquisition', in John Milton's words, 'for thinking in astronomy otherwise than the Franciscan and Dominican licensers thought'.

In his *Areopagitica* of 1644 Milton launches one of history's most impassioned and articulate assaults on censorship. He attacks the government's policy of licensing of books – in effect, pre-publication censorship, or what would now be called 'prior restraint' – and pleads to be given 'the liberty to know, to utter, and to argue freely according to conscience, above all liberties'. In his *Lives of the Poets* (1779–81),

Art is never chaste

A long-standing artistic objection to censorship is simply that it makes art dull and insipid. Picasso insisted that true art could not thrive in the safe and sterile atmosphere created by the prudish censor: 'Art is never chaste. It ought to be forbidden to ignorant innocents, never allowed into contact with those not sufficiently prepared. Yes, art is dangerous. Where it is chaste, it is not art.' George Bernard Shaw made essentially the same point for literary art with his wry observation that censorship reaches its logical conclusion 'when nobody is allowed to read any books except the books nobody reads'. In a coda added later to his 1953 novel about censorship and book-burning, *Fahrenheit 451*, Ray Bradbury bemoans the dead hand laid on art by the world's many semi-official or self-appointed censors. Doubtless from bitter personal experience, he berates in particular the 'dimwit editor who sees himself as the source of all dreary blancmange plain porridge unleavened literature, licks his guillotine, and eyes the neck of any author who dares to speak above a whisper or write above a nursery rhyme'. In his *Areopagitica* of 1644 – perhaps the most famous of all literary attacks on censorship – Milton argues that the goodness of good books is only fully apparent to a reader who can judge them alongside bad ones. Truth, he protests, will always prevail over falsehood 'in a free and open encounter'; if evil is banished, it is impossible to 'praise a fugitive and cloistered virtue'.

Samuel Johnson, a perennial conservative, makes the opposing case. Fearful of the effects of the kind of liberty that Milton demands, he cannot see why it is 'more reasonable to leave the right of printing unrestrained, because writers may be afterwards censured, than it would be to sleep with doors unbolted, because by our laws we can hang a thief'.

> **Our liberty depends on the freedom of the press, and that cannot be limited without being lost.**
>
> **Thomas Jefferson, 1786**

Liberty or safety? The liberal commitment to freedom of expression is most notably underwritten by the First Amendment (1791) to the US Constitution, which includes the provision that 'Congress shall make no law . . . abridging the freedom of speech, or of the press'. In practice, however, while there may be a presumption against any kind of prior restraint, there is a range of laws intended to punish those who abuse this freedom by publishing or otherwise expressing views that society regards as unacceptable. Laws against libel, obscenity, blasphemy and various kinds of incitement are all censorious in that they penalize those who cross the boundaries set in a particular jurisdiction. Every society thus condones some level of censorship. In certain circumstances such control may be regarded as relatively uncontroversial – if it is exercised in time of war, for instance, or in order to protect national security. Even then, however, there will be many who proclaim, with Benjamin Franklin, that those who 'can give up essential liberty to obtain a little temporary safety deserve neither liberty nor safety'.

> **Woe to that nation whose literature is disturbed by the intervention of power. Because that is not just a violation against freedom of the press, it is the closing down of a nation's heart, the excision of its memory.**
>
> **Alexander Solzhenitsyn, 1970**

the condensed idea
Protecting the servants

45 Evolution

On 16 September 1835 the British survey ship HMS *Beagle* made landfall on the Galapagos, a group of volcanic islands in the Pacific scattered like so many heaps of cinder on either side of the equator. On board was a 26-year-old English naturalist named Charles Darwin. The gruelling five-year expedition had given the young Darwin every opportunity to indulge his passion for exploring, observing and collecting specimens. He had already seen much that had impressed him deeply, yet he was still filled with awe by the unique geology, flora and fauna of the Galapagos, whose wonders included ground finches and mockingbirds, seaweed-eating iguanas, and giant tortoises.

The inspiration Darwin derived from these extraordinary encounters, on the Galapagos and elsewhere, helped him to formulate a theory that offered a compelling solution to what remained to most biologists the 'mystery of mysteries': the origin of the innumerable species of life on earth and an explanation of its astonishing diversity. Darwin's theory of evolution by natural selection has since established itself as the cornerstone and unifying principle of the biological sciences. And its significance extends far beyond the confines of science. No other scientific theory has forced humans to make so radical a reappraisal of their own position in the world and their relationship to other living things.

The origin of species When the *Beagle* entered Falmouth harbour on 2 October 1836, the young naturalist on board, weighed down by thousands of specimens and reams of notes, was beset by many riddles prompted by his journey. Again and again, he had been brought face to

timeline

1809	Dec. 1831–Oct. 1836
Darwin born in Shrewsbury, England	The voyage of the *Beagle*

face with the wondrous beauty and dreadful brutality of nature – not least of human nature. All he had seen helped to reinforce his sense of the impermanence of the environment and of the vast time scales over which the seemingly unchanging features of the earth had come and gone. Yet, in spite of the awesome scale of the undertaking, within a year of his return Darwin had begun to formulate the ideas that would eventually define his theory of evolution.

It was more than two decades, however, before Darwin would publish (in 1859) the classic statement of the theory: the momentous *On the Origin of Species by Means of Natural Selection, or the Preservation of Favoured Races in the Struggle for Life*. The long delay has usually been attributed to the author's anxieties about the public reception that would greet his ideas. It is true that the orthodox scientific view in Darwin's day was that each species was immutable and the product of an independent act of divine creation. But the idea of evolution itself – or 'descent with modification', as Darwin called it – was not new. Many, including the naturalist's own grandfather, Erasmus Darwin, had speculated on the notion that the various kinds of plants and animals might be derived from earlier forms and share common ancestors. Such thinking was widely condemned on theological grounds, as it appeared to displace God from his central role in creation, but without any explanation of how such modification might occur, it remained mere speculation. Indeed, the ideas of natural theology – in particular, the so-called 'argument from design', which inferred the existence of a creator from the wonderful complexity and order of the natural world – were generally held to be decisive in favour of the orthodox view.

> **❛I am almost convinced . . . that species are not (it is like confessing a murder) immutable . . . I think I have found out (here's presumption!) the simple way by which species become exquisitely adapted to various ends.❜**
>
> **Charles Darwin, letter to J.D. Hooker, 1844**

Natural selection Darwin's genius was in effect to undermine the argument from design by providing an alternative mechanism that could account for the 'perfection of structure and coadaptation' of living things. He went to extraordinary pains to gather evidence to support his theory and to anticipate likely objections and criticisms – it is this effort that

Sept. 1835	1859	1882
The *Beagle* reaches the Galapagos Islands	First edition of the *Origin of Species* published	Darwin dies in Downe, Kent

> **Evolution advances, not by *a priori* design, but by the selection of what works best out of whatever choices offer. We are the products of editing, rather than of authorship.**

George Wald, 1957

accounts for the long years he spent 'patiently accumulating and reflecting on all sorts of facts'. Most notably, in his own view, he made 'a careful study of domesticated animals and cultivated plants', where he saw a process (which he called 'artificial selection') closely analogous to the natural mechanism he proposed. In the end, though, the attraction of his theory was its simplicity and its capacity to reconcile otherwise-baffling facts, such as the existence of fossils and the geographical distribution of plants and animals.

In the *Origin*, Darwin succinctly summarizes natural selection as follows:

'As many more individuals of each species are born than can possibly survive; and as, consequently, there is a frequently recurring struggle for

The survival of the fattest

The 'struggle for existence' that lies at the heart of Darwin's theory, with its stern implications of the strong prevailing over the weak, proved highly suggestive to many, who sought to apply its lessons in areas far beyond its original and proper provenance. Most pernicious of all was the development of social Darwinism by theorists such as the British philosopher Herbert Spencer. In the years following Darwin's death in 1882, Spencer, an energetic and effective propagandist for evolutionism, promoted the idea of applying (or rather misapplying) the principles of natural selection to an alleged process of evolution in groups, races and human societies. The 'survival of the fittest' (a phrase coined by Spencer himself) became a harsh dogma that was used to justify, in the name of human improvement, 'natural' inequalities in class, wealth and welfare; intervention by the state to assist those who were afflicted by poverty or were 'unfit' in other ways was castigated as interference in the necessary biological 'weeding out' of weak and unworthy elements. At its most perverted, social Darwinism could be used to bolster the imperialist and racist ideologies of fascist regimes.

existence, it follows that any being, if it vary however slightly in any manner profitable to itself, under the complex and sometimes varying conditions of life, will have a better chance of surviving, and thus be naturally selected. From the strong principle of inheritance, any selected variety will tend to propagate its new and modified form.'

This epoch-making development in biological thought thus came down to the combination of a few simple ideas: variety, heredity, competition and selection. In nature, resources such as food and mates are limited, so there will always be competition for access to them. As all individuals are different from one another, some will inevitably be better equipped than others to prevail in life's struggles, and it is these individuals that will (on average) live longer and produce more offspring. And, to the extent that the characteristics that help an individual survive and succeed can be passed on to its offspring, those characteristics will persist and become more common in the population. So it is that, by minute and gradual changes over innumerable generations, animals and plants become better adapted to their surroundings; some species or kinds disappear, to be replaced by others that have proved more successful in the struggle for existence.

> **Variation, whatever may be its cause, and however it may be limited, is the essential phenomenon of Evolution. Variation, in fact, *is* Evolution.**
>
> **William Bateson, 1894**

The fifth ape In the first edition of the *Origin*, Darwin offers no more than hints of the implications of his theory in its application to humans. He was acutely conscious of the uproar that would follow the suggestion that the difference between humans and (other) animals was one of degree only, not kind, and hence that man was not the special and favoured object of divine creation. The public furore came anyway and has blazed away ever since. Indeed, as the target of Creationists and Intelligent Design theorists, the theory of evolution, or 'Darwinism', is today as contentious in some quarters as it has ever been. Among the vast majority of scientists, however, the theory is unquestioned and its significance beyond doubt. As the evolutionary biologist Theodosius Dobzhansky starkly put it: 'Nothing in biology makes sense except in the light of evolution.'

the condensed idea
Survival of the fittest

46 Gaia

'This book . . . is about a search for life, and the quest for Gaia is an attempt to find the largest living creature on earth. Our journey may reveal no more than the almost infinite variety of living forms which have proliferated over the earth's surface under the transparent case of the air and which constitute the biosphere. But if Gaia does exist, then we may find ourselves and all other living things to be parts and partners of a vast being who in her entirety has the power to maintain our planet as a fit and comfortable habitat for life.'

With these portentous words, the British independent scientist James Lovelock began, in 1979, his pioneering book *Gaia: A New Look at Life on Earth*. The search, which for him had started more than a decade earlier, faced formidable obstacles, most of them set in his path by his professional colleagues. At that time the prevailing view among scientists was that life on earth was in essence a vastly improbable accident; life was 'a quiet passenger' that had 'hitched a ride on this rock ball in its journey through space and time'. It was this very improbability – the miniscule odds that exactly the right conditions for life should exist and continue to exist – that inspired Lovelock to develop the concept of Gaia: the idea that it is life itself that maintains the conditions necessary for its own survival.

In the decades following its first public appearance in 1979, the Gaia hypothesis was much refined, not least by Lovelock himself in a series of follow-up books. At the core of the thesis is the idea of self-regulation, or homeostasis, a property he believes belongs to the entire system that comprises 'all life tightly coupled with the air, the oceans, and the surface rocks'. Through various feedback mechanisms, these components work together to regulate the climate, the gaseous balance of the atmosphere

timeline

1979

James Lovelock's *Gaia: A New Look at Life on Earth* published and the chemical composition of the ocean in such a way as to produce and maintain a physical environment that is optimally adjusted to life. At the suggestion of his friend and neighbour William Golding, the Nobel Prize-winning novelist, Lovelock named this complex entity 'Gaia', after the ancient Greek goddess of the earth.

A stable planet of unstable parts The seeds of what would eventually grow into Gaia were set in 1965, when Lovelock was working on the NASA space programme as a part of a team whose task was to detect whether there was life on Mars. A general characteristic of living organisms, he recognized, is to reverse or reduce entropy – in other words, to move their environment away from chemical equilibrium. Earth-based analysis of the atmospheres of Mars and Venus showed that both were close to equilibrium and hence that the planets themselves were probably lifeless. Once it became clear just how different our planet is from its two dead neighbours, Lovelock's mind was 'filled with wonderings about the nature of the Earth'.

The earth is in an extreme state of chemical disequilibrium. Unlike the atmospheres of Mars and Venus, which are made up almost entirely of carbon dioxide, the earth's atmosphere is just over one-fifth oxygen, with a trace quantity (about 350 parts per million) of carbon dioxide. The oxygen level is optimal for supporting animal respiration, while the tiny percentage of carbon dioxide is essential to drive the life-supporting process of photosynthesis but not so much (human activity aside) to trigger a potentially

A living gaia?

It is not always clear or consistent in Lovelock's writings exactly what status he is claiming for the complex of living and non-living elements which he calls Gaia. In the introduction to the original 1979 book he describes it as a 'living creature', and elsewhere he often refers to it as an organism or a 'superorganism'. As Lovelock himself recognized, it is the suggestion that the system as a whole is in some sense alive that originally alienated many of his scientific colleagues; and he has sometimes complained that what he intended to be a metaphor has been misunderstood, at times wilfully, by his fellow scientists. On the other hand, his ambivalence in this regard may in part be strategic, for the vision of a living Gaia has struck a resonant chord with many non-scientists and become a potent unifying symbol in the green and environmental movements.

> ❝ Our destiny is not dependent merely on what we do for ourselves but also on what we do for Gaia as a whole. If we endanger her, she will dispense with us in the interests of a higher value – life itself. ❞

Václav Havel, 1994

catastrophic greenhouse effect. Again, in spite of solar output having risen by a quarter since the earth's formation, the planet's surface temperature has remained constant, close to a global average of around 15°C – an ideal level for terrestrial life. It was the remarkable constancy of these and other parameters, maintained against expectation over hundreds of millions of years, that led Lovelock to suggest that our 'stable planet made of unstable parts' might have been brought to such a state and kept there by the combined regulatory activity of the living and non-living components.

Beyond Daisyworld Much of the early criticism of Lovelock's theory focused on its supposed teleological assumptions – on the way that Gaia seemed to have a capacity for foresight and future planning. What appeared to be lacking were plausible evolutionary paths that could explain how the necessary regulatory feedback mechanisms could have arisen in the first place. This criticism set much of the agenda for the development of the Gaia theory over the following decades.

The first product of these efforts was Daisyworld, a simulated ecosystem consisting initially of just two species of daisy, black and white. Each species has a different environment-modifying characteristic – white daisies reduce the ambient temperature, black daisies increase it; and each thereby determines its own relative abundance. In spite of the input of solar energy rising (as on earth), the model suggests that the surface temperature can be kept close to the optimal level merely by the interplay of the two kinds of daisy. The inference, then, is that modification of the environment can be achieved purely by means of competition and natural selection at the level of the individual.

Real-world feedback mechanisms supposedly analogous to those in Daisyworld have since been studied intensively. A notable example is a mechanism whereby marine phytoplankton is claimed to have a climate-cooling effect. These organisms produce a gas called dimethyl sulfide (DMS) which forms aerosol droplets in the atmosphere; these have the effect of making clouds more reflective and hence increase the amount of solar radiation scattered back into space. Growth of the phytoplankton (and hence DMS production) increases with temperature, so the system as a whole functions like a thermostat to keep the temperature constant.

The legacy of Gaia The message of Gaia has sometimes become obscured by the rhetoric and lobbying of both supporters and opponents. Some of the animosity towards the symbolism of Gaia, not least the name itself, remains, but the many serious implications of the theory itself have left their mark. In the past, earth scientists, climatologists and other experts within their own disciplines tended to approach the complexity of the environment as something to be analysed and reduced into simpler, more manageable parts. Now, this complexity is widely recognized as fundamental to the system. In a new, more holistic approach, the focus of much research has moved to the earth as a unitary system – to the major feedback mechanisms within environmental systems and to their role in maintaining long-term global stability. Today, at a time when we are faced with the unprecedented threats of climate change and global warming, the deepest lesson of Gaia – that the health of our world depends on taking a planetary perspective – seems more relevant and pressing than ever.

Apocalypse soon

The tone of 21st-century Lovelock has grown markedly more apocalyptic than his earlier avatars, and in the press he is often portrayed as a latter-day Jeremiah or prophet of doom. Gaia theory is inherently holistic, insisting that the system as a whole is far more significant than its constituent parts, so it is no surprise to hear Lovelock describing humans as 'just another species, neither the owners nor the stewards of this planet'. In his most recent work he has suggested that *Homo sapiens* has become the earth's infection: 'We have given Gaia a fever and soon her condition will worsen to a state like a coma. She has been there before and recovered, but it took more than 100,000 years. We are responsible and will suffer the consequences.' The implication is that the Earth is likely to survive, however badly we treat it, but that its survival does not necessarily include us.

the condensed idea
The quest for Mother Earth

47 Chaos

One day in the winter of 1961 Edward Lorenz, a meteorologist at the Massachusetts Institute of Technology, was running simple weather simulations through a program he had devised for his cumbersome vacuum-tube computer. He wanted to repeat and extend one particular run, but rather than start from scratch – always a time-consuming business – he started half-way through, taking the initial values from a print-out of the previous run. He broke off for a coffee, leaving the computer running, and came back expecting to find that the second half of the original simulation had been duplicated. Instead, to his astonishment, he discovered that what was supposed to be a re-run bore little resemblance to the previous version.

Lorenz's first thought was that a tube had blown, but then the truth began to dawn on him. It wasn't a matter of a computer malfunction. The figures he had typed in for the second run had been rounded by the computer – on the print-out but not in its memory – from six decimal places to three. He had assumed that such a tiny discrepancy – about one part in a thousand – would make no difference to something on the scale of a meteorological projection. But it had. A minute difference in the initial conditions had caused a major difference in outcome.

Scientific models It is in response to the huge complexity of nature – climate being a prime example – that scientists devise models. Models are simplified approximations of the real world that allow regularities to be discerned and described mathematically (i.e. by mathematical equations). It is assumed that such models behave deterministically: that a future state

timeline

of the model can be derived fully, in principle at least, by applying appropriate equations to data describing the current state. This procedure can be 'iterated' – repeated again and again using the output of one run as the input for the next – to move the forecast further and further into the future.

It was this kind of method that Lorenz was following in running his simulation program in winter 1961. The fact that, after just a few iterations, the program had produced two wildly different outcomes from practically identical input data cast doubt over the whole methodology. His model had apparently behaved unpredictably and produced random results: it had exhibited – in a terminology that did not yet exist – chaotic behaviour.

Seagulls and butterflies So why did Lorenz's climate simulation behave chaotically?

The mathematical equations used in weather forecasting describe the atmospheric motions of the relevant variables, such as temperature, humidity, wind speed and wind direction. An important characteristic of these variables is that they are interdependent: for instance, the level of

A spanner in Newton's clockworks

In the 1960s most scientists, like Edward Lorenz in 1961, would have assumed that a tiny discrepancy in the starting data fed into a system would be inconsequential. Before the full implications of chaos were recognized, the orthodox scientific view was that the world conformed, in broad terms, to the mechanistic, deterministic model that Isaac Newton had proposed nearly 300 years earlier. On this view, the reason phenomena such as the weather are hard to predict is simply that they are extremely complicated; but prediction would be possible, in principle at least, if all the relevant physical processes were fully understood and all the necessary data available. As a corollary to this, it was readily assumed that the reliability of a forecast or other output would reflect the quality of the input. This kind of assumption was blown out of the water by the emergence of chaos.

1961	1960s	1975	1977
Accident sets Edward Lorenz on the path of chaotic systems	US mathematician Stephen Smale develops topological models of nonlinear systems	US mathematician James Yorke coins the term 'chaos'. Polish-born mathematician Benoît Mandelbrot coins the term 'fractal'	First international conference on chaos convenes in Como, Italy

humidity is affected by temperature, but the temperature is itself affected by humidity. In mathematical terms, this means that these variables are in effect functions *of themselves*, so the relations between them have to be described by so-called 'nonlinear' equations. Put simply, these are equations that cannot be represented by straight lines on graphs.

It turns out that one of the properties of nonlinear equations is that they exhibit the kind of sensitivity to initial conditions that had caused Lorenz such a shock in 1961. He went on to demonstrate that sensitivity of this kind was not merely a consequence of complexity by showing that it also occurred in a much simpler model (of convection) that could be described by just three nonlinear equations. In 1963 Lorenz recorded a colleague's remark that, if his ideas were correct, 'one flap of a seagull's wings would be enough to alter the course of the weather forever'. By 1972 the beast behind the requisite atmospheric disturbance had shrunk, as was reflected in the title of Lorenz's paper of that year: 'Does the flap of a butterfly's wings in Brazil set off a tornado in Texas?' The 'butterfly effect' had been born.

Making sense of disorder The butterfly effect has been warmly embraced by popular culture, but its true implications are often not properly understood. Usually it is used as a loose metaphor for the way

Order within disorder

'It turns out that an eerie type of chaos can lurk just behind a façade of order,' observed US scientist and author Douglas Hofstadter in 1985, 'and yet, deep inside the chaos lurks an even eerier type of order.' Chaotic systems may be unpredictable but they are not indeterminate. Nor are they disordered or chaotic in the popular sense. As early as 1963 Lorenz's simple model of convection, plotted in three dimensions, revealed an astonishing abstract pattern in the midst of chaos: a complex double whorl or spiral – not unlike the wings of a butterfly – in which the lines never follow the same path or intersect. The Lorenz attractor, as the image was later called, was the first of many topological models of chaotic systems in which the plots were folded and stretched in space to reproduce the unpredictable fate or trajectory of a nonlinear system. In the 1970s Benoît Mandelbrot and others developed a new 'fractal' geometry in which order within disorder is reproduced by mesmerizing irregular figures that exhibit the strange property of 'self-similarity', in which their irregularity is repeated over and over at different scales and dimensions.

momentous events can be triggered by apparently trivial ones, but its significance goes far beyond this. The flap of a butterfly's wings is only the cause of a tornado in the weak sense that the tornado might not have happened if the flap had not occurred first. But there are millions of other butterflies, and billions of other factors, all of which may be no less relevant in bringing about the tornado. One implication is the staggering sensitivity of the system to tiny events within it. Another implication, following from the first, is the practical impossibility of identifying the causes of any event in the system. Indeed, given that infinitesimally small events may bring about gross effects and that such tiny events may be beyond our powers of detection *in principle*, it may follow that the system, though fully deterministic, is entirely unpredictable.

Lorenz drew the conclusion that long-term weather forecasting may be impossible in principle, but the implications of chaos run much deeper. The network of innumerable and interconnected factors that together determine global climate is by no means exceptional. Indeed, the great majority of physical and biological systems are of this kind, so scientific attempts to explain them mathematically are bound to involve non-linearity; and hence they have the potential to show chaotic behaviour. From its origins in meteorology, chaos theory has spread to a wide variety of disciplines whose only link is that they deal with apparent disorder: turbulence in fluid dynamics; species fluctuation in population dynamics; disease cycles in epidemiology; heart fibrillations in human physiology; planetary and stellar motion in astronomy; traffic flow in urban engineering. In a more philosophical sense, the capacity of chaos to reveal the mesmeric and (some would say) beautiful order underlying the apparent disorder of nature gives us new hope of understanding and coping with the highly suggestive randomness of the universe.

> ‘**Today even our *clocks* are not made of clockwork – so why should our world be?**’
>
> **Ian Stewart,
> British mathematician, 1989**

the condensed idea
The butterfly effect

48 Relativity

'Time travels in divers paces with divers persons.' Rosalind's remark to her lover in Shakespeare's *As You Like It* reflects a common sentiment, one captured in a famous epitaph in Chester Cathedral: 'when I was a babe and wept and slept, Time crept ... But as I older grew, Time flew.' For most of human history, alongside this subjective experience of time's ebb and flow, there was another, sterner kind of time: the regular ticking of nature's clock, a universal metronome marking life's passage, the same for everyone, everywhere, at all times. Then suddenly, in 1905, it became apparent that Rosalind's conception of time was almost exactly correct.

The idea of a paradigm shift is overused today, but it can be applied, literally and precisely, to the twin theories of relativity developed in the early years of the 20th century by the German-born physicist Albert Einstein. The central insight of these theories is that we live in a four-dimensional universe in which mass, space and time are relative, not absolute, in character. The consequences that flow from this have revolutionized the practice of physics. Investigation of the elementary particles from which all matter (including us) is made would be impossible in the absence of relativistic ideas. So, too, would the study of the fundamental processes that have created and shaped the universe. Relativity theory has also fuelled technological progress. Space exploration, including its many commercial spin-offs, such as satellite technology and the Global Positioning System, depends critically on relativistic calculation. More sinisterly, without Einstein's revolutionary ideas, harnessing the energy of the atom to generate nuclear power and to build weapons of mass destruction would not have been possible.

timeline

1687

Classical laws of motion and gravity
enunciated by Isaac Newton

Physics before Einstein In his *Principia Mathematica* (1687), Isaac Newton defined space and time as absolute concepts that remain unaffected by external influences. 'Absolute, true and mathematical time, of itself and from its own nature, flows uniformly without reference to anything external', while 'absolute space . . . remains always similar and immovable.' Operating within a universe so described, Newton's laws of motion and gravity remained largely unchallenged for nearly 200 years.

Towards the end of the 19th century, however, anomalies began to emerge in attempts to describe the behaviour of light. In 1873 the Scottish physicist James Clerk Maxwell published his electromagnetic theory, which predicted that light would travel through empty space at a finite speed of 186,000 miles per second. Then, in 1887, Albert Michelson and Edward Morley carried out a highly publicized experiment which showed, unexpectedly, that measurements of the speed of light remained constant and unaffected by the velocity of the earth's rotation – in apparent defiance of Newtonian mechanics.

The special theory of relativity Imagine that you are on a train travelling at a constant speed in a straight line (suppose, too, that it is a somewhat idealized train in which there are no bumps or vibrations caused by its movement). If you can see nothing outside the train, your experience will be indistinguishable from being on a train at rest. If, for instance, you played catch with a ball, it would be exactly the same as if the train were stationary. Furthermore, if all you could see outside the train was a second (also idealized) train, moving alongside on a parallel track at exactly the same speed, it would be impossible to tell that either train was moving. It is only if your train changes speed or direction that you will be able to tell that you are moving.

In technical terms, your train is your 'reference frame', and so long as it remains at constant speed in a straight line, it is described as an 'inertial frame'. Einstein's solution to the difficulties encountered in dealing with the behaviour of light was, first, to insist, uncontroversially, that the laws of nature are the same for everyone, in all inertial frames; and second, to extend this to the propagation of light, so that the speed of light is

1905	**1916**	**1919**
Einstein's special theory gives relativistic account of space, time, mass and energy	General theory explains gravity as a consequence of the geometry of space–time	Bending of starlight by the Sun's gravity observed by Arthur Eddington

constant for all observers, irrespective of their relative motion. Although running counter to common sense, this second postulate is in fact no more than an acceptance of the clues offered by Maxwell's theory and the Michelson–Morley observations.

Imagine now that you set up a simple clock-like device on the train. This consists of two mirrors facing each other and separated by a vertical rod, and 'ticks' of the clock are marked by a beam of light bouncing back and forth between the mirrors. In your reference frame – on the moving train – you observe the light beam bouncing vertically up and down; but an observer in a different frame – say, an observer sitting on a platform – will see the light beam follow a zig-zag path. As the speed of light is constant in all frames, as per Einstein's second postulate, the beam will take longer to travel the longer zig-zag path. In other words, for the observer on the platform, the ticks of the clock are slower!

In our everyday experience, where things travel at tiny fractions of the speed of light, the phenomenon of time dilation is not apparent. It has been demonstrated repeatedly, however, in the case of subatomic particles,

$$E = Mc^2$$

A further consequence of Einstein's special theory is the equivalence of mass and energy. Essentially two aspects of the same thing, they are related by the famous equation $E = mc^2$ – 'energy (E) equals mass (m) multiplied by the speed of light (c) squared'. Like space and time, they are also relativistic, with the mass of a body increasing with speed and approaching infinity as it nears the speed of light. It would take an infinite amount of energy, however, to accelerate a physical body to this speed, which is why the speed of light is the theoretical speed limit for the universe. Because the speed of light squared is a huge number, the energy–mass equation means that a small amount of mass can be converted into a vast amount of energy – a fact spectacularly confirmed by nuclear weapons, which convert less than one percent of their mass into energy. In 1931 Einstein warned, with tragic irony, that scientists must do everything to ensure that their creations are 'a blessing and not a curse to mankind'. Fifteen years later – in the aftermath of Hiroshima and Nagasaki – he wrote solemnly: 'The unleashed power of the atom has changed everything save our modes of thinking and we thus drift toward unparalleled catastrophe.'

which travel at speeds close to the speed of light. One consequence of time dilation is that simultaneity, too, becomes relative – events that are simultaneous in one frame may not be so in another. And a similar line of thought leads to space contraction: the length of an object contracts along its direction of motion. As time and space thus become fluid and malleable, they become entwined and lose their separate identity. In their place is a union of space and time: a four-dimensional space–time continuum, in which time is the fourth dimension.

The general theory Newton's theory of gravity violates special relativity, in that it involves a mysterious 'action at a distance' by which objects such as the Sun and the earth exert an instantaneous pulling force on each other. To develop a satisfactory new system, Einstein formulated his general theory of relativity, moving beyond the special theory by taking into account non-inertial reference frames – i.e. frames that are accelerating in relation to one another. In this context his great insight was the principle of equivalence, which recognizes that physical effects due to gravity are indistinguishable from those due to acceleration. Imagine you are in a broken lift that is falling freely to earth. You will not feel your own weight, because both you and the lift enclosure are accelerating downwards at the same rate. So, unless you can refer to a different frame – in other words, see something in the world outside the lift – it will be impossible for you to tell that you are in a gravitational field.

Now consider the behaviour of a light beam moving through the lift, parallel to the floor. If the lift were stationary, the light would travel through it in a straight line. But as the lift is accelerating downwards, the light beam will be bent upwards. So, given that light is bent in an accelerated frame, it should, according to the principle of equivalence, also be bent by gravity. Clearly, light travelling in a 'straight line' must mean something different in the vicinity of a gravitational mass. Developing the idea of combined space–time derived from the special theory, Einstein concluded that space–time itself had become distorted or curved. Gravity, he saw, was a phenomenon arising from the shape of space–time itself – from the very geometry of the universe.

> **When a man sits with a pretty girl for an hour, it seems like a minute. But let him sit on a hot stove for a minute and it's longer than any hour. That's relativity.**
>
> **Albert Einstein, *c.*1954**

the condensed idea
The merging of space and time

49 Quantum mechanics

A cat is placed in a steel box. Also in the box, out of the cat's reach, there is a Geiger counter and a tiny bit of a radioactive substance – a piece so small that there is a 50% chance that in the course of one hour one of its atoms will decay. If this happens, the release of radiation will be detected by the Geiger counter, which will trigger a spring mechanism that causes a hammer to break a small flask containing hydrocyanic acid. The deadly gas will then escape and kill the cat.

So, if the box is opened after an hour, there is a 50:50 chance that the cat will be dead. But things are not as simple as they seem. For modern physics tells us that the behaviour of matter and energy on atomic and subatomic scales – including the radioactive material sharing the box with the cat – is most accurately described in terms of quantum mechanics. And according to the view of the quantum world most widely held by physicists today, the motion and interaction of atoms and subatomic particles are essentially indeterminate until they are measured. In the case of the cat, the atom is in a 'superposition' of two possible states – decayed and not decayed – and it remains in this unresolved state until an observation is made. Until this time, the quantum event has an essentially fuzzy or indefinite character that can be described only in terms of the probability of possible outcomes. While such indeterminacy may not seem intolerably odd in the microscopic world, it is harder to stomach when its bizarre consequences visit the world of our everyday experience. And in this case, until the box is opened, it seems that the cat is in some sense both dead and alive!

timeline

1900	1905	1913
Planck assumes quantized energy to explain radiation from hot bodies	Einstein uses quantized light particles (photons) to explain photoelectric effect	Bohr proposes a new atomic structure based on quantum principles

Schrödinger's cat The thought experiment outlined above was first devised in 1935 by one of the pioneers of quantum mechanics, the Austrian physicist Erwin Schrödinger. Far from wishing to promote the idea of dead-and-alive cats, his aim was to demonstrate the absurdity of the orthodox understanding of the quantum world. The problem that Schrödinger focused on – the so-called 'measurement problem' – is but one of the great oddities thrown up by this most peculiar branch of science. Yet, in spite of its deeply counterintuitive aspects, quantum mechanics has proved to be a massively successful model whose results have been validated experimentally on innumerable occasions. Recognized, along with Einstein's theories of relativity, as the crowning achievement of 20th-century science, it underpins virtually every aspect of the current practice of physics. It has also had a profound practical impact on technology, with applications ranging from superconductors to super-fast computing.

How, then, should we reconcile the quantum world with the world of our everyday experience? Does the bizarre behaviour of atoms and subatomic particles oblige us to reappraise our understanding of reality?

> When it comes to atoms, language can be used only as in poetry. The poet, too, is not nearly so concerned with describing facts as with creating images.
>
> **Niels Bohr,** undated

From desperation to hope At the beginning of the 20th century, physicists' understanding of the world had in most respects diverged little from the classical path begun more than 200 years earlier by Isaac Newton. With respect to light, there was near-consensus that its behaviour could best be interpreted in terms of its observed wave-like properties. While this worked well for phenomena such as diffraction and interference, it manifestly failed to explain others, including the absorption and emission of light. It was chiefly in response to such failures that the first steps into the quantum world were taken.

One notable failure of the prevailing classical view was its inability to explain so-called 'black-body radiation': the way hot bodies radiate heat, glowing red, yellow and finally white as they grow hotter. It was to address this apparent anomaly that the German physicist Max Planck was driven

1924	**1925**	**1926**	**1927**
Louis de Broglie establishes the concept of wave–particle duality	Matrix mechanics formulated by Werner Heisenberg	Schrödinger's wave equation provides foundation of wave mechanics	Uncertainty principle formulated by Heisenberg

to what he himself described as an 'act of desperation'. Essentially as a 'fix' to make the equations describing black-body radiation work, Planck made the bold assumption that the radiation (energy) emitted by a hot body is emitted not continuously but in discrete packets, which he called 'quanta' (from the Latin meaning 'amounts').

While Planck himself did not suppose that his assumption was a reflection of an underlying reality, five years later Einstein successfully applied a similar method to another problem that had proved resistant to solution within classical mechanics: the photoelectric effect – the way a metal surface produces electricity when light is shone on it. Inspired by Planck's

Quantum quandaries

'If anybody says he can think about quantum theory *without* getting giddy,' suggested Niels Bohr, 'it merely shows that he hasn't understood the first thing about it!' The indeterminacy at the core of quantum mechanics is neatly encapsulated in Werner Heisenberg's uncertainty principle (1927), which states that both the position and the momentum of a subatomic particle cannot be measured precisely at the same time: the more precisely one quantity is known, the less precise the other will be. Many have taken the randomness inherent in the quantum world to undermine the notion of physical determinism and so salvage the concept of human free will. Others, however, including de Broglie in 1962, have sensibly urged caution: 'It is far safer and wiser that the physicist remain on the solid ground of theoretical physics itself and eschew the shifting sands of philosophic extrapolations.'

The weird behaviour of matter at quantum scales has consistently provoked debate about the broader implications of the new physics for our ordinary understanding of reality. Especially perplexing is the measurement problem: the idea that the character of a quantum state is not 'fixed' until it is measured; the state is essentially indeterminate, a combination of possible outcomes, until such time as the process of measurement determines which one counts as actual. The orthodox view among physicists has long been the so-called Copenhagen interpretation, which is attributed mainly to Bohr, who was based in the Danish capital. This amounts, in effect, to the claim that the indeterminacy that we observe in nature is fundamental: basically, we should accept it as such and see where the calculations take us. Einstein, for one, was not prepared to take so sanguine a view. He maintained that quantum mechanics must be incomplete and that if the 'hidden variables' were known, a more compliant classical and deterministic reality would become apparent.

'quantization of energy', Einstein's solution depended on the crucial assumption that light is made up of discrete entities (i.e. quanta) called photons. Further confirmation of Planck's hypothesis came in 1913, when the Danish physicist Niels Bohr proposed a new structure of the atom which used quantum principles to explain its stability while absorbing and radiating energy.

Wave–particle duality Light, then, was presenting a puzzle and a challenge. While the classical wave theory demonstrably worked in some areas, the approaches taken by Planck, Einstein and Bohr only succeeded by ascribing *particle*-like behaviour to light. It was becoming increasingly clear that at the level of elementary particles, it was no longer possible to sustain the sharp classical distinction between waves (radiating through space, carrying energy only) and particles (moving from place to place, carrying mass and energy). So what was light: wave or particle?

The answer that eventually emerged was that, in some strange sense, it was both. Electromagnetic radiation (including visible light) and the elementary particles of which matter is composed exhibit so-called 'wave–particle duality'. Recognition of this idea – arguably the most fundamental concept in quantum mechanics – was formally made by the French physicist Louis de Broglie in 1924. Just as Einstein had earlier proposed that radiation can display particle-like behaviour, so now de Broglie argued that matter – electrons and other particles – could exhibit wave-like properties.

In an extraordinary flurry of activity in the mid-1920s, a number of (mainly) German physicists succeeded in formulating the mathematical basis of quantum mechanics. In 1925 Werner Heisenberg developed an approach known as matrix mechanics; and in the following year Schrödinger formulated wave mechanics, demonstrating at the same time that his method was mathematically equivalent to Heisenberg's. In this dramatically new account of the elementary nature of matter, the classical picture of electrons as discrete particles in orbit around a nucleus had been replaced by ghostly halos smeared (like Schrödinger's cat) across probabilistically defined paths.

the condensed idea
The strange poetry of atoms

50 The Big Bang

It is frustrating that probably the most significant moment in the history of the universe – its first – is cloaked in almost complete darkness. True, total ignorance envelops only the first one-millionth of a second (approximately) of the universe's existence – cosmologists have many theories about what happened over the subsequent 13,700,000,000 years. Still, our lack of knowledge of the instant of the universe's supposed creation – the Big Bang – is profound indeed. Not only is it unknown what happened in that initial tiny fraction of a second; it is not even clear that it happened at all!

Among today's scientists, the Big Bang cosmology is the most widely accepted view of the origin and evolution of the universe. According to this theory, the universe originated in a catastrophic event in which all matter, infinitely compressed at that instant into a single dimensionless point, began to expand and cool extremely rapidly. It was this explosion that put in train the sequence of events that resulted, approximately 13.7 billion years later, in the vast structure of innumerable stars and galaxies that exists today. The concept of an expanding universe is now acknowledged to be the unifying theme of modern cosmology.

The uncertainty in this account concerns not so much the subsequent evolution – although the details of this are naturally the focus of intense speculation – as the Big Bang itself. The idea of an 'initial singularity', as the Big Bang is more formally called, follows, with apparent inevitability, from Einstein's general theory of relativity. The various cosmological models that have been derived in this way all feature a singularity in which the density and temperature of matter and the curvature of space–time are

timeline

1916	1910s–20s	1920s
General theory of relativity published by Albert Einstein	Vesto Slipher makes redshift observations of receding nebulae	Expanding universe proposed by Alexander Friedmann and Georges Lemaître

infinite; from this point expansion begins, with matter becoming less dense and cooling in the process. The difficulty arises because physicists today doubt that the equations of general relativity would remain valid in the extreme physical conditions that would obtain at the moment of singularity. At such high densities, it is now widely believed, the normal laws of physics will cease to apply and general relativity will need to be replaced by a more complete theory of a kind known generically as 'quantum gravity'. So-called 'superstring theory' is a leading candidate for such a role, but it is unknown whether this or any of its rivals will predict a singularity. So, while the majority of cosmologists favour the idea of a single hot Big Bang, a number of alternative, non-singular cosmologies have been proposed.

Standing the test of time There is no doubt, at least, that the current universe *looks* as if it underwent a Big Bang-type explosion in the past, and there is compelling evidence to suggest that it did. The most important strand of this evidence is the fact of expansion, which is implied in the equations of general relativity, first published by Einstein in 1916. Indeed, Einstein himself recognized this implication, but to salvage his own belief that the universe was static, he introduced a compensatory pressure called the 'cosmological constant' – a move which he later described as his 'biggest blunder'. Observational evidence of expansion, accumulated sporadically during the 1910s and 1920s, culminated in 1929 in the formulation by US astronomer Edwin Hubble of his eponymous law. Hubble, assisted in particular by Milton Humason, observed that the light emanating from nearby galaxies was 'redshifted' – it had moved to the red end of the colour spectrum. A phenomenon analogous to the Doppler effect in sound, this indicated that the light waves were stretched and

> **You don't have to search far to locate where the Big Bang occurred, for it took place where you are now as well as everywhere else; in the beginning, all locations we now see as separate were the same location.**
>
> Brian Greene, US superstring theorist, 1999

1929	**mid 1940s**	**1948**	**1965**
Hubble's law relates velocity of receding galaxies to their distance from observer	Synthesis of light elements in Big Bang explained by George Gamow and others	Cosmic microwave background (CMB) predicted by Ralph Alpher and Robert Herman	Existence of CMB confirmed by Arno Penzias and Robert Wilson

hence that the galaxies involved were travelling away from our galaxy. Repeated measurements showed that the velocities at which the galaxies were receding were proportional to their distance – the essence of Hubble's law.

When something expands, we normally think of it as occupying space; expansion, in this sense, is expansion in or through space. But at the instant of the Big Bang, there was no space 'outside' to expand into: the subsequent expansion was (and is) the expansion *of* space and occurred

God and the beginning of time

It seems entirely natural to wonder what happened *before* the Big Bang. The question has been posed, especially though not exclusively, by the theologically motivated, who wish to explore the relation of God to the moment of the universe's creation. In fact, though, the question itself is essentially meaningless, because both space *and time* were created at the moment of the Big Bang. In the analogy used by the British physicist Stephen Hawking, it is like asking what lies north of the North Pole – a question that is generally acknowledged to make no logical sense. In his celebrated 1988 book *A Brief History of Time*, Hawking explains the concepts involved more fully:

'One may say that time had a beginning at the Big Bang, in the sense that earlier times simply would not be defined. It should be emphasized that this beginning in time is very different from those that had been considered previously. In an unchanging universe a beginning in time is something that has to be imposed by some being outside the universe; there is no physical necessity for a beginning. One can imagine that God created the universe at literally any time in the past. On the other hand, if the universe is expanding, there may be physical reasons why there had to be a beginning. One could still imagine that God created the universe at the instant of the Big Bang, or even afterwards in just such a way as to make it look as though there had been a Big Bang, but it would be meaningless to suppose that it was created before the Big Bang. An expanding universe does not preclude a creator, but it does place limits on when he might have carried out his job!'

everywhere at once. The galactic recession that Hubble observed is not a matter of galaxies moving away from us *through* space. They and we remain in broadly the same positions relative to each other and everything else; it is the space between us that expands and carries us apart. This kind of expansion has been compared to the swelling-up of a fruitcake in which all the raisins, corresponding to galaxies, get further and further apart as the cake cooks; except that, in the case of the universe, as there is no outside, there is no edge and no centre. This is one aspect of the so-called 'cosmological principle', according to which the universe is essentially the same in all directions and its expansion is the same for all observers: there is no privileged position for us or any other notional observer.

Apart from the recession of galaxies, there are two other especially important strands of evidence in support of the hot Big Bang cosmology. According to the theory, the atomic nuclei of lighter elements, especially hydrogen and helium, would form in the first few instants after the bang, when temperatures had fallen to a few billion degrees. The abundances of these elements detected in the universe today accord closely with the levels predicted by the theory. Even more direct evidence that the universe went through a hot, dense phase is provided by the cosmic microwave background (CMB). This low-energy radiation, a relic of the hot early universe, suffuses all space, bathing the earth in a faint glow that comes from all directions. The existence of the CMB was predicted, as a remnant of the Big Bang, in 1948 and detected somewhat fortuitously in 1965. The discovery of the CMB not only provided further corroboration of the Big Bang cosmology but largely put paid to its main rival at that time, the steady state theory. This, no more than other rival theories, was unable to provide as satisfactory an account of the various strands of empirical evidence. The Big Bang, having so far rebuffed all major challengers, remains the cornerstone of modern cosmology.

the condensed idea
The beginning of
space and time

Glossary

Absolutism In ethics, the view that certain actions are right or wrong under any circumstances; in politics, the principle that a government's rights and powers are unrestricted.

Aesthetics The branch of philosophy concerned with the arts, including the nature and definition of works of art and the justification of artistic judgement and criticism.

American Revolution The political and military struggle, ending in 1781, in which North American colonists freed themselves from British control.

Classical Relating to ancient Greek or Latin culture or civilization; in art and architecture, influenced by Greek or Roman forms or principles; in physics (= Newtonian), relating to the theories in place before the development of the theories of relativity and quantum mechanics.

Consequentialism In philosophy, the view that the rightness of actions should be judged purely in relation to their effectiveness in bringing about certain desirable ends.

Contingent Describing something that happens to be true but might have been otherwise. By contrast, a necessary truth is one that could not have been otherwise.

Darwinian Relating to the English biologist Charles Darwin (1809–82) or to his theory of evolution by natural selection.

Determinism The theory that every event has a prior cause, and hence that every state of the world is necessitated or determined by a previous state. The extent to which determinism undermines our freedom of action constitutes the problem of free will.

Dogmatism Insistence on the truth of certain principles, with a concomitant unwillingness to consider the views of others.

Dualism In philosophy, the view that mind (or soul) and matter (or body) are distinct. Opposed to dualism are idealism or immaterialism (minds and ideas are all there is) and physicalism or materialism (bodies and matter are all there is).

Dynamics The branch of physics concerned with motion of bodies.

Egoism In philosophy, the view that people are as a matter of fact motivated by self-interest (psychological egoism) or that they should be so motivated (ethical egoism).

Empirical Describing a concept or belief that is based on experience (the evidence of the senses).

Empiricism The view that all knowledge is based on, or inextricably tied to, experience derived from the senses.

Enlightenment The 'Age of Reason', the period of Western historical thought, beginning in the late 17th century and driven by the Scientific Revolution, in which the power of reason was elevated over the authority of religion and tradition.

Fatalism The view that whatever will be will be and hence that it makes no difference how we act.

Free will *see under* Determinism.

French Revolution The overthrow of the absolute monarchy in France, achieved with escalating bloodshed between 1789 and 1799; sometimes considered the first modern revolution, because it transformed the nature of society and introduced radically new political ideologies.

Glorious Revolution The replacement on the English throne, in 1689, of the Catholic monarch James II by his Protestant daughter Mary and her husband William of Orange; the bloodless coup marked the end of absolutism and the beginning of constitutional government in England.

Humanism Any view in which human affairs are accorded primary importance; in particular, the Renaissance movement in which human dignity was elevated over religious dogma.

Idealism *see under* Dualism.

Immaterialism *see under* Dualism.

Industrial Revolution Social and economic transformation of agrarian societies into industrial, urbanized ones. Beginning in 18th-century Britain, the process was driven successively by the development of steam power, the advent of factory production and the construction of railways.

Libertarianism In philosophy, the view that determinism is false and that human choices are genuinely free; in politics, extreme liberalism that advocates a minimal role for the state, unfettered exercise of the free market, etc.

Marxist Relating to the thought of the German political philosopher Karl Marx (1818–83), the founder (with Friedrich Engels) of modern communism.

Materialism A tendency to hold material possessions and physical comforts above spiritual values; *see also under* Dualism.

Mechanics In physics, the study of the interactions between matter and the forces acting on it.

Medieval Relating to the Middle Ages, the period of European history extending from the fall of the Western Roman Empire in the 5th century AD to the start of the Renaissance in the 15th.

Metaphysics The branch of philosophy that deals with the nature or structure of reality, generally focusing on notions such as being, substance and causation.

Modern Relating to the period of Western history extending from (roughly) the 15th century till the present day; the earlier part of this period, till around 1800, is often referred to as 'early modern'.

Naturalism In philosophy, the view that everything (including moral concepts) can be explained in terms of 'facts of nature' that are in principle discoverable by science; in art, a style of representation that emphasizes accuracy of depiction.

Newtonian Relating to the work of Isaac Newton (1642–1727) and, by extension, to classical physics generally; *see also under* Classical.

Objectivism In ethics and aesthetics, the view that values and properties such as goodness and beauty are inherent in objects and exist independently of human apprehension of them.

Physicalism *see under* Dualism.

Pragmatism In philosophy, the view that beliefs or principles should be evaluated by how successful they are in practice.

Rationalism The view that knowledge (or some knowledge) can be acquired other than through the use of the senses, by exercise of our unaided powers of reasoning.

Realism In ethics and aesthetics, the view that values and properties really exist 'out there' in the world, independently of our knowing or experiencing them; in art, a style that seeks to represent people or things as they actually are.

Reformation Religious movement in 16th-century Europe calling for reform of the Roman Catholic church and leading to the emergence of Protestantism.

Renaissance Revival of European art and literature, extending from the 14th to 16th centuries, inspired by the rediscovery of classical models.

Subjectivism In ethics and aesthetics, the view that value is grounded not in external reality but in our beliefs about it or emotional responses to it.

Transcendental Belonging to a spiritual or non-physical realm, and hence lying beyond the scope of sense experience.

Index

Quercus Publishing Plc
21 Bloomsbury Square
London
WC1A 2NS

First published in 2009

A catalogue record of this book is available from the British Library

ISBN: 978 1 84724 986 9

Printed and bound in China

10 9 8 7 6 5 4 3 2 1

Prepared by *specialist* publishing services ltd, Montgomery